Movies, Miniseries, and Multiculturalism

T0406908

About the Authors

Lillian Comas-Díaz, PhD, has written extensively about cultural competence, psychotherapy, feminism of color, liberation psychology, and psychospirituality. She is past director of the Yale University Hispanic Clinic, and a past director of the American Psychological Association's Office of Ethnic Minority Affairs.

Rehman Abdulrehman, PhD, is a clinical and consulting psychologist and the author of *Developing Anti-Racist Cultural Competence*. He was a TEDx speaker on "Resolving Unconscious Bias" and his work is focused on catalyzing insight-oriented change. He is also a published poet and creative writer and an avid fan of great television and Star Wars.

Danny Wedding, PhD, MPH, has written extensively about films in two previous books, *Movies and Mental Illness* and *Positive Psychology at the Movies*. He edited PsycCRITIQUES, the American Psychological Association's journal of book and film reviews, for 12 years and now reviews movies for Hogrefe Spotlights titled "A Clinical Psychologist Goes to the Movies." Danny is a first-generation high school graduate who went on to use the GI Bill to complete a PhD in clinical psychology. He directed the Missouri Institute of Mental Health (MIMH) for 19 years, and taught in both Thailand and South Korea as a Fulbright Senior Scholar, as well as at other universities around the globe. Having retired from academic life, he now focuses on his passions, including movies.

Movies, Miniseries, and Multiculturalism

Using Films and Television to Understand Culture and Social Justice

Lillian Comas-Díaz

Rehman Abdulrehman

Danny Wedding

 hogrefe

Library of Congress of Congress Cataloging in Publication information for the print version of this book is available via the Library of Congress Marc Database under the Library of Congress Control Number 2025937929

Library and Archives Canada Cataloguing in Publication
Title: Movies, miniseries, and multiculturalism : using films and television to understand culture and social justice / Lillian Comas-Díaz, Rehman Abdulrehman, Danny Wedding.
Names: Comas-Díaz, Lillian, author | Abdulrehman, Rehman, author. | Wedding, Danny, author.
Description: Includes bibliographical references and index.
Identifiers: Canadiana (print) 20250217120 | Canadiana (ebook) 20250217821 | ISBN 9780889374942 (softcover) | ISBN 9781616764944 (PDF) | ISBN 9781613344941 (EPUB)
Subjects: LCSH: Multiculturalism in motion pictures. | LCSH: Culture in motion pictures. | LCSH: Social problems in motion pictures. | LCSH: Social justice in motion pictures.
Classification: LCC PN1995.9.M79 C66 2025 | DDC 791.43/6529—dc23

The authors and publisher have made every effort to ensure that the information contained in this text is in accord with the current state of scientific knowledge, recommendations, and practice at the time of publication. In spite of this diligence, errors cannot be completely excluded. Also, due to changing regulations and continuing research, information may become outdated at any point. The authors and publisher disclaim any responsibility for any consequences which may follow from the use of information presented in this book.

Registered trademarks are not noted specifically as such in this publication. The use of descriptive names, registered names, and trademarks does not imply, even in the absence of a specific statement, that such names are exempt from the relevant protective laws and regulations and therefore free for general use.

The cover image is an agency photo depicting models. Use of the photo on this publication does not imply any connection between the content of this publication and any person depicted in the cover image.
Cover image: © Drazen Zigic – iStock.com

PUBLISHING OFFICES

USA:	Hogrefe Publishing Corporation, 44 Merrimac St., Newburyport, MA 01950 Phone 978 255 3700; E-mail customersupport@hogrefe.com
EUROPE:	Hogrefe Publishing GmbH, Merkelstr. 3, 37085 Göttingen, Germany Phone +49 551 99950 0, Fax +49 551 99950 111; E-mail publishing@hogrefe.com

SALES & DISTRIBUTION

USA:	Hogrefe Publishing, Customer Services Department, 30 Amberwood Parkway, Ashland, OH 44805 Phone 800 228 3749, Fax 419 281 6883; E-mail customersupport@hogrefe.com
UK:	Hogrefe Ltd, Hogrefe House, Albion Place, Oxford, OX1 1QZ Phone +44 186 579 7920; E-mail customersupport@hogrefe.co.uk
EUROPE:	Hogrefe Publishing, Merkelstr. 3, 37085 Göttingen, Germany Phone +49 551 99950 0, Fax +49 551 99950 111; E-mail publishing@hogrefe.com

OTHER OFFICES

CANADA:	Hogrefe Publishing Corporation, 82 Laird Drive, East York, Ontario, M4G 3V1
SWITZERLAND:	Hogrefe Publishing, Länggass-Strasse 76, 3012 Bern

Printed and bound in the USA

ISBN 978-0-88937-494-2 (print) · ISBN 978-1-61676-494-4 (PDF) · ISBN 978-1-61334-494-1 (EPUB)
https://doi.org/10.1027/00494-000

Contents

Foreword

Narratives of Liberation, Narratives of Oppression, or Both: Considering Media Psychology and Multicultural Psychology

As an African American woman, poet, filmmaker, minister, and psychologist, I appreciate the power of story. I am recommending this book to you because it exemplifies the ways that stories can give voice and visibility to the neglected, underserved, and marginalized. More specifically, the authors show how stories can shift mindsets, open hearts, and empower the disenfranchised. Films and television series can take the form of artivism – art and activism – with an intentional commitment to promote healing and liberation. On the contrary, media can also be and has been used to stereotype, justify harm, dehumanize, and erase. In this powerful and innovative book, media analysis is utilized to illuminate important themes of multicultural psychology including but not limited to notions of identity, belonging, justice, and transformation.

My relationship with the co-authors spans over two decades. I have worked with them in advocating for mental health rights, access, and quality globally. I have also learned from them and taught with them key aspects of global psychology both through peer-reviewed publications and also peer-reviewed and invited convention addresses. They are leaders in the field of global psychology in practice, research, consultation, education, and training who have published thought-provoking and field-shifting texts on multicultural psychology, global psychology, and intersectional liberation psychology. I am pleased to share that one of them, Dr. Lillian Comas-Diaz, was the co-strategist for my campaign to become the 2023 president of the American Psychological Association. She helped to maximize the mobilization and actualization of my dreams to disseminate decolonial, liberation, and intersectional feminist psychology through the American Psychological Association.

To begin this journey in which the authors have crafted a book that will engage you intellectually and culturally, I invite you to think about one of your favorite films. Some factors to consider are: (1) In what ways does the main character reflect your identities and in what ways are they different? (2) Whose voice is central in the film and whose voice is marginalized? (3) Who is presented as desirable, attractive, smart, capable, and popular and who is not? And (4) if the film were to motivate or inspire you to take some sort of action what would that action be and who would benefit from it? I know some of us may think, "It's not that deep. I just like it because it's funny or romantic or exciting." On some level that is accurate and simultaneously there is always a deeper story regarding what appeals to us and why. Media is a tool of communication and it is effective in presenting and convincing the public of particular narratives. Millions of dollars are spent to present the message, whether it is a G-rated children's animation or porn. The writer, producer, director, editor, distributor, casting director, and cast are cooperating to create and disseminate messages that shape and influence us.

Throughout this book, the authors demonstrate the ways that media is a very influential socializing agent and can be empowering to some and disempowering to others. Consider how people of a particular race, gender, sexuality, body type, religion, age, disability, and even accent are depicted. What does the leading lady, criminal, comedy relief character typically look like and how does that mirror the way persons of a similar background are often treated in society? These media depictions can stretch us and cause us to decolonize our minds or they can reinforce stereotypes that we have been fed all of our lives.

Within these pages, the authors illuminate the fact that to adopt a critical lens and to advance your media literacy, it is helpful to consider not only who is positioned in front of the camera but also who is behind the film. It may not surprise you to know that White men in the United States are usually the ones given the opportunity to green light film projects. In this way, their taste, assumptions, political perspectives, and comfort level can often determine whether diverse stories are told and which stories are widely distributed. To amplify the need to look beyond the culture of the cast, consider if the cast is all Asian but the writer, producer, director, and editor are all White. The ways this Asian American story is told will be curated from an outsider's perspective. Likewise, if a lesbian love story is written, directed, produced, and edited by straight White men it will shift the narrative to fit their gaze instead of the gaze of those who are supposedly at the center of the narrative. Of course, you can imagine or simply recall how people who don't subscribe to a faith tradition have depicted practitioners of Indigenous Religions, Jews,

Christians, and Muslims in film. These examples highlight the fact that while representation on the screen matters, it is not sufficient. You can have diverse people on the screen and still promote and perpetuate harmful, stereotypical narratives. Humanity, nuance, voice, and agency are all important parts of creating liberating narratives. People, families, and communities don't have to be perfect to be liberating but they do need to display a full range of emotion, connection, possibility, and choices.

The authors illuminate the fact that looking at multicultural psychology from the vantage point of liberation psychology also calls for us to not only consider the feelings, thoughts, and behaviors of individuals but also reflect on the socio-political and even intergenerational context of characters. For example, to tell a narrative of youth involved in gang activity and to present them as just making bad choices without any framework regarding poverty, discrimination, and intergenerational oppression is to tell a fraction of the story. Multicultural film analysis requires that we enter the world of the story which gives space and voice to the various interlocking systems affecting the characters as well as their internal and interpersonal worlds. Before you conclude that this is asking too much of the filmmaker, think about a film that you have seen that you feel did an effective job of bringing you into both the psychological world of the characters and the larger society that is shaping their lives. Even when this is not done effectively, you as viewer can be empowered to ask those critical questions, interrogate the narrative, and pull the insights out of the narrative. In this way, the liberating aspect of the film is not only about the story that is told, the way it is told, but also the way in which it is consumed. Promoting media literacy is an important role that psychologists can play in addition to using media in teaching, practice, research, and consultation.

In narrative therapy, clients are encouraged to not only think about how other people have shaped their lives, ranging from abusers to mentors, but also to consider their voice and agency. In light of this, the authors of this groundbreaking book show us the importance of not just being passive recipients of the messages presented overtly and covertly but also viewing media from an empowered and liberating vantage point. Finally, in appreciation of this captivating book, I invite you to consider your current or future role as a content creator. Whether you are active on social media, take pictures of memorable events, or engage in creative writing, make a commitment to using your voice and vision to promote liberating messages. We are all worthy of stories that honor our truth, dignity, and humanity. The authors have the training and decades of experience to guide us on this thoughtful journey through media and multicultural psychology. This text is one I will use for myself, my clients, and my students. I recommend it strongly if you are committed to growing your knowledge and application of psychology in a way that will enhance people's lives.

Thema Bryant, PhD
2023 President of the American Psychological Association

Preface

> "Movies are something people see all over the world –
> because there is a certain need for it."
>
> Wim Wenders

Do you like movies? Do you like television miniseries? Would you like to know more about culture and multiculturalism? If your answer is *yes* to these questions, this book is for you. We wrote *Movies, Miniseries, and Multiculturalism* to help you understand multiculturalism through films and miniseries.

We are mental health professionals who love movies and television. We do not separate being psychologists from being cinephiles. These two identities inform and enrich our lives and work.

Ang Lee, the 2006 Oscar winner for Best Director, declared that movies are a way of understanding the world and ourselves. In our experience, movies and miniseries also can be therapeutic, and we sometimes prescribe films for our patients to watch. We believe we deepen our knowledge and understanding of human behavior when we watch films and miniseries. In short, *movies teach us about life*. No wonder actress Audrey Hepburn said that everything she learned, she learned from the movies.

Since human behavior is culturally rooted, films and miniseries expand our knowledge of self and others. Because multiculturalism promotes transformation as well as an openness to others (Fowers & Davidov, 2006), it helps to understand our cultural embeddedness and to embrace flexibility (Comas-Díaz, 2024). When we watch multicultural films and miniseries, we unconsciously, preconsciously, and consciously witness ourselves and others. Movies help us reflect on who we are as well as on who others are. Since multiculturalism supports the integration of multiple healing systems (Fowers & Davidov, 2006), watching multicultural films and miniseries nurtures healing. According to film director Tim Burton, films are like therapy. Watching multicultural films and miniseries not only reflects who we are, but more importantly, it nurtures who we are becoming. Multicultural movies and miniseries promote growth and transformation, and watching multicultural movies and miniseries illuminates multiple ways of being in the world. In our experience, watching multicultural films and miniseries can be enlightening and promote personal growth. Entertainment media is much like initially seeing an iceberg, and realizing most of it is submerged; watching multicultural films and miniseries, thinking about them, and discussing them with friends, family, and colleagues help us appreciate the deeper aspects of life's iceberg.

> I think cinema, movies, and magic have always been closely associated. The very earliest people who made film were magicians.
>
> Francis Ford Coppola

We are three different individuals connected by our profession (clinical psychology) and our love of films and miniseries. Like Italian American film director Francis Ford Coppola, we strongly believe that movies *are* magic. We share this perspective even though we are culturally different from each other. Our positionalities further explain our differences.

Lillian

I am a Latinx cisgender mixed-race decolonial liberation feminist woman. I was born in Chicago and was transplanted to Puerto Rico at age 6. Like many Puerto Ricans, my parents engaged in circular migration between the island and the continental United States with my younger brother David. I remained on the island living with my maternal grandparents. My parents and David moved back to the island, and we were reunited as a nuclear family. Growing up in Puerto Rico was a blessing. I was exposed to multiple intersecting cultures including those of the Caribbean, Spain, and North, Central, and South America. We lived in the beautiful little town of Yabucoa, located on the eastern south coast of the island, and we had gorgeous views of the Caribbean Sea and the mountains. However, living in a colony taught me the realities of oppression, and it nurtured a thirst for social justice, decolonization, and liberation. Movies became an elixir. Yabucoa had a movie theater, and Henry, the theater owner, loved movies, especially foreign movies. Movies were a panacea. Accompanied by David, cousins, and close friends, I went every weekend to watch serious cinema from all around the world. This experience whetted my appetite for movies. Growing up in Puerto Rico and watching movies nurtured my "harbor mind." Harbor mind refers to the ability to manage multiple realities resulting in pluralism (Nicolson, 2023). My harbor mind encouraged multiculturalism as well as the engagement in critical consciousness, liberation, and decolonization. I returned to the continental United States to work and to complete a doctoral degree in clinical psychology. I remained there and met my husband, Fred, an American man who experienced significant ethnocultural translocation. As lovers of movies, we enjoy watching and talking about movies. This practice blends magic into our shared lives.

Rehman

I am a Muslim Canadian of Zanzibari descent with a mixed ethnic heritage. Following the Zanzibar revolution, my parents and large portions of my family fled to the mainland of the now amalgamated country of Tanzania, and I was born and lived in Dar es Salaam until I was 7 years old. I remember our neighbor, nicknamed Baby, in Dar es Salaam having an entire room dedicated to organized and categorized Betamax video cassettes of movies, and my being in awe of the rows and rows of towering stories organized on shelves. I remember sitting down with her to watch a film on the Holocaust. The images of men, women, and children, naked and being forced into the gas chambers, are seared into my mind, and I realize now how impactful film was in creating an awareness of social justice for me even as a child. I also remember my parents taking me to the drive-in theaters in the heat of African summers and seeing Bambi's mother die from a hunter's gun. Once again, the issue of social justice became salient for me. I also remember moving to Canada when I was 7, my parents having adopted an old but large console television in a wooden box, with a whole 13 channels. But at that time in Canada, movies were a luxury for immigrants, and instead I followed television and early Saturday morning cartoons, accompanied by sugary cereal and milk. These were hopeful shows about superheroes who were defenders of justice (all of them White). Although those shows did not have people that looked like me, they made me feel very Canadian and a part of a culture I had only read about in books as a child in Dar es Salaam. When I fast-forward to the present, my young son watches many of those series and shows today, delving deeper into stories with more diverse casts that now include people like him. And he is better for it, as his generation has an opportunity to learn about social justice, with characters that look, act, and feel like him (and me). And so naturally, as film has increasingly moved toward miniseries and television to tell more in-depth narratives infused with nuances of culture and social justice, it also made sense for us to review television miniseries that can allow us to share experiences with a broader audience like never before.

Just as film and television have been an important part of my life, so too has psychology. I've had the pleasure to return "home" to teach and develop mental health resources in low-resource settings in both Dar es Salaam and Zanzibar with three universities in the region. I've served on the International Relations Committee for the American Psychological Association and been the chair of this committee. And I've helped larger media organizations such as the Canadian Broadcasting Corporation and Google/YouTube address issues of inclusion and bias so they can improve the inclusion of stories watched by my son and others like him.

Stories, one way or another, have become a significant part of my work. Narrative storytelling is important in therapy, in workshops, and in training but also in relaying humanity. I've had the honor to give a TEDx talk on unconscious bias, exploring the question, "But Where Are You Really From?" You now know the answer. I've been a published poet, and still write poetry. I wrote a book titled *Developing Anti-Racist Cultural Competence* (Abdulrehman, 2024), and a newly released novel about the supernatural folklore of the jinn in Zanzibari and Arab culture, entitled *Jinn in the Family* (Abdulrehman, 2025). I am also the editor of a new anthology of poetry for people of color, which is currently in progress, titled *The Poetry of Angry Black and Brown People*. I was also a guest editor for a *Consulting Psychology Journal* special edition, titled "Beyond the generic Brown: South Asian and Arab people in the workplace."

Danny

I am a 76-year-old cisgender White guy who knows far less about multiculturalism than my two colleagues (both of whom have international reputations for their multicultural work). However, I knew I needed to learn more about culture, and working with Lillian and Rehman has been a tremendous learning experience.

I am also an enthusiastic film aficionado, and my love of films is reflected in the current book, in two editions of *Positive Psychology at the Movies* (Niemiec & Wedding, 2013), and in five editions of *Movies and Mental Illness* (Wedding, 2024).

My passion for film grew out of my neurotic need to be *accomplishing something*; simply enjoying good films wasn't enough, so I got in the habit of taking notes while watching movies, and these notes eventually turned into books, chapters, and articles. Both of my previous movie books have been translated into multiple languages.

I have also loved being a peripatetic psychologist, and my love of film has supported considerable international travel. I lectured widely on movies during two Senior Scholar Fulbrights: The first involved teaching psychotherapy to psychiatry residents at the Chiang Mai University School of Medicine (Thailand); 10 years later a second Fulbright allowed me to spend a year teaching graduate students in psychology at Yonsei University in Seoul, South Korea. Like all Fulbright Scholars, I was expected to lecture widely, and I did, presenting at universities in Thailand, Cambodia, Australia, New Zealand, South Korea, China, Okinawa, and mainland Japan. Most of these talks were about movies.

I was delighted to learn that many of my Thai and Korean students had watched – and loved – dozens of movies that I had enjoyed, and I cherish the long discussions with my students about whether given films (e.g., *A Beautiful Mind*) present accurate portrayals of mental illness, addiction, or developmental disabilities. I have always secretly wanted to be a film critic; being a psychologist who writes about movies is almost as good! (And I've finally gotten there – my reviews of psychologically relevant films can be found by Googling "A Clinical Psychologist Goes to the Movies.")

We genuinely appreciate the hundreds of colleagues who have taken time to recommend movies to include in this book. Some of the films are dated (e.g., *Walkabout*); however, each film discussed is included because we believe watching the film will make you more culturally sensitive, sophisticated, and literate – in short, more *multicultural*!

All three of us also spent considerable time using Rotten Tomatoes and the Internet Movie DataBase (iMDB) to identify films and television miniseries that would provide a good springboard for multicultural learning and meaningful class discussions. Once word got out that we were writing a book about movies and multiculturalism, our colleagues brought dozens of recommendations for films that could potentially be good teaching tools.

Despite our cultural differences, sharing a mutual passion for movies and miniseries helped us navigate these differences, enriching our lives and infusing this book with multicultural content. And we believed that a book like this was necessary to promote discussion of multicultural narratives in film and television. As Toni Morrison said, "If there is a book you want to read, and it hasn't been written yet, then you must write it." So we did.

Our goal is to help you expand your multicultural knowledge. Specifically, we aim to help you develop a taste for multiculturalism while you are being entertained. Since the world is becoming more multicultural, this volume can help you to better understand yourself and others through the lens of movies and miniseries. We aimed to summon magic in this book – we hope we have succeeded.

Lillian Comas-Díaz
Washington, DC, USA

Rehman Abdulrehman
Winnipeg, Manitoba, Canada

Danny Wedding
West Linn, Oregon, USA

References

Abdulrehman, R. (2024). *Developing anti-racist cultural competence.* Hogrefe. https://doi.org/10.1027/00515-000

Abdulrehman, R. Y. (2025). *Jinn in the family.* Lead With Diversity Press.

Comas-Díaz, L. (2024). Multiculturalism: A paradigmatic force in psychology. *Journal of Consulting and Clinical Psychology, 92*(4), 199–201. https://doi.org/10.1037/ccp0000876

Fowers, B. J., & Davidov, B. J. (2006). The virtue of multiculturalism: Personal transformation, character, and openness to the other. *American Psychologist, 61*(6), 581–594. https://doi.org/10.1037/0003-066X.61.6.581

Nicolson, A. (2023). *How to be: Life lessons from the early Greeks.* Picador.

Niemiec, R., & Wedding, D. (2013). *Positive psychology at the movies: Using films to promote character strengths and well-being* (2nd ed.). Hogrefe.

Wedding, D. (2024). *Movies and mental illness: Using films to understand psychopathology* (5th ed.). Hogrefe.

Chapter 1
Family

Troy: It's not easy for me to admit that I've been standing in the same place for 18 years! Rose: Well, I've been standing with you! I gave 18 years of my life to stand in the same spot as you!

A married couple grapples with the struggles involved in relationships and life in *Fences*.

Questions to Consider While Watching
Fences (2016)

- How did a history of slavery influence the development of African American families?
- How do patriarchal and matriarchal families differ from each other? Can you give examples of each?
- Are African American families more likely to be matrilineal? Is this one? How so?
- How did urban migration from the rural South to the North affect Black families?
- Troy and Rose live in Pittsburg. Does racism take different forms in the North and the South?
- Troy makes just enough money as a garbage collector to barely get by in the 1950s. How does the average wage of African Americans today compare to that of White Americans?
- Have marriage rates or practices in African American families changed since the 1950s? How do they differ from other cultural groups?
- Why doesn't Rose simply leave Troy after his refusal to give up his relationship with another woman?

- How do the film's frequent references to food (e.g., pig's feet) help establish cultural identity?
- In what ways is the concept of "fences" important for this film? Do Rose and Troy relate to the fence Troy is building in different ways?
- Are African Americans in the United States more likely than other ethnic groups to be – or to have been – incarcerated? If so, why?
- The play was written by August Wilson (an African American who also wrote *The Piano Lesson*). Could a White playwright have written the play, or would this be cultural appropriation?
- Why do women (like several portrayed in the films discussed) stay in abusive relationships?
- If two parents speak different languages in addition to the one they share as a family, is there any compelling reason to ensure their children grow up to be bilingual?
- Do all cultures celebrate holidays?
- Why are mealtimes especially important for families?

Families and Culture

In the novel *Anna Karenina*, Leo Tolstoy famously wrote, "Happy families are all alike; every unhappy family is unhappy in its own way."

We're not so sure.

Family structures, traditions, and values vary widely across nations, regions, cultures, and subcultures, and anyone at all interested in understanding cultural differences will have to be sensitive to the ways in which different cultural groups define themselves as family units. The relationship between a father and his children may be dramatically different in a Hmong family, for example, than in a White family living in a suburban neighborhood in a New England community.

Families and *Fences*

Fences is a widely acclaimed 2016 film directed by Denzel Washington – who also performs as Troy Maxson, the male lead, a complicated but funny and engaging man who earns a living and supports his family as a garbage collector in downtown Pittsburg. He is married to Rose (Viola Davis), and they live with their teenage son Cory, a young man with a promising potential career as a football player. *Fences* is a film adaptation of August Wilson's Pulitzer Prize-winning play with the same name, and the movie brings together many of the actors who performed in the play. Viola Davis and Denzel Washington both received Tony Awards for their roles in the Broadway play.

Troy is a complicated 53-year-old man whose life is defined by profound regret that he was once a gifted baseball player in the Negro league, but he grew too old for baseball before Jackie Robinson broke the color barrier and Black men were permitted to play on major league (White) teams. There are multiple baseball metaphors throughout the film, mixed with Troy's musings about growing old and his inevitable – and all too rapidly approaching – death. At one point, he remarks, "Death ain't nothing but a fastball on the outside corner." Surprisingly, and because of motives that are never fully clear for the viewer, Troy finds little pleasure in his son's success as a high school athlete, and he refuses to let his son meet with college football recruiters, instead insisting that he continue working in a low-paying and insignificant after-school job.

Troy has another son, Lyons, who only drops by to see the family on Fridays, the day Troy gets paid. He needs $10, but his father rejects the request, instead giving his pay to Rose (who subsequently gives Lyons the money he needs). Lyons is a gifted musician, but these talents aren't appreciated by his father. During one scene, Troy laments not being able to get credit to buy furniture and having to pay $10 every month for 15 years to avoid having his furniture repossessed; Rose points out the story isn't true, but the interaction underscores the kind of exploitation associated with an inability to get credit experienced by many members of minority communities.

Troy is embittered because Black men are only permitted to lift the trash they collect, and the preferred and easier jobs as drivers are always given to Whites. He has filed a formal complaint, ignoring the advice of his best friend, Bono. This type of blatant discrimination was widespread and tolerated in cities like Pittsburgh in 1950s America.

Most families experience tension, and this family is no exception. In addition to the tensions between father and son, the already complicated

Bono: Your daddy got a promotion on the rubbish. He gonna be the first colored driver. Ain't got to do nothin' but sit up there and read the paper, like them white fellas.

Lyons: Hey, Pop, if you knew how to read, you'd be all right.

Bono: Nah, nah. You mean if the nigger knew how to drive, he'd be all right. Been fighting with them people about driving and ain't even got a license.

Denzel Washington's character aspires to a better job with higher pay in the award-winning movie *Fences*.

Figure 1.1.   *Fences* (2016, Paramount Pictures). Produced by Molly Allen, Todd Black, Eli Bush, Allegra Clegg et al. Directed by Denzel Washington. *Fences* provides a moving portrayal of the complex challenges faced by a loving couple coping with racism, poverty, discrimination, adultery, family tensions, and the protagonist's personal demons.

relationship between Troy and Rose is threatened by Troy's history of infidelity and especially by a new and substantive relationship he develops with another woman who subsequently bears his daughter. Troy's mistress dies during the delivery, and Rose – despite some misgivings – agrees to adopt and raise the child, and she subsequently experiences great happiness from her continuing role as a mother. Rose notes, "I'll take care of your baby for you. 'Cause, like you say, she innocent. You can't visit the sins of the father upon the child. Motherless child's got a hard time."

Gadsden et al. (2015) provide an excellent overview of the role of fathers in African American communities.

Movies About Families That Will Teach You About Culture

There are literally *thousands* of films that revolve around family dynamics, but we believe some are especially useful in helping you understand how families are an integral part of every cultural group, differing in traditions, patterns of interaction between generations, and power dynamics. *Fences* is an excellent place to start; here are some other films that will help you learn about multiculturalism.

Prejudice, Discrimination, Oppression, Racism, and Ethnocentrism

American History X (1998) is a powerful film about racism and hate. It stars Edward Norton in the role of Derek Vineyard, a man released from prison after serving 3 years for killing two Black men who had attempted to break into his food truck. Vineyard had been a Neo Nazi skinhead, someone taught to hate Black people and other racialized people by his father (who was eventually killed by a Black man). Derek's younger brother, Danny, is following in his older brother's footsteps, but Derek has changed while in prison, and he tries to dissuade his brother from embracing the hate that had consumed his life and resulted in his incarceration. The film includes a scene of unforgettable cruelty in which Derek stomps on a Black man's head after forcing him to bite into a curb, and it illustrates the ways in which racialized groups band together in a prison setting. The many ways in which racism affects Black families is described by St. Jean and Feagin (1998).

Seth: Who do you hate, Danny?

Danny Vinyard: I hate anyone that isn't White Protestant.

Seth: Why?

Danny Vinyard: They're a burden to the advancement of the White race. Some of them are all right, I guess...

A racist White Nationalist attempts to justify his bigotry in *American History X*.

Cultural Identity, Acculturation, Assimilation

The Hundred-Foot Journey (2014) is a delightful film that we highly recommend. This film is directed by Lasse Hallström and stars Helen Mirren. It opens with a scene of senseless political violence in which an Indian family's restaurant is burned to the ground, and the mother – the restaurant's main cook – is burned to death. Led by a stern but loving father, the family leaves India and wanders around Europe looking for a new home. When their van breaks down in the south of France, the family settles in Saint-Antonin-Noble-Val and opens an Indian restaurant called *"Le Maison Mumbai."* Unfortunately, the restaurant is across the street from a very snooty French restaurant run by Helen Mirren's character, Madame Mallory. Her restaurant, *"Le Saule Pleureur,"* has one Michelin star, and Madam Mallory is determined to get a second one. She deeply resents the newcomers who have opened their restaurant across the street from hers, and she does everything possible to see that they fail. However, her sous chef, Marguerite, becomes romantically involved with Hassan, the Indian man who is the main chef for Maison Mumbai. Marguerite befriended the family when their van initially broke down, and she is consistently supportive (although a bit frustrated when Hassan, who eventually comes to work for Madame Mallory, is clearly the better person to become head chef, leading the way to the second Michelin star). Hassan has been fascinated by food since childhood, and he has a sense of taste that is the gastronomic equivalent of perfect pitch in a musician. There are numerous clashes between Indian and French cultural habits and practices in the film; for example, Papa Kadam is determined to bargain hard for the best possible rate for a night's lodging in a hotel, and he refuses to listen to his son who tells him this type of negotiation simply doesn't happen in France. There are also racial tensions and misunderstandings that have to be overcome as romantic relationships develop between Marguerite and Hassan, and – eventually – between the domineering father and Madam Mallory.

> **Madame Mallory:** What is this flavor that is fighting against the chicken?
>
> **Hassan:** I added some spices for flavor to the sauce, and coriander for garnish and freshness.
>
> **Madame Mallory:** But why change a recipe that is 200 years old?
>
> **Hassan:** Because, madam, maybe 200 years is long enough.
>
> An Indian chef attempts to improve on classic French recipies in *The Hundred-Foot Journey*.

The film offers a good example of Indian family life, and it illustrates some of the challenges associated with assimilation into a new and often foreign culture. Morris et al. (2015) describe an approach to understanding families and culture that they describe as "polycultural psychology"; this approach emphasizes the interaction of various cultural influences and the fact that a given individual may have multiple cultural identities.

Value Conflicts, Value Orientations

Black or White (2014) is a film based on real events. It tells the story of an affluent White grandfather (played by Kevin Costner) left alone to raise his biracial granddaughter (Jillian Estell) after his wife is killed in a car wreck. His resolve is pitted against the will of the maternal grandmother (Rowena Jeffers, played by Octavia Spencer), who seeks custody, believing her granddaughter should be brought up by a Black family and taught to appreciate Black values, beliefs and customs while surrounded by "her own people." Grandparents often play a pivotal role in Black families, and it is not uncommon for grandparents to fill the role of parents when a child's parents cannot fill their expected role. The film nicely illustrates this grandmother's

Figure 1.2. *Black or White* (2014, BlackWhite, Sunlight, Treehouse Films, Venture Forth). Produced by Robert Ogden Barnum, Bryan Binder, Mike Binder, Kevin Costner et al. Directed by Mike Binder. *Black or White* stars Kevin Costner, seen here learning to brush his Black granddaughter's hair.

> **Elliot Anderson:** So, yes, we're different, you and I. You want to submit that? Submit it. We have different skin colors. Is that the first thing I notice when I see a black man, the color of his skin? Yes. Submit away. Because I can go ahead and submit that that's the first thing you see when you see a white guy. Now, I don't know why that is any more than I know why when I see a good-looking woman the first things I notice are her breasts, because I do. But if I move on to my next thought quick enough, I'm not a pervert, all right? I'm not a bad guy. I'm just mildly flawed. It's the same thing with race. It's not my first thoughts that count, it's my second, third, and fourth thought, and each and every case I'm in, it comes down to the same thing: the action and interaction I'm having with the person that I'm interacting with!

> Kevin Costner's character acknowledges the
> salience of race in *Black or White*.

commitment to raising her granddaughter and her role as the family matriarch. The situation is complicated by the fact that Reggie, the biological father, is addicted to crack and Elliot Anderson (Kevin Costner's character) is a functional alcoholic. It is never clear how Anderson's daughter became involved with her Black boyfriend, but the film leaves the viewer guessing that she was also addicted to crack cocaine, and she died during childbirth. Anderson is a privileged and wealthy attorney who can send his granddaughter to one of the finest private schools in Los Angeles; however, he is also a lonely and isolated man who can never offer his granddaughter the kind of loving support found in her Black grandmother's extended family home. A custody hearing is scheduled, presided over by a Black female judge. Reggie, the biological father, also is hoping to gain a daughter, but any credibility he might have had as a potential father figure is lost when the judge realizes he is unable to spell his daughter's name. Anyone interested in learning more about the challenges associated with transracial adoption can benefit from reading *Parenting in Transracial Adoption: Real Questions and Real Answers* (Hoyt-Oliver et al., 2016).

Social Norms and Norm Violations

Social norms are profoundly important. They inform us about what to eat and how to eat it; whom and when and how to marry; where we should live and who we should be living with; and how much we should be paid for the work we do. We don't burp or fart in public (at least in Western societies) – and we're embarrassed when we do – because of social norms.

Solomon Asch (1956) demonstrated the salience of social norms in a series of classic studies that pitted the normative opinions of confederates against objective reality (judgments of the length of a line). Social norms inevitably won out over common sense and good judgment.

We rarely take time to think about these norms, but they define the warp and woof of our existence. They are most often conveyed informally (e.g., no one typically *tells* us how men and women are expected to behave differently – we just *know*). Often, roles and norms are conveyed most powerfully through the media.

Tomboy (2011) is a charming French film that deals with sexual identity issues in a 10-year-old child, Laure, who has just moved to a new neighborhood with her parents and her 6-year-old sister. Laure has always dressed like a boy, and she has a boy's haircut, so the children in her new neighborhood assume she is a boy. Laure likes the assumption the other children make, so she impulsively introduces herself as "Mikael" and she is accepted as the newest kid in the neighborhood – a new boy. The summer progresses quite happily, but Mikael's situation becomes more complicated when an attractive neighborhood girl named Lisa begins to pay attention to the new neighbor. When school starts, Mikael's deception becomes apparent, and she has to deal with disapproving parents and teachers who are clearly uncomfortable with gender ambiguity. This is a beautiful film, and it is highly recommended.

Rayan: We hear you're a girl. We're gonna check that.

Lisa: Stop it! What do you think you're doing?

Rayan: We're gonna check if she's really a girl.

Lisa: Leave him alone.

Rayan: You're right. It's YOU who'll check.

Lisa: No, I won't.

Rayan: If she's a girl, then you kissed her. It's disgusting. Right?

Lisa: Yes, it's disgusting.

Rayan: Then, you're gonna do it.

[*Lisa pulls down Laure's pants*]

Two friends experience a tense and awkward confrontation in the film *Tomboy*.

Figure 1.3. ◦ *Tomboy* (2011, Hold Up Films, Arte France Cinéma, Lilies Films). Produced by Rémi Burah, Bénédicte Couvreur, & Tiphaine Perin. Directed by Céline Sciamma. A 10-year-old girl moves to a new neighborhood and adopts an identity as Mickael, a transgender boy. The film beautifully illustrates the tensions involved in being a transgender child.

Films like *Tomboy* underscore how very much our lives are anchored in our assumptions about gender. Typically, the very first thing a new parent is told about their newborn child is its gender ("It's a boy!"); if not told, it is often the first question that a parent asks. Gender is even embedded in our language (e.g., we don't have dedicated, single, gender-neutral pronoun in English), and phrases like "female neurosurgeon" still remind us that most neurosurgeons are men.

Readers who want to learn more about working with transgender clients will benefit from reading *Affirmative Counseling for Transgender and Gender Diverse Clients* by lore dickey and Jae Puckett (2023).

Stereotyping

Crash is a 2004 film starring Sandra Bullock, Don Cheadle, and Matt Dillon. It is a powerful film that offers compelling illustrations for how families are affected by race, racial bias, and stereotypes about race.

Crash (not to be confused with the 1996 David Cronenberg film with the same title) takes place over 36 hours in multiple settings in Los Angeles; the film involves numerous people, all of whom have interlocking lives. Although addressing racial tension, the film refuses to pander to popular stereotypes of racial groups while still showing how these stereotypes affect the lives of those people who hold them. The movie opens with two Black men discussing whether Black people tip less in restaurants (and whether this practice is the cause or the effect of the poor service they receive in White restaurants). Almost immediately after this discussion, the two men carjack an expensive SUV. The car is owned by a White district attorney and his wife, Jean Cabot (played by Sandra Bullock), and the wife's already entrenched racial biases are only solidified after the car-jacking incident. In a subsequent scene, Bullock's privileged character is clearly annoyed with her Latina housekeeper, although deeply fond of her at the same time. Jean appears depressed, and she reports, "I am angry all the time... and I don't know why."

Somewhat later a Black film director and his Black wife are stopped and frisked by two White police officers, and the wife is clearly and inappropriately sexually assaulted during the search. The husband does nothing, having learned early in life that Black men don't question White police officers. The wife is furious with her husband's failure to confront the abusive police officer, and she finds the situation clearly supports her belief that her successful husband is an "**Oreo cookie**" (i.e., black on the outside, but clearly white inside). The White police officer who was sexually inappropriate during the search is concerned about his sick father and tries to get assistance for him; however, he becomes frustrated when he must deal with a social service worker named Shaniqua, somebody presumably Black. In a dramatic scene,

Anthony: You see any White people in there waiting an hour and thirty-two minutes for a plate of spaghetti? Huh? And how many cups of coffee did we get?

Peter: You don't drink coffee and I didn't want any.

Anthony: That woman poured cup after cup to every single White person around us. Did she even ask you if you wanted any?

Peter: We didn't get any coffee that you didn't want and I didn't order, and this is evidence of racial discrimination? Did you happen to notice our waitress was Black?

Anthony: And Black women don't think in stereotypes? You tell me something man. When was the last time you met one who didn't think she knew everything about your lazy ass? Before you even open your mouth, huh?

Two Black men discuss poor service in a restaurant and wonder if it reflects racism in the film *Crash*.

the sexist Sergeant Ryan (played by Matt Dillon) winds up saving the life of Christine, the same woman he had earlier sexually assaulted.

Other vignettes include a Hispanic locksmith committed to keeping his young daughter safe in a dangerous neighborhood, an East Asian man (a Korean identified as "just another Chinaman") involved in trafficking, and an angry Persian shopkeeper who hires someone to defend his store after his shop is repeatedly robbed and the police do nothing. The man who sells the gun to the shopkeeper and his daughter becomes angry when they speak Farsi in his presence, and he can't understand what they are saying.

As the film ends, we realize that everyone's life relates to the lives of everyone else in the film, and the movie makes the point that we are all struggling, sentient beings who face similar challenges and have similar fears. We can't think of a better film to get viewers to examine their own stereotypes and biases. Hoxha et al. (2007) examined the impact of the movie *Crash* as an experiential tool in a graduate-level multicultural counseling class at Loyola University Chicago. The authors found:

> *Crash* appeared to be an effective teaching tool for enhancing knowledge and awareness. The movie helped students to: see the impact of stereotypes on others (53% strongly agree), to learn about their own biases (63% agree), and the small group discussions helped them increase their own self-awareness (60% strongly agree).
>
> ... When students were asked in an open-ended question [about] what they learned from the movie, several key themes emerged, such as facts about stereotypes (e.g., how common stereotypes are, how others are hurt by them), how stereotypes manifest in our society (they can be expressed verbally or nonverbally), actions the students wanted to take personally to counteract stereotypes or change society, and awareness of stereotypes and biases the students hold personally. (n.p.)

Indigenous People

Once Were Warriors (1994) is a powerful film about the life of a modern-day Māori family living in a slum in Auckland, New Zealand. Jake, the father, is an alcoholic who abuses everyone in his family when he is drunk, which is often, but who is loving, kind, and generous to Beth, his wife, and to his five children when he is sober. He is unable to hold a job because of his alcoholism, and his estranged son has joined a Māori street gang.

It is interesting to note the influence of American culture on this Māori family; for example, there are pictures of Mike Tyson and Malcolm X in Beth

Beth Heke: You raped a 13-year-old girl and sat here drinking with her father while the rest of us buried her!

Bully: You should learn to control your Missus.

Beth Heke: Sneaking around the house laying your filthy fucking hands on my baby!

> A mother confronts the man who raped her daughter in the
> New Zealand film *Once Were Warriors.*

and Jake's bedroom. Jack blames his wife for tolerating his abuse ("You know what I'm like when I'm drunk"), and it is hard to understand why Beth doesn't leave an intolerable situation. However, although the family is clearly dysfunctional, it is also one in which the members love each other, and Beth's enduring and long-suffering love for her abusive husband is the glue that holds the family together.

Jake's 13-year-old daughter, Grace, spends more time with her boyfriend than with her family. One night she is raped by a drunken family friend, but

Figure 1.4.   *Once Were Warriors* (1994, Communicado Productions). Produced by Andrew Mason and Robin Scholes. Directed by Lee Tamahori. This is a powerful film that illustrates the challenges associated with alcoholism, domestic abuse, and life in a Māori community in Aotearoa (New Zealand).

her father insists that she continue to show respect to the friend. Grace, depressed, alone, and discouraged, dies by suicide by hanging herself in the family's backyard. Neither parent knows about the rape until they read about it in Grace's diary. Beth brings the diary to a bar to show Jake, who proceeds to beat his friend (the rapist) to death.

The film's title deliberately contrasts the proud history of Māori warriors with the lives of contemporary Māori people, many of whom now live in urban slums, having lost much of their cultural identity. This movie ranks with our all-time favorite New Zealand films (the other two are *The Piano* and *Heavenly Creatures*).

Additional Films About Families

Literally thousands of movies have revolved around the joys – and oftentimes the tensions – associated with being a part of a family. While we can't discuss all of these, we can point you to some of our favorites. They include *Wonder* (2017), *Akeelah and the Bee* (2006), *Remember the Titans* (2000), *Big Fish* (2003), *Little Miss Sunshine* (2006), *The Boy Who Harnessed the Wind* (2019), *Wadjda* (2012), *King Richard* (2021), and *Ruby Bridges* (1998). Older favorite films that celebrate families include *Pelle the Conqueror* (1987) and *Antonio's Line* (1995). We also enjoy films that celebrate non-traditional families like *The Kids Are All Right* (2010), *All About My Mother* (1999), *Captain Fantastic* (2016), *Love, Simon* (2018), and *Tell Me That You Love Me, Junie Moon* (1970). More recently, Danny watched and wrote about *Ghostlight* (2024), a movie that celebrates the way that the arts can help a grieving family heal (Wedding, 2024).

While most films demonstrate the positive influence of families, others document the deleterious effects of bad parenting. Examples include *Dolores Claiborne* (1995), *Mommie Dearest* (1981), *Nuts* (1987), *Prince of Tides* (1991), *Ordinary People* (1980), *The Florida Project* (2017), *August: Osage County* (2013), *Running With Scissors* (2006), *This Boy's Life* (1993), *The Glass Castle* (2017), *Hillbilly Elegy* (2020), and *Dead Poets Society* (1989).

Tanner et al. (2003, p. 355) identified themes about couples and families in 23 Disney animated classic films and isolated four overarching themes:
(a) Family relationships are a strong priority.
(b) Families are diverse, but the diversity is often simplified.
(c) Fathers are elevated, while mothers are marginalized.
(d) Couple relationships are created by "love at first sight," are easily maintained, and are often characterized by gender-based power differentials.

Hu et al. (2022, n.p.) examined the ways in which English-language films could be used to enhance language learning in Chinese students. They note that films can "intuitively show the humanistic style, historical geography, cultures, and customs of English countries, and then cultivate students' western cultural literacy."

Dunham and Dermer (2020) have identified ways films can be used in working with African American families. Likewise, Dermer and Hutchings (2000) have written about the ways in which movies can be incorporated in family therapy, and they include a helpful list of relevant films. When assessing the appropriateness for including cinematherapy when treating a family, they recommend the following steps:

1. Identify presenting problems and goals for therapy.
2. Assess strengths (i.e., interests, hobbies, activities, type of employment).
3. Determine clients' ability to understand the content of the film and recognize similarities and differences between themselves and the characters.
4. Take into account issues of diversity (i.e., culture, race, ethnicity, socioeconomic status, sexual orientation, and gender) when choosing a film.
5. Based on assessment, match clients with movies.

Critical Thinking Questions About Families and Culture

- How did your family treat mealtimes? Was it a significant part of your own cultural heritage?
- Can you share a traditional dish from your culture and its significance?
- Do cultural dishes change if you've immigrated to another country?
- What holidays did your family celebrate?
- If you or your family don't celebrate Christmas, how do you feel about it being the central holiday to the year when other cultural holidays from non-White groups are ignored in cultural calendars?
- What particular challenges do multigenerational families face?
- Were gender roles clearly defined in your own family?
- Do you have family heirlooms that have been passed down across generations in your family?
- What is the significance of birth order? Does this significance vary across cultures?
- Is it disrespectful to ask someone, "What is your cultural background?" or "Where are you from?" (e.g., asking a person of Asian descent what part of Asia their ancestors came from)?

Further Exploration

If you only have time for one article, read:

Van Hook, J., & Glick, J. E. (2020). Spanning borders, cultures, and generations: A decade of research on immigrant families. *Journal of Marriage and Family, 82*(1), 224–243. https://doi.org/10.1111/jomf.12621

If you have time for one chapter, read:

Chuang, S. S. (2019). The complexities of immigration and families: Theoretical perspectives and current issues. In B. H. Fiese, M. Celano, K. Deater-Deckard, E. N. Jouriles, & M. A. Whisman (Eds.), *APA handbook of contemporary family psychology: Applications and broad impact of family psychology* (pp. 437–455). American Psychological Association. https://doi.org/10.1037/0000100-027

If you have time to read a book about families and culture, make it:

Hays, P. A. (2022). *Addressing cultural complexities in counseling and clinical practice: An intersectional approach* (4th ed.). American Psychological Association. https://doi.org/10.1037/0000277-011

References

Asch, S. E. (1956). Studies of independence and conformity: A minority of one against a unanimous majority. *Psychological Monographs: General and Applied, 70*, 1–170.

Dermer, S. B., & Hutchings, J. B. (2000). Utilizing movies in family therapy: Applications for individuals, couples, and families. *American Journal of Family Therapy, 28*(2), 163–180. https://doi.org/10.1080/019261800261734

dickey, l., & Puckett, J. (2023). *Affirmative therapy with transsexual and gender nonconforming patients*. Hogrefe.

Dunham, S. M., & Dermer, S. B. (2020). Cinematherapy with African American couples. *Journal of Clinical Psychology, 76*(8), 1472–1482. https://doi.org/10.1002/jclp.22999

Gadsden, V. L., Davis, J. E., & Johnson, C. J. (2015). African American fathers and families within cultural and historical perspective. In J. L. Roopnarine (Ed.), *Fathers across cultures: The importance, roles, and diverse practices of dads* (pp. 155–182). Praeger/ABC-CLIO.

Hoxha, D., Speight, S. L., Gomez, K. L., Steele, J., Merle, C., & Moallem, I. B. (2007). *Crash: A preliminary investigation of an experiential exercise* [Conference session]. APA 115th Annual Convention, San Francisco, CA, United States.

Hoyt-Oliver, J., Straughan, H. H., & Schooler, J. E. (2016). *Parenting in transracial adoption: Real questions and real answers*. Praeger/ABC-CLIO. https://doi.org/10.5040/9798400695247

Hu, N., Li, S., Li, L., & Xu, H. (2022). The educational function of English children's movies from the perspective of multiculturalism under deep learning and artificial intelligence. *Frontiers in Psychology, 12*, Article 759094. https://doi.org/10.3389/fpsyg.2021.759094

Morris, M. W., Chiu, C.-y., & Liu, Z. (2015). Polycultural psychology. *Annual Review of Psychology, 66,* 631–659. https://doi.org/10.1146/annurev-psych-010814-015001

St. Jean, Y., & Feagin, J. R. (1998). The family costs of White racism: The case of African American families. *Journal of Comparative Family Studies, 29*(2), 297–312. https://doi.org/10.3138/jcfs.29.2.297

Tanner, L. R., Haddock, S. A., Zimmerman, T. S., & Lund, L. K. (2003). Images of couples and families in Disney feature-length animated films. *American Journal of Family Therapy, 31*(5), 355–373. https://doi.org/10.1080/01926180390223987

Wedding, D. (2024, November). A clinical psychologist goes to the movies, Part 3: *Ghostlight*. Hogrefe. https://www.hogrefe.com/eu/article/a-clinical-psychologist-goes-to-the-movies-part-3-1

Chapter 2
Relationships

"Man, I told you not to go in that house."

Chris gets advice from his friend Rod, who believes nothing good can come from his buddy's decision to meet his White girlfriend's parents in *Get Out*.

Questions to Consider While Watching
Get Out (2017)

- Are interracial relationships becoming more accepted in the United States?
- Are there differences in the ways a Black/White relationship is perceived as compared to an Asian/White relationship?
- Does the thought of a Black man having sex with a White woman leave you feeling more uncomfortable than a White man having sex with a Black woman? Why?
- Are Black men fetishized for their anatomy, but not seen as appropriate long-term romantic partners? Why or why not?
- Can you identify at least five examples of microaggressions in the film?
- Why does Rose's father's insistence that "I would have voted for Obama a third time if I could" leave Chris feeling so uncomfortable?
- Is the scene where a White police officer insists on seeing Chris's driver's license, even though he was only a passenger, realistic? Are there data documenting Blacks are treated differently when stopped by police officers (i.e., is "driving while Black" a real phenomenon)?
- Is the portrayal of hypnosis in the film realistic?
- What first gives away the fact that Walter the groundskeeper and Georgina the maid are somehow different from other Black people?
- What is the basis for cultural stereotypes about the sexual appetites and prowess of Black men?

- How does the opening scene in the film relate to the experiences of Trayvon Martin and other young Black men shot by police officers?
- Did the racial tensions portrayed so vividly in *Get Out* play a role in the 2016 and 2024 Presidential elections, or even global politics and human rights violations in the Middle East?
- Jordan Peele is biracial. How might this cultural background have prepared him to make this film?
- Jordan Peele is married to a White Jewish woman, and along with other celebrities, signed an open letter to President Biden in 2023, thanking him for the financial support of Israel's military incursion and what some like Amnesty International are calling genocide of Palestinians following the events of October 7, 2023. He was criticized for this, as many felt he ignored systemic oppression of people of color, even though he made a powerful film about racism and system oppression, *Get Out*. Is this criticism fair? Why or why not?
- Do Black men have a cultural obligation to date Black women? Does the same obligation apply to Black women? Why or why not?
- In the United States, there are almost three times as many interracial marriages between Black men and White women than there are between Black women and White men. What accounts for this disparity?
- What is the significance of skin color in the African American community?
- Rachel Dolezal identified as a Black woman and achieved a leadership position in the National Association for the Advancement of Colored People (NAACP). However, she was later "outed" as a White woman with two white parents (Brubaker, 2016). Can someone "take on" a cultural identity by choice?

Relationships and Culture

Love is one of the most profound human emotions, and it is complicated in almost everyone's life. However, there are often particular challenges in relationships when cultures collide. This can occur because of race or ethnicity, gender, sexual orientation, age, religion, political affiliation, or socioeconomic class. The situation is further complicated because we have multiple cultural identities, and they may change as we grow up or grow older. Some couples may joyously celebrate multiple holidays (Christmas, Rosh Hashanah, Eid, Diwali, etc.), but for other families the decision to spend the holidays with only one cultural group from their multicultural family may be a source of considerable conflict. Negotiating the parameters of an intercultural relationship may become even more difficult when children are involved, and families have to decide whether their children are going to grow up attending to one cultural or religious practice over another; with a specific worry that due to White supremacy, Christian or White culture is more likely to win out. As an alternative, Abdulrehman and Williams (2025) explore the idea of a more intersectional approach of having statutory holidays that reflect all cultural communities in the #CelebrateEverything initiative.

Relationships and *Get Out*

Get Out (2017) is well-known comedian Jordan Peele's directorial debut; it is a stunning first film and a major commercial success. Peele became the first Black writer–director to earn more than $100 million theatrically with a debut feature.

Although there are funny moments, most notably the comic relief provided by the main character's best friend, Rod Williams (played by Lil Rel Howery), the film belongs in the horror genre, and it pays homage to other classic horror films including *Rosemary's Baby*, *The Stepford Wives*, and the original *Invasion of the Body Snatchers*.

Get Out revolves around a romantic biracial relationship between Chris Washington (played by Daniel Kaluuya) and Rose Armitage (Allison Williams). Chris is a photographer, and Rose initially seems to be an independent, freethinking, and liberal woman who is genuinely in love with Chris. She explains that her parents are eager to meet the new man in her life, but she acknowledges that she has not yet told them he is a Black man. Chris is

Rod Williams: Then he sent me some weird pictures… I'm like man that's Andre Hayworth… this dude been missing for 6 months. Right? So I do all my research you know cause as a TSA agent… you know, you guys are detectives, you know, I got the same training. We might know more than y'all sometimes, you know cause we are dealing with some terrorist shit, so… but that's a totally different story. So look I, I go do my… my detective work, right? And I start putting pieces together. And see this is what I came up with. Their probably abducting Black people, brain-washing them and making them slaves. Or sex slaves. Not just regular slaves, but sex slaves and shit. See? I don't know if it's the hypnosis that's making them slaves or what not, but all I know is they already got two brothas we know and there could be a whole bunch of brothas they got already. What's the next move?

A TSA agent expresses his concerns for his missing friend in *Get Out*.

anxious about meeting her White parents, despite her assurances that they are politically liberal and will be entirely comfortable with the relationship. Chris's anxiety is heightened after conversations with his best friend Rob, who feels that Chris shouldn't be dating a White woman, much less going to her childhood home to meet her parents.

Chris and Rose clearly come from very different backgrounds; Chris was orphaned at the age of 11 when his mother was killed in a car wreck, while Rose led a privileged life in an affluent suburb as the daughter of a neurosurgeon father and a psychiatrist mother. On their way to Rose's home, she accidently kills a deer, and she becomes indignant when a police officer interviews both her and Chris, insisting on seeing his driver's license as well as hers. She is adamant that he has no right to ask for his identification because she was driving, and he was only a passenger. This interaction between a Black man and a White police officer sets the stage for a series of Black/White exchanges still to come.

Chris is uncomfortable throughout the visit with Rose's family, and he seeks out the only two Black people who are available to him: the groundskeeper (Marcus Henderson) and the maid (Betty Gabriel). Rose's father, Dean Armitage (Bradley Whitford), apologizes for the blatant racism apparent in a White couple being waited on by two Black servants; however, he explains that they had both worked for his parents, and after they died, he "didn't have the heart to fire them." These two individuals, however, respond like polite zombies, and there is nothing Black about them. At a subsequent social event,

Figure 2.1.   *Get Out* (2017, Universal Pictures). Produced by Jason Blum, Marcei Brown, Phillip Dawe, Gerard DiNardi, et al. Directed by Jordan Peele. Chris is pleased to discover another African American at a party, only to realize that this man has become a sexual slave.

another Black man is present with his older, affluent White wife; however, he too is oddly and overly polite, and nothing like the Black brother Chris was looking for. The film hints at the fact that the Black husband exists for little else than giving sexual pleasure to the White woman he married, and on whom he now seemingly dotes.

Although Chris is educated, sophisticated, and a gifted photographer, everyone at the party held in his honor seems only to be able to acknowledge him in physical terms, noting his fortunate "genetic makeup" and alluding to his presumed sexual prowess. The guests go out of their way to acknowledge the accomplishments of Jesse Owens and Tiger Woods, but their praise for Blacks only extends to athletes and musicians. (Dean, the father, notes that his father was a contender for the 1936 Olympic games, and he would have competed had he not been beaten for a slot on the US Olympic team by Jesse Owens. This scene subtly underscores the racist view that Blacks have displaced many Whites in employment and academic situations.)

The film's ending is surprising, dramatic, and unforgettable. We won't spoil it for you here, but we strongly encourage you to watch this splendid film, noting everything it has to say about racism, culture, and the complexity of mixed cultural relationships.

Movies About Relationships That Will Teach You About Culture

Relationships – happy, sad, romantic, jaded, doomed, or enduring – are the very stuff movies are made of, and you will find a plethora of films that will teach you about how relationships are affected by cultural identity. In the following sections, we will introduce you to a few of our favorite films that relate to multiculturalism.

Prejudice, Discrimination, Oppression, Racism, and Ethnocentrism

Monster's Ball (2002) is a powerful film about family dysfunction in three generations of prison guards, and the film illustrates how two suffering people – a White man and a Black woman – can use a sexual relationship to assuage the almost unbearable pain that results from the death of their children. The film stars Billy Bob Thornton as Hank Grotowski, a middle-aged prison guard. His father, a racist and tyrannical patriarch, is Buck (Peter Boyle), and his adult son is Sonny (Heath Ledger). Buck and Hank share a home after Hank's mother kills herself. Hank and his son both work on death row, and both share their father's racist views, although the intensity of hate and racism is attenuated in each successive generation. Hank criticizes his son for becoming ill and vomiting while accompanying an inmate to his execution; this criticism leads to a tense interaction between father and son. Sonny pulls a gun on his father, remarking "You hate me, don't you?" Hank confirms that this is true ("Yes, I hate you. Always have."). Sonny replies, "Well, I always loved you," before shooting himself in the head. Hank quits his job at the prison after his son's suicide.

The man whose execution was botched because of Sonny's illness was Lawrence Musgrove (Sean "Diddy" Combs), married to Leticia Musgrove, played by Halle Berry. After his execution, Leticia supports herself and her son by waiting tables at a local restaurant. However, she is unable to earn enough to pay her rent, and in addition, she has to bring her obese son to work with her to control his eating disorder. She is frequently late for work because her car is constantly breaking down. Once this happens, she and her son must walk home in the rain, and her son is struck by a hit-and-run driver and badly injured. Several people drive by without stopping to assist, as Hank does initially. However, he has a change of heart and comes back to drive Leticia and her son to the hospital where the boy is declared dead. Since no one else knows what to do next, Hank drives Leticia home.

Hank frequents the restaurant where Leticia works, and he gets in the habit of driving her home because she doesn't have a car. On one of these trips, it becomes clear to each that both of them have lost their sons. Leticia invites Hank into her home for a drink, and they find temporary relief from their pain by getting drunk and becoming lovers. However, the film is not about interracial love, but rather about the fact that suffering is an integral part of the human condition, and sometimes others can help us ease the almost unbearable pain associated with simply living our lives.

What the hell those niggers doing out there? I said something to you. You hear me? .... Damn porch monkeys. Be moving in here soon. Sitting next to me. Watching my TV. There was a time when they knew their place. Wasn't none of this mixing going on. Your mother, she hated them niggers, too. Tell them to get the hell off my property.

Buck, Hank's racist Dad, is incensed that two Black children have come to visit his grandson in *Monster's Ball*.

Figure 2.2.   *Monster's Ball* (2001, Lion's Gate, Lee Daniels Productions). Produced by Milo Addica, Michael Burns, Lee Daniels, Eric Kopeloff, et al. Directed by Marc Forster. *Monster's Ball* stars Billy Bob Thronton and Halle Berry; Thornton's character is a racist prison guard who develops an unlikely romantic relationship with Berry's character, a Black woman whose husband has just been executed in the prison and whose son has been killed in a tragic traffic accident.

At one point in the film, Hank's father, Buck, has an ugly, racist encounter with Leticia and tells her Hank is only sleeping with her because he wanted to experience sex with a Black woman. Hank has the bigoted old man put in a nursing home and invites Leticia to move in with him. One day while Hank is away, she discovers some drawings her husband had made while in prison and realizes that Hank was involved in her husband's execution. However, this discovery does not lead to the expected confrontation. Instead, she wearily greets Hank with ice cream when he returns home. As they sit on the porch, eating their ice cream, Hank remarks, "I think we're going to be alright."

Monster's Ball (a British term for a convict's last night before his execution) shows us two deeply flawed human beings struggling to find relief from the pain of existence. However, the film is also worth viewing in part because it demonstrates how very ugly racism can be, and how shared suffering can bring at least temporary relief from pain and help two people get past a

Meena: What about me? What about me? I've never asked you for anything! Never expected anything! I'm 24 years old, and I'm still here! Stuck here! You think I'm happy? I love him. That's not a crime, is it?

Kinnu: You call this love? When all you have done is bring such shame upon our heads?

Meena: I didn't do anything! They barged in!

Jay: Don't answer back! At least have the decency to be sorry!

Meena: I am sorry about this mess, but I'm not sorry I'm in love with him.

> Meena's Indian parents are convinced that her love for a Black man will bring shame upon the family in *Mississippi Masala*.

history of racial stereotyping. Billy Bob Thornton is unforgettable as the suffering father, and Halle Berry won an Oscar for Best Actress in a Leading Role for playing Leticia.

Cultural Identity, Acculturation, Assimilation

Mississippi Masala (1991) is a somewhat dated but still powerful film starring Denzel Washington as Demetrius, an ambitious young Black man who owns a carpet cleaning business, and Sarit Choudhury as Meena, the beautiful 24-year-old daughter of a prosperous Indian couple who had to leave their home and property in Uganda when Idi Amin came to power and forced all emigrants to leave the country in 1972 because he desired a pure "Black Africa." (The British brought Indian workers to Uganda to help build railroads; many stayed and became prosperous landowners who were often more successful and more wealthy than indigenous people in Uganda.) *Masala* is a Hindu word referring to mixed spices, a mixture producing richer flavor than could ever be produced by a single spice.

Jay, Meena's father, is a proud man who was trained as a lawyer; however, after emigrating to the United States, he is reduced to owning a small, shabby roadside motel in Greenwood, Mississippi, with his wife and daughter cleaning toilets and making beds. He deeply resents having his property confiscated and being expelled from his home in Uganda, and his hatred extends well past Idi Amin to all Blacks.

There is a close, cohesive, and extended Indian network in Greenwood, and the entire community becomes concerned when a romantic relationship develops between Demetrius and Meena. The Black community is initially friendly, but eventually just as concerned about this complicated interracial relationship, especially after the Indians boycott Demetrius's rug cleaning business.

Like many Indians, Meena's parents had expected her to marry someone in the Greenwood Indian community, preferably someone of their choosing. However, they are concerned that she might be "too dark" to find a suitable husband, demonstrating colorism in many communities of color, including the South Asian community. The folly of her parents' obsession with her skin tone is underscored by her infatuation with the much darker Demetrius; however, she is warned that a woman who needs a husband can be poor and light-skinned, or rich and dark-skinned – but *never* poor and dark-skinned! The significance of skin color is reviewed in a scholarly book by Kimberly Norwood titled *Color Matters: Skin Tone Bias and the Myth of a Postracial America* (2014). Writing in *PsycCRITIQUES*, Martha Banks (2014, n.p.) noted:

> *Colorism*, similar to racism, is an ongoing consequence of the myth of White superiority, manifested as "the allocation of privilege and disadvantage according to the lightness or darkness of one's skin" . . . and "the tendency to perceive or

Figure 2.3.   *Mississippi Masala* (1992, Studio Canal Souss, Black River Productions, Channel Four Films, Mirabai Films, Cinecom Pictures, Movie Works). Produced by Lydia Dean Pilcher, Mitch Epstein, Mira Nair, and Michael Nozik. Directed by Mira Nair. Food is always an integral part of culture. *Mississippi Masala* revolves around the intersection of three distinct cultures in three parts of the world: India, Uganda, and Mississippi. This powerful movie deals with racism, class struggle, colorism, displacement, and interracial love.

behave toward members of a racial category based on the lightness or darkness of their skin tone" …. In the United States, educational opportunities, employment, incarceration, and wealth can be linked to skin tone, with definite advantages for people with lighter skin.

Value Conflicts, Value Orientations

Me Before You (2016) is a serious film about the value of life, what's important in life, and the question of one's right to choose to end one's life. The film, an adaptation of Jojo Moyes's best-selling novel, juxtaposes the almost perfect life of a handsome bachelor, Will Traynor, with the life of the protagonist after a traffic accident results in him becoming quadriplegic. He responds to his new situation with bitterness, making life miserable for himself and everyone around him. He has had a variety of caretakers, most of whom quit shortly after starting employment. This changes, somewhat and only slowly, after Lou enters the picture. She is funny, high spirited, and spunky, and she gives as good as she gets. She won't tolerate abuse from Will, and she effectively uses humor to diffuse his despondency and his omnipresent ill humor. Gradually, a bond develops between the two of them, and eventually a love relationship.

Will had made a previous suicide attempt, slashing his wrists, and he still has scars to show for it. However, he made a pact with his parents to live for 6 months, after which they will agree to let him fly to Switzerland to terminate his life if he still insists. Lou learns about this agreement, and she does her best to convince him that (a) she needs him in her life, and (b) life could be rich and rewarding for the two of them if they were together. However, he remains adamant. Lou initially refuses to accompany Will to Switzerland, wanting no part of an assisted suicide. However, he eventually changes her mind, they fly to Switzerland, and she is with him for the final moments of his life. The film ends with Lou in Paris on a favorite street corner, one Will had previously loved and visited often in his fantasy life. He has left her a sizable amount of money with the admonition to live life fully because it is precious.

Me Before You contrasts the beliefs and values of Will's parents, friends, and his new lover with his own value system, one that tells him life is not worth living in a wheelchair, even if deeply loved by family, friends, and a wonderful romantic partner. The viewer finds himself or herself thinking about autonomy, independence, and the freedom of individuals to make fundamental decisions about life – like when to end it. Emanuel et al. (2016)

Will Traynor: I have to tell you something.

Lou Clark: I know. I know about Switzerland, I have known for months. Listen I know this is not how you would have chosen it, but I can make you happy.

Will Traynor: No.

Lou Clark: What?

Will Traynor: No Clarke. This could be a good life, but it's not my life, it's not even close. You never saw be before. I loved my life. I really loved it. I can't be the kind of man who just accepts this.

Lou Clark: You're not giving it a chance, you're not giving me a chance. I have become a whole new person these last six months because of you.

Will Traynor: I know and that's why I can't have you tied to me. I don't want you to miss all the things that someone else can give you. And selfishly I don't what you to look at me one day and feel even the tiniest bit of regret or pity.

Lou Clark: I would never think that!

Will Traynor: You don't know that. I can't watch you wondering around the annex in your crazy dresses. Or see you naked and not be able to... oh Clarke if you have any idea what I want to do to you right now. I can't live like this.

Lou Clark: Please Will! Please!

Will Traynor: Shh. Listen, this, tonight being with you is the most wonderful thing you could have ever done for me. But I need it to end here. No more pain and exhaustion and waking up every morning already wishing it was over. It's not going to get better than this. The doctors know it and I know it. When we get back, I'm going to Switzerland so I'm asking you if you feel the things you say you feel. Come with me.

> A quadriplegic man insists on his right to end his own life when and where he chooses in *Me Before You*.

examined laws and practices for physician-assisted suicide and found that public acceptance was widespread and growing:

> Currently, euthanasia or physician-assisted suicide can be legally practiced in the Netherlands, Belgium, Luxembourg, Colombia, and Canada (Quebec since 2014, nationally as of June 2016). Physician-assisted suicide, excluding euthanasia, is legal in 5 US states (Oregon, Washington, Montana, Vermont, and California) and Switzerland. Public support for euthanasia and physician-assisted suicide in the United States has plateaued since the 1990s (range, 47%–69%). (p. 79)

More recently, the acronym **MAID (medical assistance in dying)** has been widely adopted. MAID is defined as "the practice of a clinician prescribing lethal drugs in response to a direct request from the patient, with a shared understanding that the patient intends to use the medication to bring about the patient's death" (Hanif et al., 2024, p. 347).

Social Norms and Norm Violations

We can't think of a better film to illustrate how relationships are affected by a refusal to accept cultural and societal norms than *Captain Fantastic* (2016). This film revolves around an iconoclastic family led by Ben (played by Viggo Mortensen), the father of six children he and his wife Leslie are raising in the Pacific Northwest. The family rejects celebrating Christmas because it is a bourgeois holiday; instead, they have developed their own holidays (e.g., celebrating "Noam Chomsky Day" because he is "a living humanitarian who's done so much to promote human rights and understanding").

It is an unconventional way to raise children and represents home schooling in the extreme, but all the children seem to be precocious and well educated, able to both kill wild animals and recite Karl Marx. However, there are

Ben: [*commandeering the eulogy from the minister*] First of all, Leslie practiced Buddhism, which to her was a philosophy and not an organized religion. In fact, Leslie abhorred all organized religions. To her, they were the most dangerous fairy tales ever invented, designed to elicit blind obedience and strike fear into the hearts of the innocent and the uninformed. To her, the only thing worse than death would have been the knowledge that her rotting flesh was to be trapped for all eternity inside a big box, and buried in the middle of a fucking golf course. Although the absurdity of being eulogized by someone that didn't even know her has exactly the kind of comedic flourish that Leslie would have cherished. If nothing else, she had a sense of humor. I want to read something to all of you, so you'll know what I mean.

[*pulling out a piece of paper*]

Ben: Leslie's last will and testament. And I quote, "in the event of my death, I, Leslie Abigail Cash, as a Buddhist, wish to be cremated. My funeral, such as it is, shall be a celebration of the life cycle, with music and dancing. After, it is my expressed desire that my ashes shall be taken to a nondescript location, preferably public and heavily populated. At which point my ashes, promptly and unceremoniously, are to be flushed down the nearest toilet."

A grieving but unwelcome husband crashes his wife's funeral in *Captain Fantastic*.

Figure 2.4. *Captain Fantastic* (1992, Electric City Entertainment, ShivHans Pictures). Produced by Declan Baldwin, Samantha Housmen, Lynette Howell Taylor, Monica Levinson, et al. Directed by Matt Ross. An iconoclastic father arrives at a funeral with his six children to ensure his wife won't have to spend eternity in a box, in the provocative film *Captain Fantastic*.

clear and dramatic gaps in their education; this is seen most clearly when Bodevan, the oldest teenage son, kisses a girl for the first time and deeply moved by the moment, promptly proposes marriage.

We only see the mother in flashback moments, because she has been hospitalized for bipolar disorder and is away from the family. While in the hospital, she kills herself, and Ben conveys this information to his children bluntly and as a simple matter of fact, although he is clearly shaken by the news. Much of the tension in the film results from the clashing values of the family – and especially Ben – and his wife's family, led convincingly by Jack, played by Frank Langella, a conventional, successful, and religious individual appalled by the life his son-in-law shares with his grandchildren. Jack and his wife live a very ordinary life in a wealthy White suburb, and they are proud of their very conventional other daughter and her very conventional husband and children. Ben won't let Leslie's sister use euphemisms at the dinner table to describe her sister's "passing"; instead, he insists on bluntly reminding his children that their mother's death resulted from suicide. When the sister expresses concern about the fact that Ben's children don't attend regular schools, Ben quizzes her children and his on the meaning of the Bill of Rights. His children have memorized it, and her children struggle to guess what it is and why it might be important.

Jack insists that his daughter will have a conventional burial following a church service – even though she was a committed Buddhist who wanted to be cremated. He also consults with an attorney in an attempt to have Ben's children taken away from him. Ben is told he is not welcome at his wife's funeral, but he shows up anyway, sporting a red blazer and red trousers that stand in marked contrast with the black and gray suits that fill the pews.

The family is thrown out of the church, but only after Ben makes a moving speech about how much his Buddhist wife loved life and how she would have hated the ceremony (presided over by a Christian minister she had never met). Although she is buried according to her father's wishes, the family eventually goes to the cemetery, recovers her body, and gives her the cremation and the kind of burial ceremony she wanted all along. After the cremation, the family flushes her ashes down a nearby toilet.

Stereotyping

Heath Ledger and Jake Gyllenhaal co-star in the 2005 film *Brokeback Mountain* about two cowboys who spend long days and nights together herding sheep on Brokeback Mountain in Wyoming, eventually becoming lovers. Ledger plays the role of Ennis Del Mar; Gyllenhaal's character is Jack Twist. Ang Lee won an Oscar for his directing, and the film also resulted in Academy Awards for Best Writing–Adapted Screenplay and Best Achievement in Music Written for Motion Pictures. The film also received two Golden Globe Awards for Best Motion Picture and Best Director.

The two men in the film grow closer as friends throughout the film, and they become sexually intimate after a night of heavy drinking when they must share a tent and a sleeping bag to avoid freezing. They are happy sexual partners throughout their time on the mountain, but part ways when the summer ends. Both go on to marry and have children, and they don't see each other for several years (Jack moves to Texas while Ennis remains in Wyoming). After 4 years, Jack, who has maintained his attraction to men, writes to Ennis and they agree to meet. They greet each other with a passionate kiss that is seen by Ennis's wife, Alma, who is disgusted by what she witnesses. Jack and Ennis maintain their passion for each other during a series of fishing trips; Alma, who recognizes that these are likely sexual adventures, divorces Ennis

Ennis Del Mar: I tell ya there... there were these two old guys ranched up together, down home. Earl and Rich. And they was the joke of town, even though they were pretty tough ol' birds. Anyway they... they found Earl dead in an irrigation ditch. Took a tire iron to 'im. Spurred him up, drug him 'round by his dick 'till it pulled off.

Jack Twist: You seen this?

Ennis Del Mar: I wasn't... nine years old. My daddy, he made sure me and brother seen it. Hell for all I know, he done the job.

Ennis describes a childhood memory to Jake
in *Brokeback Mountain*.

and takes custody of their children. Jack and Ennis consider living together on a ranch, but Ennis realizes the risk involved in being "outed" as two gay men ("This thing gets hold of us at the wrong time and wrong place and we're dead"). Jack continues an active homosexual lifestyle, spending much of his time in gay Mexican bars. He eventually dies accidentally, and Ennis visits Lauren, the cowgirl who was the mother of Jack's son. Ennis gets to see and hold two of their blood-stained shirts, one hung over the other. He brings the shirts back to his mobile home, where he keeps them, often taking them out to think about how different his life might have been.

The film is powerful in its repudiation of many traditional stereotypes about gay men. Neither character is effeminate in any way as older stereotypes would suggest – in fact, they are the antithesis of femininity in their respective roles as rancher and rodeo rider. Both characters reject their homosexual identity (Ennis remarks "You know I ain't queer" and Jack replies "Me neither") and they reject any idea they sit somewhere on a spectrum of sexuality, feeling they need to choose between one end or the other of a sexual dichotomy. Both men are married and have children, like many other men who have sex with other men. The story is especially tragic insofar as we sense that these two men love one another and there is a deep sense of connection; however, they cannot be who they really are or even acknowledge the extent of their love for one another. Ennis's fears about being murdered if he and Jack are discovered to be lovers are reality based and realistic.

Homophobia is very real, and it can be lethal. A gay student, Matthew Shepard, was murdered near Laramie, Wyoming, on October 6, 1998. Writing about *Brokeback Mountain* in *PsycCRITIQUES* (n.p.), the late psychologist Ilene Serlin (2006) noted:

Because everything else in the cowboys' life changed, but their love lasted all their life, I see this film as showing the enduring power of love. The director set out to sympathetically portray the challenges of two men in love and the human need to live an authentic life. To this end, he succeeds magnificently. ... In short, *Brokeback Mountain* introduces many complex psychological issues that would be valuable for psychologists to see and understand.

Indigenous People

Dances With Wolves (1990) stars Kevin Costner as Lieutenant John Dunbar, a Union soldier in the Civil War. He is sent to a desolate site in the Dakotas frontier where he makes friends with the local Sioux Indians. Gradually, he relinquishes the habits, beliefs, and attitudes associated with his former military life and adopts the life of the Sioux people, who give him the name "Dances With Wolves." Only two people know of Dunbar's assignment to the remote outpost; one is scalped and killed, and the other dies by suicide, so there is no official record of this officer's posting. While living among the Sioux, Dunbar becomes romantically involved with "Stands With a Fist," a White woman, recently widowed, who had been captured as a child and raised by a Sioux tribe. She speaks both Lakota and English, and she can translate for Dunbar.

Lieutenant Dunbar divides his time between the fort and the tribe, and he keeps a detailed journal. He warns the Sioux about the fact that White men will come to conquer the lands of the Sioux; they will come "as many as the stars in the sky." Returning to the fort to retrieve his journal, he discovers that it is now occupied by soldiers. He is captured and treated as a traitor, but later he is rescued by his Sioux tribe. Realizing that his presence puts the tribe in danger, he and his wife leave. The film is a sensitive and respectful portrayal of the Sioux people, and it turns the Western genre on its head.

John Dunbar: Who would do such a thing? The field was proof enough that it was a people without value and without soul, with no regard for Sioux rights. The wagon tracks leading away left little doubt and my heart sank as I knew it could only be White hunters. Voices that had been joyous all morning were now as silent as the dead buffalo left to rot in this valley, killed only for their tongues and the price of their hides.

Lt. John Dunbar reacts to the pillage and destruction caused by White hunters in *Dances With Wolves*.

Dances With Wolves was strikingly successful, winning nine Academy Awards, including an award for Best Picture; Costner also took home an Oscar for Best Director. It is a sensitive film that will help you understand the Sioux people and the ways in which culture affects relationships.

Additional Films About Relationships and Culture

One is hard pressed to identify films that *don't* deal with relationships and culture in some way. However, some movies are especially poignant and powerful, and we believe you can expand your appreciation for how relationships are affected by culture if you take time to watch several of the following films: *Australia Day* (2017), *Love Actually* (2003), *Fargo* (1996), *The Green Mile* (1999), *Parasite* (2019), *The Dreamers* (2003), *The Killing of a Sacred Deer* (2017), *Gran Torino* (2008), *Oldboy* (2003), *Dogtooth* (2009), *The Wonder* (2022), *Hereditary* (2018), *Thirteen* (2003), and *Little Miss Sunshine* (2006).

Numerous television series address relationships as well: Some of our favorites are *Yellowstone, Peaky Blinders, The Sopranos, Game of Thrones, Shameless, Breaking Bad, Better Call Saul, Adolescence, This is Us*, and *Succession*.

Critical Thinking Questions About Relationships and Culture

- How important is language in a relationship? Can a loving couple achieve happiness if they cannot directly communicate using a common language?
- How is sexual jealousy expressed in different cultures?
- How do cultural groups differ in their expectations of monogamy and fidelity for men and women?
- Does interracial marriage diminish the salience of culture? Why is marriage outside of one's cultural group so threatening?
- Would you support **MAID** (physician-assisted suicide) for someone you loved?
- How did marriage equality eventually succeed in the United States? Why is gay marriage now legal when it was once so threatening for so many?
- Is divorce more common or less common when couples marry across racial or ethnic boundaries?
- Do you accept the widely held belief that interracial children tend to be especially attractive?

- What is the relationship between anti-miscegenation laws and Nazi ideology?
- *Loving v. Virginia* (1967) was a Supreme Court decision that banned laws prohibiting interracial marriage. Given the court's 2022 decision to overturn the precedent established by *Roe v. Wade*, is there some chance the Supreme Court or individual states may try to once again outlaw interracial marriage? If this happens, how will you respond?

Further Exploration

If you only have time to read one article about relationships and culture, make it:

Kuperberg, A., & Padgett, J. E. (2016). The role of culture in explaining college students' selection into hookups, dates, and long-term romantic relationships. *Journal of Social and Personal Relationships, 33*(8), 1070–1096.

If you have time to read one chapter, make it:

DeLoach, C.' D., Petersen-Coleman, M. K., & Young, S. J. (2013). Love and intimacy issues with intercultural black couples. In K. M. Helm & J. Carlson (Eds.), *Love, intimacy, and the African American couple* (pp. 123–147). Routledge/Taylor & Francis Group.

If you have time to read a whole book, make it:

Kağitçibaşi, Ç. (2007). *Family, self, and human development across cultures: Theories and applications* (2nd ed.). Lawrence Erlbaum Associates Publishers.

References

Abdulrehman, R., & Williams, M. (2025). Celebrate everything: A conversation about equity in federal holidays. In H. C. Peters & M. Luke (Eds.) *Anti-oppressive supervision interventions: Navigating critical praxis*. Routledge/Taylor & Francis.

Banks, M. E. (2014). Colorism: (Still) getting away with racism [Review of the book Color Matters: Skin Tone Bias and the Myth of a Post-Racial America, edited by K. J. Norwood]. *PsycCRITIQUES, 59*(36).

Brubaker, R. (2016). The Dolezal affair: Race, gender, and the micropolitics of identity. *Ethnic and Racial Studies, 39*(3), 414–448. https://doi.org/10.1080/01419870.2015.10 84430

Emanuel, E. J., Onwuteaka-Philipsen, B. D., Urwin, J. W., & Cohen, J. (2016). Attitudes and practices of euthanasia and physician-assisted suicide in the United States, Canada, and Europe. *JAMA: Journal of the American Medical Association, 316*(1), 79–90. https://doi.org/10.1001/jama.2016.8499

Hanif, H., McNiel, D. E., Weithorn, L., & Binder, R. L. (2024). Legal implications of psychiatric assessment for medical aid in dying. *Journal of the American Academy of Psychiatry and the Law, 52*(3), 347–357.

Norwood, K. J. (Ed.). (2014). *New directions in American history. Color matters: Skin tone bias and the myth of a postracial America.* Routledge/Taylor & Francis Group.

Serlin, I. A. (2006). Brokeback Mountain: A gay and a universal love story [Review of the media Brokeback Mountain (2005), by A. Lee]. *PsycCRITIQUES, 51*(11).

Chapter 3
Sex and Sexuality

Little: [*innocently*] **What's a faggot?**
Juan: **A faggot is... a word used to make gay
people feel bad.** [*pause*]
Little: **Am I a faggot?**
Juan: **No. You're not a faggot. You can be gay, but
you don't have to let nobody call you a faggot.**

A child tries to make sense of sexuality in *Moonlight*.

Questions to Consider While Watching
Moonlight (2016)

- How did Chiron's relationship with his mother affect his psychosexual development?
- Why does Juan take an interest in Chiron?
- How does Chiron's mother display her love for her son, despite her addiction?
- How common is it for effeminate boys to be bullied?
- At what age does sexual orientation most often become apparent?
- What are the connections between homosexuality and race?
- Is homosexuality found in every country and culture?
- At what age do gay children first realize that they are different?
- What does it mean to be on the "down low?"
- What is the significance of the film's title?
- Does *Moonlight* perpetuate a stereotype by suggesting that poor Black males escape poverty by selling drugs?

- How common is homophobia in the Black community? In the White community? In the Latinx community? In other ethnic communities?
- Did this movie deserve the Academy Award for Best Picture? If so, what makes it special?

Sexuality and Culture

There are literally thousands of films that touch on the intersection of sexuality and culture, and we have picked a few of our favorites to share in this chapter. However, both sexuality and culture are complex and multifaceted, and each interacts with the other in myriad ways. It is also important to realize even within Western and White culture, there are negative beliefs toward marginalized groups such as gay, bisexual, queer, and transgender people. As such, we have ensured the discussion of culture addresses sex, sexuality, and gender in films from all these angles, including in White communities. As some of these films address intersecting challenges on issues of culture and sexuality, it is important to not jump to judgmental stereotypical beliefs before informing ourselves about people and cultures in question. Rather, we must watch these films knowing that different cultures have unique challenges and experiences when it comes to sex and sexuality. These stories help us understand the experiences of people in communities we may not otherwise be aware of and build more relatable experiences that unite instead of divide. We hope you will enjoy – and learn from – watching the films we discuss.

Sexuality and *Moonlight*

Toxic and rigid views of masculinity and sexuality prevent many men from being aware of where on the spectrum of sexuality they fall, in part because of racist stereotypes of Black men, power dynamics, and colonialism (Jones & Ferguson, 2020). Negative views toward homosexuality or any form of sex between men (e.g., sex on the "down low") in the Black community are common (Quinn, et al., 2015). This is why movies such as *Moonlight* are important to understanding the experiences that link ethnicity, culture, and sexuality.

Moonlight (2016) is a provocative coming of age film that traces the lifespan of a young Black boy growing up in Miami, coming to terms with being gay in the Black community. The protagonist, Chiron, is seen at three

Figure 3.1.   *Moonlight* (2016, A24). Produced by Adele Romanski, Dede Gardner, and Jeremy Kleiner. Directed by Barry Jenkins. *Moonlight* underscores the importance of a male role model in the development of a young gay boy. In this scene, Juan, a father figure, is teaching Chiron how to swim.

developmental stages: childhood, adolescence, and young adulthood. The first act, titled "Little," shows Chiron running from other boys who yell out, "Get his gay ass" as they chase and torment the 10-year-old child. Chiron's mother loves her son, but she is an addict dealing with her own demons; however, she knows full well her son is different from other boys, at one point yelling "You're a faggot!" prompting Chiron's query in the epigraph.

The second act, "Chiron," shows an older, tormented teenager. He established a brief but meaningful relationship with a friend, Kevin, and the two boys sit on the beach and share a kiss and Chiron's first sexual experience. Chiron feels tremendous guilt after being masturbated by his friend, suggesting he has internalized much of the homophobia he has been exposed to his entire life. We later see Chiron retaliate against his tormentors, breaking a chair over the head of one of his fellow students in an unforgettable scene.

At some point you gotta decide for yourself who you gonna be. Can't let nobody make that decision for you.

Juan, a father figure, gives advice to Chiron in *Moonlight*.

Chiron is sent to jail following this event, which marks his transition from uncertain adolescence into a mature, confident gay Black man.

The third act, "Black," shows Chiron as an attractive and muscular man who has achieved success as a drug dealer (like his role model Juan). However, Chiron has never accepted his homosexuality. When he reunites with Kevin (from act one), Chiron remarks, "You're the only one... I haven't really touched anyone since." The film ends with the suggestion that Chiron and Kevin have the potential to establish a meaningful and loving relationship, and the final shot shows a young Chiron staring out at the ocean, possibly reflecting on the long journey necessary to establish a positive identity as a gay and proud Black man. It is noteworthy that *Moonlight* had an all-Black cast, and it received an unexpected Academy Award as Best Picture in 2016.

Prejudice, Discrimination, Oppression, Racism, and Ethnocentrism

Birthday Girl (2001) stars Nicole Kidman as a Russian grifter who seduces men online through a dating website called "From Russia with Love." John, a lonely bank teller working in a London suburb, has given up on British girls and signs up for the website. He eventually connects with Kidman's character, Nadia. After an online relationship develops, John arranges to bring Nadia to Britain as a "mail-order bride." When he meets her at the airport, John is disturbed to discover that she speaks no English; she replies "yes" to every question he asks, including "Are you a giraffe?" She also smokes, and John has explicitly asked for a nonsmoker. Although he initially attempts to cancel his order and send Nadia back, John finds her to be a willing, enthusiastic, and exciting lover, providing the sexual adventure John had longed for but could never find. It soon becomes clear that John is falling in love with Nadia. The plot thickens when Sophia's cousins arrive, without invitation, and the viewer learns that Sophia knows the two intruders and is romantically and sexually involved with one cousin (and possibly both). Somewhat implausibly, John steals a great deal of money from his bank to meet the ransom demands of the trio. The three Russians have a history of working together with similar scams; however, this attempted scam falls apart when John and Nadia surprisingly team up to foil the swindle. Although the film is somewhat uneven and unsure about whether it is a drama or romantic comedy, it works, in part because of the skill of Kidman, who convincingly plays her role, despite not knowing the Russian language.

International dating has become increasingly common with the development of easy and inexpensive channels of communication. Sites like International Cupid, Bumpy–International Dating, Filipino Cupid, and Sakura Date promise to link potential romantic partners, most often linking Western men with Asian, Russian, or Latin women. Zhigalova (2024) has reported the (surprising) data that the divorce rate resulting from "mail-order marriages" is *lower* than that for more traditional marriages in the United States (around 35%–40%, while the overall US divorce rate is 48%). This certainly raises the question of financial and cultural power between a mail-order bride from a non-Western and sometimes non-White community and their Western husband who purchased them. It also raises concerns over sex trafficking and abuse. In addition, women seeking marriage partners online often come from countries like Russia and the Ukraine with very high divorce rates, and women participating on these sites tend to be young (21–25 years old). The most popular country for men seeking mail-order brides is the Philippines (even though the practice is illegal), and thousands of Filipina women from the Philippines enter the United States each year on a K-1 visa and get married to American men after their arrival. After arriving, individuals holding a K-1 visa must marry within 90 days; if a marriage does not occur, the visa holder must leave the country (USAGov, 2024). This highlights the issue of power the men have over these women of color.

Internet dating sites like Tinder have become a favored means of meeting new people and potentially hold promise as a way to significantly expand the range of potential romantic and sexual partners. For example, Aldana and Salazar (2024) note:

> Generally, in our day-to-day in-person lives, we interact with individuals with similar social characteristics, so we have fewer chances to connect with others who are different from us and build less homogamous relationships. Accordingly, coupling with a person from the same racial background is more usual. Online dating could be changing this pattern since it increases the possibility of meeting strangers without the intervention of previously known social ties, and this seems to have extended the presence of interracial couples ... However, racially homogeneous patterns also occur in the online dating context, and there is a hierarchy that prioritizes Whiteness. (p. 1)

Thomas (2020) found that couples who meet through a dating platform are over 1.5 times more likely to be in an interracial relationship. That said, there are meaningful differences across racial groups (Curington et al., 2021); in general, Black women are the least likely to be selected or matched on dating sites and hookup apps, followed closely behind by Black men, although in one study most White men rationalized their preference for White women in "colorblind racist rhetoric that drew upon language couched in cultural incompatibility, relied on stereotypes and generalizations that often conflated race with social class, and attributed their racial preferences to family values and regional demographic restrictions" (Peck et al., 2021, p. 304).

Race and **skin color** are likely to be especially salient variables on dating sites like Tinder and Grindr because there are relatively few cues to support dating decisions, but photos are almost always provided, and these images may be the single most important factor influencing one's decisions about potential sexual partners. Hunter (2007) has documented that racialized groups are stratified and disadvantaged based on how light their skin appears. This is especially problematic in the gay community (Chen, 2024). Tsunokai et al. (2019) assessed over 2,000 dating profiles and found darker-skinned Asians were more likely to state a preference to date African Americans and Latino/Latinas compared to their lighter-skinned counterparts.

Women's bodies are becoming a global commodity, and both men and women can be exploited by international dating sites, although few connections are likely to wind up as badly as that in *Birthday Girl*. Pornographic websites often offer large sections devoted specifically to Asian, Latin, or African women. However, fetishizing people of color seldom leads to equal rights.

While few reliable data are available about the extent to which international brides purchased online are abused, it seems clear that many of these women are economically, psychologically, and linguistically dependent on the men they marry, and instances of domestic abuse are frequently found in these relationships, along with occasional instances of sexual slavery. Starr and Adams (2016), in an article titled "The Domestic Exotic: Mail-Order Brides and the Paradox of Globalized Intimacies," noted:

> The discourse utilized by international dating websites [constructs] foreign women as available and desirable mates within the global marriage market and, by extension, narrate Western men, whose lack of romantic success is assumed to be the fault of feminism, as the preferred marital partners on the global stage. It is through this reading that the "domestic exotic" is created and fleshed out. She is not a physical being, but a fictive marketing entity juxtaposed against the similarly fictive Western woman who has grown unappreciative, corpulent, and career-minded through the deleterious effects of feminism. (p. 954)

Cultural Identity, Acculturation, Assimilation

Halal Love (and Sex) (2015) is set in the cosmopolitan city of Beirut and follows the love and sex lives of four Lebanese couples. Lebanon is a diverse country that is 67% Muslim (with about equal numbers of Sunni and Shia) and around 32% Christian. There are also many Syrian and Palestinian refugees in Lebanon. The film's dialogue is Arabic (with English subtitles); although the film focuses on Lebanon, it can be generalized to Muslim couples throughout the Middle East.

While stereotypes of Muslims and Arabs suggest they are stringent and sexually oppressed, we see through the four couples in this film that their sexual reality is complex and multifaceted. Each couple navigates social norms based on culture and religion, just as in many other global communities. In fact, the film illustrates practices like many of those found in Italian and Latin communities, even though the religions in those communities are predominately Christian.

Halal Love (and Sex) portrays Lebanese, Arab, and Muslim culture and illustrates how couples navigate those cultural and religious norms in real life. The film also helps us challenge stereotypes about Arab men being controlling and committed to polygamy. One of the women, Awatef (played by Mirna Moukarzel), grows weary of her affectionate husband's advances, and actively works to bring a second wife into the household to help her placate her amorous husband. Her husband, Salim (played by Ali Sammoury), is incensed and vehemently opposed. "Are you mad? You should be ashamed!" "What woman tells her husband she is looking for a second wife?!" "You've definitely lost it! I'm married! I don't want a second wife!" But despite his objections, Awatef persists, seeking out and bringing home a young woman who agrees, based on promises of the size and skill of Salim's "nunu." Awatef's silver lining is she gets help with raising the kids and with the housework. "I need a wife!" she proclaims. Without Salim's consent, Awatef brings home Bardot, a beautiful woman named after the actress Bridget Bardot. (Interestingly, the real Bridget Bardot is an animal activist who has been fined by the French government four times for making anti-Muslim slurs following the Muslim feast of *Eid al-Adha*.) After a little time, Awatef notices Salim and Bardot becoming close, and even more problematic to her, Bardot is patient with and wins the favor of Awatef's daughters. Realizing what she is losing, she shuts Bardot out of her house and her family.

Views of polygamy in Muslim culture often unfairly focus on men and their seemingly insatiable sexual desires (Musawah, 2024). But Salim only desires Awatef, and he becomes angry when Awatef proposes that he take on

Figure 3.2.   *Halal Love (and Sex)* (2015, Razor Film Produktion). Produced by Lara Chekerdijan, Rania Haddad, Abla Khoury, Gerhard Meixner, et al. Directed by Assad Fouladkar. Loubna (Darine Hamze) gets her divorce papers and celebrates with her married lover. The two arrange for a temporary (pleasure) marriage (*nikah mut'ah*), which is allowed in some Muslim sects.

a second wife. It is also interesting that Western views of romantic and sexual relationships have broadened recently, and many couples now are in open or polyamorous relationships. Yet Arab Muslim families that engage in polygamy often experience prejudice because of ethnicity, culture, and faith (Pew Research Center, 2024). The portrayals of Awatef, Salim, and Bardot lend levity and context to their decision, which in this case is woman led, and allow the viewer to see love and sex from a slightly different perspective.

Although much of the tension in *Halal Love (and Sex)* appears to revolve around decisions to marry and divorce, tension also rises from questions about staying in or leaving a problematic relationship. These are common and relatable issues for couples everywhere. For example, Loubna, played by Darine Hamze, is torn between remaining in Beirut with her married lover, Abou Ahmad (played by Rodrigue Sleiman), or immigrating to Australia to join her gay brother, and she is sorely disappointed when her visa application is turned down without explanation. As she explores her options and the viability of the relationship with this married man, she realizes he will not leave his wife, and patterns in his problematic relationship with his wife are also showing up in the relationship she has with him. "You were much more inspiring to me as a dream," Loubna tells Abou Ahmad, as she ends their relationship. Despite this, she is challenged by the cultural (not religious) concepts of reputation when her mother (played by Randa Kaadi) visits. Though Loubna defends her choices citing Islamic theology, her mother is belligerent, focusing instead on the cultural concept of reputation. "Go on, go join your gay brother. Because only a faggot would get along with a slut like you," says the mother, insulting both her children in one breath. Though subtle in this movie, the case of Loubna (a divorced woman choosing her relationships) and her brother (a gay man living abroad) highlights the difference between religion and culture. Where Loubna clearly articulates theology to support her decisions, and even though the concept of homosexuality and same-sex relations is not openly negated in the Quran or Islamic tradition (Kugle, 2010; contrary to popular Islamophobic belief), her mother is enraged because in her mind her children violated norms of Lebanese culture. Interestingly, this conflict is not exclusive to just Arab or Muslim cultures. Conflict around sexuality occurs in many cultures, including many from southern Europe, and the situation is reminiscent of a scene from a well known play by Federico Garcia Lorca, *The House of Bernarda Alba* (1936). When the mother of daughters finds out that her youngest daughter fell in love with a young man visiting the house, she screams, "Hot coals in the place she sinned!"

The film also depicts a young newlywed bride, Batoul (played by Zeinab Hind Khadra), who is married to an abusive man, Mokhtar (played by Hussein Mokaddem). Batoul ultimately makes the decision to leave him. "Now I see you for the man you really are," Batoul says. Contrary to the stereotype that women are not supported by Islamic families, Batoul's family were the ones who did not approve of the marriage and serve as primary means for social support when Mokhtar forces her to leave their home.

In every relationship depicted by this film, the relationships are women led; they either choose to engage or disengage, challenging commonly held stereotypes of Arab and Muslim women. Although there are problems with women's rights in some countries in the Middle East, this is also the case all over the world, in all societies, including Western and White communities.

Feminism and women-led or egalitarian relationships are not new to the Middle East or Islam. The prophet Muhammad's wife was his employer, was wealthier than him, had children from prior relationships, had power over him, and she proposed to him (Ali, 2015; Cevherli, 2022). *Halal Love (and Sex)* provides a culturally sensitive view of the subject, with all its challenges and nuances, and yet clearly illustrates that many Muslim homes are women led. As Awatef says in the film, "Listen, I'm the decision maker around here, and it will stay that way."

Value Conflicts, Value Orientations

A 13-year-old girl experiences emerging sexuality through sexual abuse and rigid cultural expectations in *Towelhead* (2008), demonstrating the trap many young girls face, in particular girls of color. The film was directed by Alan Ball, perhaps best known for the television series *Six Feet Under* and the movie *American Beauty* (1999). The film was likely influenced by Ball's own childhood in Marietta, Georgia, growing up as a closeted gay teenager whose sister was killed in an auto accident while driving Alan to piano practice.

Jasira, the protagonist in *Towelhead*, lives with her mother until it comes out that she has been sexually assaulted by her stepfather who had enthusiastically shaved Jasira's pubic hair at her request ("girls at the pool call me Chewbacca"). The mother, threatened and sexually jealous, sides with her boyfriend, minimizes the encounter, and becomes angry at Jasira for letting it happen; after the incident, she ships her daughter off to live in Houston with her rigid and demanding Lebanese Christian ex-husband (Jasira's father). The father is ill-prepared to cope with his daughter's puberty; for instance, Jasira is alarmed when she begins to menstruate, but her father forbids her from using tampons, claiming they are only appropriate for married women.

Jasira begins to babysit the 10-year-old boy next door, who introduces her to his father's collection of erotica. Both children are fascinated, and Jasira's interest in pornography is a precursor to her eventual abuse and rape. The rapist, a flag-waving Army reservist about to be deployed to Iran, knows sex with a child is reprehensible, but he has sex with Jasira anyway. Jasira also has – and enjoys – a more appropriate sexual encounter with her African American boyfriend; however, her father is deeply opposed to this relationship

> Usually when you read a story about a young girl who undergoes any sort of sexual abuse or assault, the implication at the end is always that she's damaged for life. But it's such a statistically common experience for so many young women (and young men) that I found it truly refreshing that Jasira is not ruined by what she goes through, but that she comes out of the experience more powerful, with a healthy sense of who she is and with her own healthy sexuality very much intact.
>
> Alan Ball, describing his decision to take on the challenges associated with directing *Towelhead* (Robinson, 2024).

(despite his own marked experiences with racism) and he forbids her to continue seeing the boy. A kindly neighbor takes Jasira in and allows her to stay after she runs away from her father's home; the neighbor is aware of the child's abuse by a neighbor, and she is determined to protect Jasira from both the rapist and her demanding, critical, and punitive father. Jasira is trapped between two adult men; they come from different cultures and ethnicities, but both abuse her in different ways.

There is a marked undercurrent of racism throughout the film. Jasira is at first confused by, and later troubled by, the derogatory terms she hears at school, including "towelhead" (conflating all Arabs and Muslims), "camel jockey," and "sand nigger." Jasira is quite innocent as she tries to make sense of the bigotry and sexual repression she sees all around her. The film also demonstrates that women and young girls are at risk of abuse and harm, from any culture, not just Arab cultures. The film ends on a hopeful note, with Jasira and her boyfriend, Thomas, reconciling and agreeing to maintain the happy sexual connection they have established.

Social Norms and Norm Violations

Will and Harper (2024) is a delightful documentary that examines some of the tensions associated with Andrew Steele's COVID-era decision to transition from his lifelong identity as a male to adopt a total identity makeover as a female (Harper Steele). Will Ferrell had known Steele since they started working together on *Saturday Night Live* in 1995. After receiving an email notifying her *Saturday Night Live* colleagues and others of her decision to transition and live life as a woman, Will Ferrell approached Harper and proposed a 17-day road trip, driving from New York city to Los Angeles, exploring some of their favorite American sites along the way. The two friends seem to have a great time, drinking beer, eating Pringles, and visiting mutual friends. They are understandably nervous at times, sensing that not every setting is benign, and not every stranger is going to be a friend. They are especially anxious in an Oklahoma bar proudly displaying banners supporting Donald Trump; somewhat surprisingly, they are received in a congenial and positive way, possibly because of the filming that was occurring and the recognition of Will Ferrell as a celebrity.

There are touching scenes in the film, most notably when Harper's children and former *Saturday Night Live* crew and cast embrace Harper and signify their strong support for this difficult decision. The love of Harper's children is palpable. There is also a less comfortable interaction with Eric

Figure 3.3.   *Will and Harper* (2024, Gloria Sanchez Productions, Wayfarer Studios, Delirio Films). Produced by Samantha Apfel, Justin Baldoni, Carolina Barlow, Andrew Calof et al. Directed by Josh Greenbaum. The trip is going well, but Will and Harper have some misgivings when they arrive at the Texas border.

Holcomb, the Republican Governor of Indiana, at a Pacers game; Holcomb is cordial and friendly on camera, but he has a history of supporting legislation that makes it a crime to provide gender-affirming care for minors.

Will and Harper is likely to make you question many of your assumptions about the trans community. Many of us think of transitioning as a privilege of youth and the prerogative of the brave and beautiful, but Harper is neither young nor beautiful – he is a witty but unattractive individual who made the decision to live as a woman in his 60s.

One of the hallmarks of a great documentary is that it leaves you thinking about the film long after you see it, and, with the best of films, you come away seeing the world somewhat differently. This film celebrates a 30-year friendship and leaves almost all viewers questioning any bias they might have held against trans people.

Readers interested in learning more about gender affirming care are referred to the book *Affirmative Therapy with Transsexual and Gender Nonconforming Patients* by lore dickey and Jae Puckett (2023).

Stereotyping

Beyto (2020) is a film that highlights the clash between personal values and cultural expectations. The movie illustrates the tensions involved when young queer immigrants must deal with traditional norms, deep cultural convictions, and the belief that homosexuality is a sin.

Beyto is a Turkish immigrant living in Switzerland who helps his family manage their shawarma restaurant. The family is happy with the Swiss life they have created and their economic security; however, they long for the traditions and practices they knew as simple shepherds in their home village.

Beyto is a competitive swimmer who gradually becomes involved in a romantic relationship with his trainer, Mike. After family friends spot Beyto and Mike in a gay pride march, Beyto is confronted by his parents in the middle of the night who demand to know if their son is gay. Beyto initially denies participating in the march and disavows his homosexuality; however, eventually he acknowledges that he is a gay man who desires to live with his lover. This admission is tremendously upsetting to Beyto's Turkish parents, who had been planning for him to adhere to tradition and marry a "nice Turkish girl." The parents plot to travel with Beyto to Ankara, where they are met by Beyto's uncle and driven to a remote village where surreptitious plans have been put in place for a wedding between Beyto and a childhood friend, Narin. Beyto reluctantly participates in the ceremony, but the marriage is never consummated, and Beyto's wife is forced to confront the fact that her marriage lacks both passion and purpose.

The family's return to a traditional village underscores the clash between traditional Turkish values and the more open traditions and values of Swiss life. Beyto's parents genuinely believe an arranged marriage (like their own) is in his best interest; in contrast, Beyto increasingly is comfortable with his identity as a gay man. Watching the film will help you understand the logic

Narin: If we move in together, I want my own room. I'm going to learn a profession and work. I'm going to go out, whenever I want … and it is none of your business. I'm not responsible for the housework, and I'm not going to cook or clean either. *If* I feel like it, I'll prepare a Turkish dish sometime. [And] I'll bring friends home … maybe even a man! Is that clear?

Mike: It sounds like a plan.

Narin lays down ground rules for her new life
in Germany with Mike in *Beyto*.

behind arranged marriages, and you will have a better sense for Turkish life and values, as well as the challenges that confront immigrants with limited knowledge of their new community and language.

The film's ending depicts Narin deciding to move to Germany with Beyto and Mike, sharing their home if not their bed. Their future is uncertain, but promising. The two men establish their identity as a happy gay couple, and Narin winds up with an opportunity to learn German and continue her education. The film's conclusion is promising, albeit a tad contrived, and suggests that true love can triumph over tradition when necessary. There is also a subtext involving women's rights and agency. Narin looks forward to a life as an independent, professional woman who can have the kind of freedom and success that would have never been possible for her in her native village.

Diamond-Smith et al. (2020) have discussed the ways in which traditional marital practices are changing around the world, with a focus on South Asia and Nepal; however, much of what they report is germane to other countries and cultures. They note:

> Marriage practices are changing, with a move towards more love marriage; this is likely to have important implications on women's status and agency, household and couple dynamics, and mental and physical health. ... Many marriages remain arranged; however, couples often talk or meet before marriage and feel that they are able to build a foundation of love before marrying. Access to technology facilitates this practice, although some couples are reluctant to admit their communication, suggesting stigma about this practice. Husbands have growing ambivalence about dowry, leading to confusion and negatively impacting relationships post-marriage. (p. 971)

The film also addresses the struggle of Muslims who are gay and shows how these individuals try to balance the belief that homosexuality is a sin with their own needs and identities. This is a challenge experienced by many and a situation that can be fraught with family conflict. Muslim scholars such as Scott Siraj al-haqq Kugle (2010), have addressed this by examining the issue of homosexuality from a faith-based perspective; this is surprising to many who have followed a cultural perspective of Islam instead of a faith-based one.

Indigenous People

A dramatic clash between two vastly different cultures is seen in the 1971 film *Walkabout*. This movie, directed by Nicolas Roeg, opens with a dramatic scene in which a British geologist father conducting research in Australia arranges

In Australia, when an Aborigine man-child reaches sixteen, he is sent out into the land. For months he must live from it. Sleep on it. Eat of its fruit and flesh. Stay alive. Even if it means killing his fellow creatures. The Aborigines call it the WALKABOUT.

Opening line from the movie *Walkabout*.

to take his 15-year-old daughter (Jenny) and his 8-year-old son (Luc – the director's son in real life) on a picnic in the Australian outback. For inexplicable reasons, the father attempts to murder his children with a handgun. Failing this, he sets his Volkswagen on fire and uses his gun to kill himself. The abandoned children are left to cope with the dangers of the outback on their own. After wandering for several days in the scorching heat, the children awaken one morning to see an Aborigine teenager standing over them. Despite the inevitable language barriers, the two children indicate their need for water, and each learns a few words in the other's language.

The film's climax occurs when the Australian teenager (David Gulpilil) sends the young British boy to fetch wood. He then paints his body and engages in an elaborate courtship dance that is ignored, but which continues

Figure 3.4.   *Walkabout* (1971, Max L. Raab Productions, Si Litvinoff Film Production). Produced by Anthony J. Hope, Si Litvinoff, and Max Raab. Directed by Nicolas Roeg. Two children lost in the Australian outback are rescued by an Aboriginal boy, and the sexual tension between the two teenagers is palpable, despite their profound cultural differences.

through the night. The next morning the two English children discover the body of the Aborigine teen hanging in a tree, apparently a result of suicide and in response to the sexual rejection he has encountered. The movie ends with a **jump cut** to an older, experienced Jenny, cooking dinner while listening to the radio. Her (proper, British) husband returns home to tell Jenny about a likely promotion, one that will allow them to vacation on Australia's Gold Coast. Although seemingly happy, Jenny still has fantasies about her time in the Outback, and she still wonders how life might have turned out had she stayed in Australia and become lovers with the Aborigine boy. The film offers a dramatic juxtaposition of Western (British) values and Australian Aboriginal culture. There are striking visual images throughout the film, which was criticized for multiple depictions of animal murder, as well as the nude scenes Jenny Agutter made while still underage.

Additional Films About Sex and Culture

It is difficult to limit our discussion to a few films that address sexuality and culture – because there are so many! Numerous films depict the inevitable intersectionality involved when sexuality is influenced by external factors like age, race, class, or gender. Some of our favorite films are listed next.

A film that is both engaging and educational is *May/December* (2023), which raises interesting questions about child sexual abuse and statutory rape. The film is loosely based on the life of Mary Kay Letourneau, a 36-year-old teacher who initiated an affair with a 12-year-old student. Letourneau was initially sentenced to 6 months in prison for second-degree rape with the condition that she no longer see her former student. The teacher and student were later found together, and a judge changed the sentence to 7 years. Letourneau wound up marrying her former student lover and having two of his children.

Other films that address the intersection of culture and sexuality include *Spa Night* (2016), a movie that illustrates Korean culture and the difficulties a closeted gay teen experiences as he comes to grips with his sexuality; *Lionhood* (2018), a film that deals with two teenage hockey players experiencing puberty; and *Brokeback Mountain* (2005), an Ang Lee film that involves two cowboys who become lovers while tending sheep on an isolated mountain (see Chapter 2). Another tremendously creative film is *Poor Things* (2023), directed by Yorgos Lanthimos, which stars Emma Stone, Willem Dafoe, and Mark Ruffalo. The admittedly implausible thesis of the film revolves around a pregnant woman who kills herself by drowning after throwing herself off a bridge. She dies, but her baby survives, and a Dr. Frankenstein-like scientist (played by Dafoe) implants the baby's brain into the mother's body, bringing her back to life. We watch with fascination while Stone's character learns to masturbate and quickly moves on to the joys of adult sexuality. Some critics have noted that Stone's character may have the body of an adult woman, but she has the brain of a child, and this brain clearly has not reached the age at which meaningful consent is possible (Wedding, 2024).

Two interesting and necessary miniseries that challenge stereotypes about sex and sexuality are *Baby Reindeer* (2024) and *We Are Lady Parts* (2021). *Baby Reindeer*, written and performed by Richard Gadd, really delves into the often ignored but common experience of male sexuality, how it is varied, and how men can also be victims of sexual abuse and stalking. This honest miniseries is a must watch, and anyone who has worked with male survivors of abuse knows these experiences are all too common. *Baby Reindeer* challenges Western notions of heteronormativity, depicting males as victims, and females as perpetrators. *We Are Lady Parts* is a British TV series created by Nida Manzoor that follows an eclectic all-female Muslim punk band as they chase their musical dreams while navigating cultural expectations and personal struggles. Through the characters and their storylines, the series portrays a nuanced and intersectional view of sexuality, emphasizing that Muslim women, like all individuals, navigate their desires and identities in complex and personal ways.

Anora (2024) won the Palme d'Or at Cannes and the 2025 Academy Award for Best Picture. The film also earned an Oscar for the Director (Sean Baker), and Mikey Madison received the Academy Award for Best Actress in a Leading Role for her stunning performance. The film addresses the seemingly happy (but hasty) marriage between Vanya, the spoiled son of a Russian oligarch, and an exotic Russian American dancer named Ani (short for Anora). The film is explicit and direct, frequently showing the lead characters joyfully cavorting and copulating. Ani's character is feisty and engaging, and she holds her own when Ivan's parents send their goons to capture the couple so the marriage can be annulled. It is striking that the film was released at a time when oligarchs (Musk, Bezos, etc.) seem to have immense political power, and when the relationship between the United States and Russia appears to have taken precedence over our commitments to NATO and our European allies. The Academy Award presentation occurred two days after a disastrous meeting between Trump, Vance, and Ukrainian President Volodymyr Zelenskyy. The meeting was intended to discuss a minerals agreement but ended abruptly without resolution. *Anora* seems prescient, and the film dramatically underscores the disregard that the superwealthy have for those less fortunate. Reviewing the film, Jacques Berlinerblau (2025, n. p.) noted:

Figure 3.5.   *Anora* (2024, Cre Film, FilmNation Entertainment). Produced by Sean Baker, Glen Basner, Alex Coco, Alison Cohen et al. Directed by Sean Baker. An exotic dancer has an affair with the son of a Russian oligarch, only to learn that ordinary rules don't apply to the super rich.

Yes, Ani is likely crying over the betrayal, violence and feelings of powerlessness she's endured. But in light of "Anora's" portrait of the elite, maybe we could think of this sobbing woman as us – the US, weeping over what the wealthiest people in the world are doing to Americans.

Additional recommended films that deserve at least honorable mention include *Call Me By Your Name* (2017), *Milk* (2008), *Y Tu Mamá También* (2001), *Boys Don't Cry* (1999), *Two Spirits* (2009), *Venus* (2006), and *Get Out* (2017).

Critical Thinking Questions About Sex and Culture

- What is the difference between a hijab, a niqab, and a burka?
- If a Muslim woman wearing a hijab extends her hand, is it appropriate to shake hands?
- Several countries, including France and Belgium, have banned face-covering clothing such as the hijab. Is this sound public policy or discrimination?
- Do governments (like Canada) have a right to ban religious symbols such as the Muslim hijab, Sikh turban, Jewish kippah, and Christian cross if worn by civil servants while they serve the public?
- What are your own views on arranged marriages? Would you have the courage to push back if your parents demanded one of you?
- When examining cultures that come from monotheistic faiths, how does the Christian Bible, the Jewish Torah, and the Muslim Quran address homosexuality?
- Is patriarchy necessarily a bad thing?
- Why is polygamy much more common than polyandry?
- How widespread is the practice of requiring a dowry before marriage?
- How did the practice of requiring dowries develop? Why do women pay dowries and not men?
- What are the major differences in the ways in which Muslim countries address sexuality? How does this differ from Christian countries? Or Israel? How about Hindu countries like India?
- Are some relationships with "mail-order brides" satisfactory? How has the internet changed this practice?
- How common are Internet hookups in the 21st century in the United States?
- Why are marriages between cousins discouraged – and sometimes illegal? Why are there still such marriages in many parts of the world, including the United States?
- In the United States, is it more common for cousins to marry in Southern states than in the rest of the country?
- How common is it for young people to live together before getting married in your culture?
- How do different cultures address the issues of masturbation and sex before marriage?

Further Exploration

If you only have time for one article, read:

Diamond-Smith, N. G., Dahal, M., Puri, M., & Weiser, S. D. (2020). Semi-arranged marriages and dowry ambivalence: Tensions in the changing landscape of marriage formation in South Asia. *Culture, Health & Sexuality, 22*(9), 971–986. https://doi.org/10.1080/13691058.2019.1646318

If you have time to read one chapter about sexuality and culture, make it:

Brettell, C. B. (2017). Marriage and migration. *Annual Review of Anthropology, 46*, 81–97. https://doi.org/10.1146/annurev-anthro-102116-041237

If you have time to read an entire book, we recommend:

Sidun, N. M., & Hume, D. L. (Eds.). (2018). *A feminist perspective on human trafficking of women and girls: Characteristics, commonalities and complexities*. Routledge/Taylor & Francis Group.

References

Aldana, A. A., & Salazar, L. (2024). Racial preferences in dating apps: An experimental approach. *The History of the Family, 29*(4), 620–640. https://doi.org/10.1080/1081602X.2024.2352547

Ali, K. (2015). Muhammad and Khadija. *Critical Muslim*. https://criticalmuslim.com/explore/issues/power/muhammad-and-khadija

Berlinerblau, J. (2025, March 2). 'Anora' is a genre-toggling romp with a hidden political message. *MSNBC*. https://www.msnbc.com/opinion/msnbc-opinion/oscars-favorite-anora-hidden-political-message-rcna194072

Cevherli, F. (2022). As a commercial genius Khadija bint Khuwaylid (RA) and her Mudarabah partnership with Prophet Muhammad (SAW). *International Journal of Islamic Economics and Finance Studies, 8*(3), 299–310. https://doi.org/10.54427/ijisef.1191298

Chen, K. A. (2024). Book reviews: Racial erotics: Gay men of color, sexual racism, and the politics of desire. *Sexualities, 27*(8), 1743–1745. https://doi.org/10.1177/13634607231191434

Curington, C. V., Lindquist, J. H., & Lin, K. H. (2021). *The dating divide: Race and desire in the era of online dating*. University of California Press.

Diamond-Smith, N. G., Dahal, M., Puri, M., & Weiser, S. D. (2020). Semi-arranged marriages and dowry ambivalence: Tensions in the changing landscape of marriage formation in South Asia. *Culture, Health & Sexuality, 22*(9), 971–986. https://doi.org/10.1080/13691058.2019.1646318

dickey, l., & Puckett, J. (2023). *Affirmative therapy with transsexual and gender nonconforming patients*. Hogrefe.

Hunter, M. (2007). The persistent problem of colorism: Skin tone, status, and inequality. *Sociology Compass, 1*(1), 237–254. https://doi.org/10.1111/j.1751-9020.2007.00006.x

Jones, B. E., & Ferguson, A. (2020). Black and gay: A historical perspective of black gay men. *Journal of Gay & Lesbian Mental Health, 24*(4), 336–359. https://doi.org/10.1080/19359705.2020.1798683

Kugle, Scott Siraj Al-Haq (2010). *Homosexuality in Islam: Critical reflection on gay, lesbian and transgender Muslims.* Oneworld Publications.

Musawah. (2024, October 20). *Global repository of Muslim family laws.* https://campaign-forjustice.musawah.org/repository/lebanon/

Peck, A. J., Berkowitz, D., & Tinkler, J. (2021). Left, right, black, and white: How white college students talk about their inter- and intra- racial swiping preferences on Tinder. *Sociological Spectrum, 41*(4), 304–321. https://doi.org/10.1080/02732173.2021.1916663

Pew Research Center (2024, October 20). *Living in polygamous households is very uncommon in most places.* https://www.pewresearch.org/short-reads/2020/12/07/polygamy-is-rare-around-the-world-and-mostly-confined-to-a-few-regions/ft_2020-12-07_polygamy_01-png/ https://doi.org/10.35629/3002-12110107

Quinn, K., Dickson-Gomez, J., DiFranceisco, W., Kelly, J. A., St. Lawrence, J. S., Amirkhanian, Y. A., & Broaddus, M. (2015). Correlates of internalized homonegativity among Black men who have sex with men. *AIDS Education and Prevention, 27*(3), 212–226. https://doi.org/10.1521/aeap.2015.27.3.212

Robinson, T. (2024, October 27). *Towelhead movie review.* https://www.ihavenet.com/towelhead-movie-review-michael-phillips.html

Starr, E., & Adams, M. (2016). The domestic exotic: Mail-order brides and the paradox of globalized intimacies. *Signs, 41*(4), 953–975. https://doi.org/10.1086/685480

Thomas, R. J. (2020). Online exogamy reconsidered: Estimating the internet's effects on racial, educational, religious, political and age assortative mating. *Social Forces, 98*(3), 1257–1286.

Tsunokai, G. T., Kposowa, A. J., Carroll, E., & Karamoko, M. (2019). The color continuum: Skin tone and online dating preferences among Asian Americans. *Journal of Social and Personal Relationships, 36*(11–12), 4027–4047. https://doi.org/10.1177/0265407519847772

USAGov. (2024, November 3). *Learn about K-1 fiancé(e) visas and sponsoring a future spouse.* https://www.usa.gov/fiance-visa#:~:text=If%20you%20are%20issued%20a,days%20and%20cannot%20be%20extended.

Wedding, D. (2024). *A clinical psychologist goes to the movies, Part 2: Poor Things.* Hogrefe Spotlight. https://www.hogrefe.com/eu/article/a-clinical-psychologist-goes-to-the-movies-part-2-1

Zhigalova, M. (2024, July 10). Mail order marriage statistics – how successful they are in 2024? *Medium.* https://medium.com/@margaritazhigalova/mail-order-marriage-statistics-327fd64ead0f

Chapter 4
Community

> "And he came on the back of a whale. A man to lead a new people. Our ancestor, Paikea. But now we are waiting for the firstborn of the new generation, for the descendant of the whale rider. For the boy who would be chief."
>
> *Whale Rider*

Questions to Consider While Watching
Whale Rider (2002)

- Do you think leadership qualities are gender specific? If so, how?
- Are there differences in style between a male leadership and a female leadership?
- Why do you think most leaders historically have been male?
- How does culture inform who can be a leader?
- How do you think Koro feels about Pai (Paikea) surviving her mother's and twin brother's death?
- How do you understand Koro's complicated relationship with his granddaughter Pai?
- Pai's father moved to Germany leaving her behind with Koro, her grandfather. How do you understand this?
- What was the effect of Koro prohibiting Pai from learning Māori martial arts?
- What do you think about how Pai circumnavigated her grandfather's prohibition?
- What is the significance of history among Indigenous communities?
- What is the function of demarcating gender roles in communities?

Community and Culture

The concept of community refers to interactions between individuals who share a set of values, beliefs, and expectations that inform their behavior. Out of this process cultural values and norms emerge to guide the behavior of community members. Indeed, culture is embedded in the concept of community. However, community is a complex construct. To illustrate, a community is more than its residents. Instead, it is a sociopsychological construct. Community members may be born in a specific physical location, or in another place. Moreover, members may have moved out of the community, hoping to return, but be unable to do so. In short, community is the unit of an efficient human group.

Community and *Whale Rider*

Based on a novel by Witi Ihimaera, *Whale Rider* (2002) is a New Zealand–German film written and directed by Niki Caro. It stars Keisha Castle-Hughes as Paikea (Pai), who was nominated for the Academy Award Best Actress category at age 13 in this extraordinary film. The movie is about a contemporary New Zealand Māori community whose members are expecting a leader to be born to lead them into greatness.

Paikea (Pai) is a 12-year-old Māori girl. She was born a twin, but her twin brother died at childbirth. Sadly, her mother also died giving birth. After this tragedy, Pai's father moved to Germany. He left the community because Koro (his father) was pressuring him to take leadership of the tribe. Disappointed with his son, Koro assumes the leadership of his community. Nanny and Koro, Pai's grandparents, raise her. Koro develops an affectionate but ambivalent relationship with his granddaughter. He carries Pai to school every day on his bicycle. Pai expresses her interest in becoming her community's leader:

> A long time ago, my ancestor Paikea came to this place on the back of a whale. Since then, in every generation of my family, the firstborn son has carried his name and become the leader of our tribe ... until now.

Koro vigorously opposes Pai's wish to become the community's leader – solely because she is female. Pai is hurt by her grandfather's rigid patriarchal position. She feels mistreated by Koro, and when her father comes to visit, she decides to go to Germany to live with him. While riding in the car with her father, Pai senses that the whales are calling her back. She changes her mind and decides to stay in the village.

Figure 4.1.   *Whale Rider* (2002, South Pacific Pictures, ApolloMedia Distribution, Pandora Filmproduktion, New Zealand Film Production Fund, et al.). Produced by John Barnett, Reinhard Brundig, John Crye, Bill Gavin, et al. Directed by Niki Caro. Māori girls were forbidden to be a Chief or learn the art of warfare.

Loyal to tradition, Koro continues to discourage Pai from becoming the leader. He hopes to find a male leader. Koro calls all the adolescent boys and instructs them on how to be a Māori. Indeed, multicultural psychological research has indicated that adolescents' strong ethnocultural identity correlates with positive psychological functioning (Umaña-Taylor & Updegraff, 2007). Koro teaches the adolescent boys how to use the *taiaha* (a fighting stick), a practice traditionally reserved for males only. Today, the *taiaha* is a cultural practice that is used to introduce the Māori culture to Māori school children (see the section on "Further Exploration" in this chapter for more information on *taiaha* and its cultural use).

Paikea: My name is Paikea Apirana, and I come from a long line of chiefs stretching all the way back to the whale rider. I'm not a prophet, but I know that our people will keep going forward, all together, with all of our strength.

Paikea delivering her speech as a descendant of the whale rider at her school in *Whale Rider.*

Pai secretly watches the *taiaha* lessons. Nanny, her grandmother, informs her that Pai's uncle won a *taiaha* competition when he was young. Pai takes secret lessons from her uncle. Hemi, a student at the cultural school, befriends Pai. They practice the *taiaha* and Pai wins a fight over Hemi.

When Koro finds out that Pai won the *taiaha* fight against Hemi, he becomes furious. Koro then throws the *rei puta* (whale tooth) into the ocean, a tradition that identifies the Māori who retrieves it as the community leader. When none of the males can retrieve the whale tooth, Koro implores the ancient whales. Pai also calls upon the ancients. While swimming, she finds the whale tooth and wants to heal the conflict between her and Koro. Pai invites her grandfather to a school event where she will deliver a speech she composed in honor of the community traditions.

Koro does not hear Pai's speech because he is late. When he arrives at the school, he notices a group of southern whales lying on the beach. The villagers try to entice the whales to go back into the water without success. Koro interprets this event as an omen regarding his failure to find a leader. He prohibits Pai from approaching the largest whale, who represents the legendary Paikea.

What happens next? Does Pai obey Koro? Will she accept her fate as a female, and renounce her wish to be a leader? Will Pai ride the whale?

Watch this evocative movie and enjoy the glorious culmination of this extraordinary story. After watching the movie, feel free to read Kevin V. Dodd's (2012) article on myth and the empowerment of women.

Movies About Community That Will Teach You About Culture

Movies about community will teach you about culture. A community may have a specific demarcated physical location, such as the remote village in Iran in the movie *The Stoning of Soraya M.* Conversely, there can be several communities within a community, like in the movie *Mixed Blood*. Moreover, communities can have a general culture, in addition to several subcultures within the overarching community. For instance, the film *In Jackson Heights* is a superb illustration of multiple communities within a major community. There are several movies that show the cultural influence of communities over their members, including the following examples.

Prejudice, Discrimination, Racism, and Ethnocentrism

Written and directed by Paul Morrissey, *Mixed Blood* (1985), is a movie about the drug trade in New York City's Lower East Side alphabet section (Avenues A, B, and C) during the 1980s. Paul Morrissey and Alan Bowne wrote the screenplay, and Morrisey revealed that he was inspired to do the movie by real community events published in daily newspapers (https://www.youtube.com/watch?v=qD4ft4kt2fo). Interestingly, this was actor John Leguizamo's first movie. Film critic Vincent Canby (1985) wrote in *The New York Times* on October 18, 1985:

> Paul Morrissey continues to be a cinema original and his *Mixed Blood*, a most orthodox look at the drug trade on New York's Lower East Side, is successively comic, brutal, primitive, and sophisticated. ... The surprise is that it [*Mixed Blood*] hasn't dated, possibly because no one else has ever successfully done anything like it. (Section C, Page 10)

Plagued with violence, this kind of *cinema verité* shows the effects of gentrification on marginalized communities in New York City's Lower East side. Among these communities, the main business is illicit drug sales. The movie is infused with Caribbean music, including songs by New York Puerto Rican Willie Colón and Héctor Lavoe. If you like classic New York salsa music, you are in for a treat. Indeed, Paul Morrisey said:

> In the case of *Mixed Blood*, the music was so vital and ... the music from countries that have a very poor standard of living, like most of the countries in the Caribbean, or even the poor countries in Africa, are so positive, and upbeat, and melodious, and musical and fun, and enjoyable ... (https://www.youtube.com/watch?v=qD4ft4kt2fo)

Rita La Punta (played by Brazilian actress Marília Pêra), a Brazilian woman, leads an adolescent drug ring called *Los Maceteros*. This name may be an allusion to *Los Macheteros* ("the Machete Wielders"; *Ejército Popular Boricua*), a clandestine Puerto Rican organization working for the independence of Puerto Rico.

Never mix blood.

Rita La Punta in *Mixed Blood*

La Punta lives in dilapidated quarters with her son Thiago (played by Richard Ulacia), who is intellectually limited but street-smart, and Toni (played by Geraldine Smith), a Brazilian prostitute who is Thiago's girlfriend. La Punta also lives with her "adopted" boys (Latinx gang members). She takes care of them and prohibits them from using drugs. La Punta adheres to the model of *Menudo* ("small change"), a Puerto Rican boy musical band, whose members retired when they reached 18 years of age. (Interestingly, singer/actor Ricky Martin was an original member of the Menudo band). In this way, La Punta only recruits young adolescents, who, due to their age, cannot be sent to jail for committing serious crimes.

The movie's title refers to Rita La Punta's belief that one should "never mix blood," indicating that she does not include members of different ethnic groups in *Los Maceteros*. This perspective reinforces an **us vs. them** position, providing a sense of in-group membership. Indeed, gang membership offers many youths of color a sense of belonging, given that they are marginalized within an oppressive racist society.

La Punta decides to expand her drug territory and invades Juan the Bullet's gang members' (the Dancers) grounds. A drug war erupts between the two gangs. At the same time, the Lower East Side community is being gentrified, and this process interferes with the illegal drug business.

Mixed Blood portrays death by murder as a normal aspect of drug life. To illustrate, early in the movie, La Punta visits a funeral parlor after the Dancers killed a *macetero*. While discussing the funeral, another *macetero* chooses the casket for his burial, in a matter-of-fact manner, expecting to be murdered in the near future.

The movie depicts **horizontal racism** among ethnic and racial drug gangs. According to liberation psychology, horizontal racism is a form of internalized racism and oppression (Martín-Baró, 1994). *Mixed Blood* is full of racist slurs and **microaggressions**, as well as homophobic insults. For instance, talking with an Asian American cop about the effects of ethnic drug gangs fighting with each other, La Punta says to a police officer: "We can always go to the Chinks for our supply, or even the Niggers, if we have to."

Mixed Blood offers a powerful illustration of **internalized racism**. For instance, while combing Thiago's hair, Toni tells him that he can pass as White if he dyes his hair blond.

An iconic scene in the movie depicts several drug lords discussing the drug wars during a meeting with local crooked policemen. There are numerous racial epithets uttered, illustrating internalized racism, as well as horizontal aggression. Simply put, **horizontal aggression** occurs when members of an oppressed group verbally and or physically attack members of other oppressed groups (including their own group; Martín-Baró, 1994). For instance, a Latinx former police officer, now a drug dealer, expresses his interracial racist frustration: "Those Koreans, with their fruit stands, open around the clock. Man, they never stop working.... Listen, we have regular hours, OK, we have a family to go home to – shit like that."

Carol (played by Linda Kerridge) is the White girlfriend of The German (played by Ulrich Berr), a drug dealer in the Lower East Side. Carol accompanies The German to a meeting at La Punta's place. Carol and Thiago eye each other. Later on, La Punta is surprised when she sees Carol walking behind Thiago out of the only bedroom in the place.

La Punta and her son Thiago occasionally share a bed. *Are there cultural and or socioeconomic differences regarding sleeping arrangements? How do you feel about a mother sharing her bed with a grown son?*

Carol invites Thiago to visit a bar outside the Lower East Side. Thiago ignores La Punta's prohibition about leaving the alphabet area community and leaves the lower east side to accompany Carol. They have a drink at a fancy establishment. However, while exiting the bar, The Dancers attack them and kill a *macetero* who was accompanying Thiago. As a result, severe negative consequences emerge. A different kind of war is declared.

Who is betrayed? Who dies? What happens to the community?

It is difficult to explain the allure of this movie, and there are no lukewarm reviews about *Mixed Blood*. Simply put, viewers either love it or hate it. Watch *Mixed Blood* and judge it for yourself.

The Hate U Give (2018), directed by George Tillman Jr., is based on Angie Thomas's book by the same title and the screenplay by Audrey Wells. Angie Thomas, who had a teen rap career, identified rappers as her biggest literary influence (Feldman, 2019). Angie Thomas is also one of the executive producers of the film.

As long as I play it cool and keep to myself, I should be fine. The ironic thing is though, at Williamson I don't have to "play it cool" – I'm cool by default because I'm one of the only Black kids there. I have to earn coolness in Garden Heights, and that's more difficult than buying retro Jordans on release day.

Funny how it works with White kids though. It's dope to be Black until it's hard to be Black.

Starr contemplates the difficulties that come with code switching when she transfers from a Black school to one that is predominately White in *The Hate U Give.*

Starr Carter (Amandla Stenberg), a 16-year-old African American adolescent girl, alternates between two communities: one rich and White, the other, poor and Black. Starr lives in Garden Heights, a fictional African American community, and studies at a rich, mostly White private school. She lives with her father, Maverick (Mav) Carter (played by Russell Hornsby), mother, Lisa Carter (played by Regina Hall), older half-brother, Seven (played by Lamar Johnson), and Sekani, her younger brother.

Managing two opposite communities, Starr exhibits **code-switching behavior**. This concept refers to the different ways individuals behave and interact according to the specific sociocultural contexts. A linguistic concept, code switching was originally coined to denote changes in language according to context. However, code-switching behavior has been extended to include racial, cultural, socioeconomic, and community contexts.

The movie begins with Maverick Carter explaining to his children what to do if the police stop them. He instructs them that they have to place their hands so that the police can see them. This instruction is an example of **racial socialization**. This multicultural psychological concept describes how people of color socialize their children about race, ethnicity, racial discrimination, and racial injustice (Hughes et al., 2006).

Starr goes to a party at her Garden Heights community and sees Khalil (played by Algee Smith), a childhood friend. They re-connect, and while talking, they hear shots, and everyone runs out of the house. Khalil's car is nearby, and he asks Starr to come along. They drive off and stop to reminisce about old times and Khalil kisses Starr. She tells him that she has a boyfriend. Khalil drives on. A White policeman stops them due to Khalil's failure to use turn signals. Starr gets anxious and tells Khali to place his hands on the car dashboard so that the cop can see his hands. The policeman asks Khalil to lower the music, and Khalil gets into a verbal confrontation. The policeman asks Khalil to step out of the car while he checks Khalil's driver's license. Standing up, Khalil leans into the car to get a hairbrush. Thinking that Khalil has a gun, the policeman shoots and kills him.

The incident became a major issue in the Garden Heights community. As a witness, Starr is quiet about the incident, and her silence disrupts her

Maverick "Mav" Carter: I ain't set a good example of a Black man for you.

Starr Carter: No, you didn't. You set a good example of what a man should be.

Starr recognizes her father's positive qualities despite his past mistakes in *The Hate U Give*.

code-switching ability to negotiate her two communities. Starr's relationships with her White friends are affected, including her relationship with Chris, her White boyfriend.

Is Chris exhibiting color blindness (the belief that race /color does not matter)? Along these lines, psychologist Stephanie Fryberg (2010) notes that White people can ignore racism, feeling comfortable with their relative White privilege in society. *Do you think Chris exhibited aversive color-blind racism* (Bonilla-Silva, 2013)? *What effect did Chris's color blindness have on Starr?* To explore this, let's examine Starr's response to Chris:

"If you don't see my blackness, you don't see me."

Deborah Son Holoien and J. Nicole Shelton (2012) conducted a study with university students examining the effects of priming White individuals with colorblind or multicultural approaches to diversity prior to interacting with ethnic minorities. The results indicated that ethnic minorities matched with Whites who had a colorblind approach to diversity showed poorer cognitive functioning on a cognitive test than those who were matched with Whites who had a multicultural approach to diversity. The findings suggest that Whites with a color-blind orientation may affect the cognitive functioning of those ethnic minorities they encounter.

King (played by Anthony Mackie), the local drug lord, threatens Starr and her family if she speaks up. Since Khalil worked for King, he fears negative consequences for his drug business. As a community, Garden Heights gets

Figure 4.2.   *The Hate U Give* (2018, Fox 2000 Pictures, State Street Pictures, TSG Entertainment, Temple Hill Entertainment). Produced by Timothy Bourne, Marty Bowen, H. H. Cooper, John Fischer, et al. Directed by George Tillman Jr. Starr must engage in code switching, altering her speech, vocabulary, and mannerisms, when she transfers to Williamson High School, so she won't be perceived as "ghetto."

organized to protest police brutality against African Americans. *Will Starr speak up? If she does, what happens to her and to her family? Will she honor her name? In other words, will she shed light into the darkness?*

The title of the movie *The Hate U Give* refers to Tupac Shakur's statement: "The hate u give little infants fucks everyone." He identified the acronym THUG LIFE as an element of liberation within the Black Panthers' movement (Massey, 2016).

Social Norms and Norm Violations: *The Stoning of Soraya M.*

The Stoning of Soraya M. (2008) is a painful, yet powerful, film based on Freidoune Sahebjam's book *La Femme Lapidée*, a true story. The film was condemned and banned in Iran. Cyrus Nowrasteh, an American with Iranian parents, directed this Persian-language American film. The film stars are Academy Award nominee Shohren Aghdashloo (as Zahra), James Caviezel (as the foreign journalist Freidoune Sahebjam), and Mozhan Marno (as Soraya M.). This movie had eight Academy Award nominations and six wins. The film's many awards include the Director's Choice Award at the 2008 Toronto International Film Festival.

Set in Iran, this shocking film tells the story of Soraya M., an innocent woman in a remote Iranian village whose unfaithful husband accused her of adultery. Freidoune Sahebjam is a journalist traveling through Iran when he encounters car trouble in a remote village. He meets Zahra, Soraya's aunt who tells him Soraya's story, shortly after her execution.

The Stoning of Soraya M. illustrates how a community betrays itself by the manipulation of a self-centered middle-aged man who wanted his wife (Soraya M.) out of the way so he can marry a 14-year-old girl. To achieve his goal, he convinces the community that Soraya is guilty of adultery. The community becomes complicit, and through its **entrenched patriarchy**, violates cultural, social, and Islamic religious norms. As a result, Soraya is condemned to death by stoning. She is buried alive to her waist in a hole in the middle of

In a world of victims and executioners, it is the job of thinking people not to side with the executioners.

Howard Zinn's opening line in *The Stoning of Soraya M.*

Figure 4.3. *The Stoning of Soraya M.* (2008, Roadside Attractions, Mpower Distribution, Mpower Pictures, Prime Meridian Pictures, Fallen Films). Produced by Todd Burns, Diane Hendricks, Jason Jones, Stephen Marinaccio, et al. Directed by Cyrus Nowrasteh. This film is a dramatic and deeply disturbing illustration of patriarchy, extreme sexism, and cruelty.

the village square. Then, a crowd composed of relatives, neighbors, and community members stone her. To make sure that Soraya is dead, her husband checks her face, and shouts: "The bitch is still alive." The mob crosses in, and Soraya is stoned until she dies.

According to director Cyrus Nowrasteh, the stoning scene was so horrendous that many people walked out of the movie theater (Hazelton, 2010). Notwithstanding the horrific stoning scene, this movie is a testament to the power of **bearing witness**. Like Freidoune Sahebjam, who bore witness to Zahra's story of Soraya's unjust murder, when you watch *The Stoning of Soraya M.*, you bear witness to the injustice committed against an innocent woman.

To **bear witness** refers to listening to painful and traumatic stories in a compassionate way that conveys empathy, support, and validation. For example,

Ebrahim: [*instructing Soyara*] When a man accuses his wife, she must prove her innocence. That is the law. On the other hand, if a wife accuses her husband, she must prove his guilt. Do you understand?

Zahra: [*to Ebrahim*] Yes, it's clear, all women are guilty, and all men are innocent.

A description of misogynous and cruel treatment
in *The Stoning of Soraya M.*

instead of passive listening mode, the trauma psychotherapist engages in the active process of bearing witness to his or her client's story (Herman, 1992).

Film director Cyrus Nowrasteh hopes that this movie's impact pressures Iran's government to change its laws that allow women convicted of adultery to be stoned to death. He wants the laws to be changed to eliminate stoning and instead use hanging, a less gruesome method of killing (Hazelton, 2010).

Cultural Identity: *In Jackson Heights*

Directed, produced, and edited by Frederick Wiseman, *In Jackson Heights* is a fascinating story showcasing the amalgamation of diverse ethnic communities living in Jackson Heights, in the Queens neighborhood of New York.

This documentary presents Latinx, Indian, Muslim, Jews, LGBTQ, undocumented immigrants, and older people in diverse facets of their daily lives. The film is in English, French, Italian, Indian, Arabic, and Spanish (with subtitles in English). Indeed, when residents speak in their native language it adds a richer sense of reality to the documentary. Although a long film, *In Jackson Heights* has a special quality, one that invites you to become immersed in the residents' day-to-day life. As such, it regales you with fascinating scenes illustrating the realities of diverse ethnic groups' activities, such as a Middle Eastern shop for threading eyebrows, an Indian hand-painting establishment, a Jewish senior center, and an undocumented Latinx community meeting, among many others.

A poignant scene in this documentary shows a Mexican woman telling her **testimonio** of how her daughter and a woman friend spent 2 weeks lost in the desert trying to get to the United States. Born in Latin America, *testimonio* is a form of life history that promotes resistance, struggle, and social–political transformation (Cienfuegos & Monelli, 1983). As a therapeutic approach, *testimonio* nurtures cultural survival, agency, and resilience (Smith, 2010–2011)?

A moving scene in the film shows a community worker preparing immigrants for their citizenship test:

"If the examiner asks you, why do you want to become a US citizen, what do you say?"

An Indian woman seeking to become an American citizen answers in Bengalese.

"I don't understand Bengalese," the community worker said. She continued: "You say: I want to vote. I want to live in a democracy. I want to live in freedom."

In Jackson Heights will fill you with hope. It shows the resilience among diverse ethnic and immigrant groups – a quality that benefits the whole

Because we came here flying or walking, dry or wet, but all equal. We got wet in the Rio Grande, those who came earlier got wet in the Atlantic. That's the difference.

> Latinx immigrant man speaking at a community meeting in *In Jackson Heights.*

community. In fact, the film is an ode to immigrant groups. *In Jackson Heights* illustrates the positive psychological qualities prevalent among immigrants and in their communities (Cobb et al., 2019).

This documentary shows how immigrants' cultural identity informs their lives. At the same time, it illustrates how they become Americans without losing their deep cultural roots. Watching *In Jackson Heights* leaves you with the feeling of having been an invisible guest in the life of diverse ethnic communities.

Stereotyping: *Slumdog Millionaire*

Slumdog Millionaire (2008), directed by Danny Boyle and written by Simon Beaufoy, was filmed in India. The main actors of the film are Dev Patel (as Jamal Malik), Freida Pinto (as Latika), Madhur Mittal (as Salim), and Anil Kapoor (as Prem).

Prem Kumar: [*starting lines*] So, Jamal, tell me something about yourself.

Jamal Malik: I work in a call center in Juhu.

Prem Kumar: Phone basher! And what type of call center would that be?

Jamal Malik: XL5 mobile phones.

Prem Kumar: Ohh ... so you're the one who calls me up every single day of my life with special offers?

Jamal Malik: Actually, I'm an assistant.

Prem Kumar: An assistant phone basher? And what does an assistant phone basher do exactly?

Jamal Malik: I get tea for people and...

Prem Kumar: Well ladies and gentlemen, Jamal Malik, ... let's play Who Wants to Be a Millionaire!

> A television game show host tries to humiliate a humble and unlikely contestant in the film *Slumdog Millionaire.*

Jamal Malik is an 18-year-old orphan from the slums of Mumbai, India. He is competing on India's version of *Who Wants to Be a Millionaire?* Jamal is one question away from winning the grand prize of 20 million rupees. When the show breaks for the night, Jamal is arrested because the policemen suspect that he is cheating on the show. How can an adolescent from the slums be knowledgeable enough to win a game show? The police stereotype Jamal because he is a member of a low caste (*dalit*) and consequently treat him as such.

The caste system was reinforced by the **British colonization of India**, and this ancient system is the longest surviving example of sociopolitical stratification. Indeed, although **caste discrimination** has been illegal since India's Independence (https://www.bbc.com/news/world-asia-india-35650616), members of the lower caste continue to be stereotyped. In the movie, the policemen beat Jamal up, hoping for a confession. To prove his innocence, Jamal tells them the story of how he and his brother Salim survived living in the slums. He narrates the scary adventures they experienced growing up and on the road. Additionally, Jamal tells them about Latika, the girl he loved and

Figure 4.4.   *Slumdog Millionaire* (2008, Searchlight Pictures, Warner Brothers, and Film4). Produced by Christian Colson, Francois Ivernel, Ivana MacKinnon, Cameron McCracken, et al. Directed by Danny Boyle and Loveleen Tandan. A lower-caste teen has the good fortune to win 20 million rupees on the Indian television show *Kaun Banega Crorepati*? (*Who Wants to Be a Millionaire?*).

lost. His stories are inspired by how Jamal, Shalim, and Latika view themselves as Alexander Dumas's *The Three Musketeers*.

Slumdog Millionaire is an engaging and heart-warming movie that is a delight to watch. This epic movie is a story of adversity, survival, coming of age, hope, and love. Jamal's stories and flashbacks reveal how he learned the answers to the game show questions. Perhaps you can learn from all your experiences how to conquer the challenges you may find in your life.

Indigenous People: *The Gods Must Be Crazy*

The Gods Must Be Crazy (1980) is a South African comedy written, directed, and produced by Jaime Uys. The film actors are the Namibian San farmer N!xau Toma (as Xi), Andrew Steyn (as Marius Weber), and Kate Thompson (as Sandra Prinsloo).

The first scene in this entertaining movie depicts a pilot tossing an empty glass bottle of Coca Cola out of the window of a flying plane. The bottle reaches the land unbroken. Xi, a San member of a Bushmen tribe from the Kalahari Desert, finds the empty bottle. His Indigenous tribe has no contact with the outside world. According to this community, the bottle is a present from the gods. As such, the gift needs to be used. Since the gift is a single bottle, the community begins to experience conflicts about its usage. As a result, Xi decides that the gift (the bottle) must be returned to the gods. Since the tribe members believe that the gods live at the end of the world, Xi embarks on an odyssey to return the gift.

This entertaining film revolves around Xi's journey to return the empty bottle at the end of the world. During his odyssey, Xi encounters several characters including Andrew Steyn, a biologist studying wildlife; M'pudi, Steyn's Land Rover mechanic; a school teacher named Kate Thompson; a group of guerrillas headed by Sam Boga; and Jack Hind, an arrogant safari tour guide.

Like Odysseus in *The Odyssey*, Xi experiences multiple adventures, incidents, and misunderstandings. At one point Xi is jailed.

"They gave him a death sentence," M'pudi says to Steyn.

"For shooting a goat?" Steyn asks.

"No, 3 months in jail. Same thing, he gonna die for sure. He never seen a wall in his life, now he got walls all round him." M'pudi says.

This amusing movie offers you a superb example of **cultural shock**. In psychology, culture shock refers to individuals' behaviors and adjustment when they move from one cultural environment to another one (Weaver, 1994).

The Gods Must Be Crazy became one of the most successful South African films. *Watch this iconic movie and see how cross-cultural interactions are portrayed, and how cross-cultural communications are managed. Witness Xi's arrival at God's Window. Finally, find out what he does next.*

Additional Films About Community and Culture

Midsommar (2019) is a remarkable horror film that illustrates life in a cult community. *Little Children* (2006) depicts a community torn apart by the arrival of a registered sex offender. *Brooklyn* (2015) traces the life of an Irish immigrant and contrasts life and love in two very different countries: Ireland and the United States. Lars von Trier's *Dogville* (2003) stars Nicole Kidman as a woman on the run from the mob who finds refuge in a small Colorado community.

Nomadland (2020) stars one of our favorite actors, Frances McDormand, who takes up life in a van-dwelling nomadic community, and *Parasite* (2019) contrasts the lives of a wealthy Korean community with that of the servants who work in that community. *Triangle of Sadness* (2022) is a satirical black comedy about celebrities on a luxury cruise ship who become stranded on an island. The film is an indictment of capitalism. *Motherless Brooklyn* (2019) stars Ed Norton as a private detective with Tourette syndrome and illustrates how a 1950s New York community responds to the disorder. *The Stepford Wives* (1975) is a compelling portrayal of the potential outcome when men control a community, and *My Big Fat Greek Wedding* (2002) and its sequels offer insight into what life is like in a Greek/American community in Chicago. *Beasts of the Southern Wild* (2012) will give you a sense for the challenges associated with life in a bayou community, as will *Where the Crawdads Sing* (2022). Part of the joy of watching movies is being exposed vicariously to communities and cultures that may be very different from your own.

Critical Thinking Questions About Community and Culture

- What is the role of myth in Indigenous communities?
- How do you feel about discrimination due to a caste system?
- Do you think people are stereotyped according to their socioeconomic class? If so, how?

- How do you describe your cultural identity?
- Were you racially socialized when you were a child? If so, how?
- Are US citizens stereotypes based on socioeconomic class? If so, can you think of examples?
- Do you associate the drug trade with specific racial or ethnic groups?
- Do you think racial socialization impacts psychological functioning? If so, how?
- What do you think about color-blindness? What about color-blind racism?
- If you are White, do you think your interactions with people of color are mediated by your orientation to diversity (color-blind or multicultural)?
- If you are a person of color, what is your reaction to your interactions with people who have a color-blind orientation to diversity?
- How would you describe the status of women in patriarchal communities?
- Do all patriarchal communities treat women the same way? If not, what are the differences?
- What are the links between systematic racism and the caste system of India (e.g., *dalits*).
- Why did India ban the classification of "untouchables"? Did the ban work?
- Have you experienced culture shock? If so, what was it like for you?

Further Exploration

If you only have time for one article, read:

Jorm, A. F. (2012). Mental health literacy: Empowering the community to take action for better mental health. *American Psychologist, 67*(3), 231–243. https://doi.org/10.1037/a0025957

If you only have time to read one chapter about communities and culture, make it:

Creak, A., Dixon, H., & Sohawon, Z. "Z." (2024). Engaging with diverse communities. In H. Sharp & L. Walker (Eds.), *Participation in children and young people's mental health: An essential guide* (pp. 148–157). Routledge.

If you have time to read a book, we recommend:

Comas-Díaz, L. (2012). *Multicultural care: A clinician's guide to cultural competence.* American Psychological Association. https://doi.org/10.1037/13491-000

To understand the role of *taiaha* in the Māori culture, watch the documentary:

Rangatira: Pita Sharples at https://www.nzonscreen.com/title/rangatira-pita-sharples-1997

To watch Paul Morrissey's discussion of his movie *Mixed Blood*, check out the YouTube video available at:

https://www.youtube.com/watch?v=qD4ft4kt2fo

Here's how Tupac inspired *The Hate You Give*:

https://www.epicreads.com/blog/tupac-thug-life-hate-u-give/

If you want to know more about Māori spirituality, read this article after watching *Whale Rider*:

"Whale Rider: The Re-enactment of Myth and the Empowerment of Women":
https://digitalcommons.unomaha.edu/cgi/viewcontent.cgi?article=1017&context=jrf

References

Bonilla-Silva, E. (2013). *Racism without racists: Color-blind racism and the persistence of racial inequality in America*. Rowman & Littlefield.

Canby, V. (1985, October 18). Screen: Tough comedy. *The New York Times*. https://www.nytimes.com/1985/10/18/movies/screen-tough-comedy.html

Cienfuegos, A. J., & Monelli, C. (1983). The testimony of political repression as the therapeutic instrument. *American Journal of Orthopsychiatry, 53*(1), 43–51. https://doi.org/10.1111/j.1939-0025.1983.tb03348.x

Cobb, C. I., Branscombe, N. R., Meca, A., Schwartz, S. J., Xie, D., Zea, M. C., Molina, L. E., & Martinez, C. R (2019). Toward a positive psychology of immigrants. *Perspectives on Psychological Science, 14*(4), 619–632. https://doi.org/10.1177/1745691619825848

Dodd, K. V. (2012). Whale Rider: The re-enactment of myth and the empowerment of women. *Journal of Religion & Film, 16*(2), Article 9. https://digitalcommons.unomaha.edu/jrf/vol16/iss2/9/ https://doi.org/10.32873/uno.dc.jrf.16.02.09

Feldman, L. (2019, February 18–25). 8 Questions: Angie Thomas. *Time Magazine*. https://time.com/5521258/angie-thomas-on-the-come-up-book

Fryberg, S. (2010). When the world is colorblind, American Indians are invisible: A diversity science approach. *Psychological Inquiry, 21*(2), 115–119. https://doi.org/10.1080/1047840X.2010.483847

Hazelton, L. (2010, October 18). The horrific execution that got a film banned. … And why the director hopes it will stop death row women from being stoned. *DailyMail.com*. https://www.dailymail.co.uk/tvshowbiz/article-1320989/The-Stoning-Soraya-M-The-horrific-execution-scene-got-film-banned.html

Herman, J. (1992). *Trauma and recovery: The aftermath of violence from domestic violence to political terror*. Basic Books.

Holoien, D. S., & Shelton, J. (2012). You deplete me: The cognitive costs of colorblindness on ethnic minorities. *Journal of Experimental Social Psychology, 48*, 562–565. https://doi.org/10.1016/j.jesp.2011.09.010

Hughes, D., Rodriguez, J. Smith, E. P., Johnson, D. J., Stevenson, H. C. & Spicer, P. (2006). Parents' ethnic-racial socialization practices: A review of research and direction for future study. *Developmental Psychology, 42*(5), 747–770. https://doi.org/10.1037/0012-1649.42.5.747

Martín-Baró, I. (1994). *Writings for a liberation psychology: Ignacio Martín-Baró* (A. Aron & S. Corne, Eds. & Trans.). Harvard University Press.

Massey, C. (2016). Tupac Shakur, THUG Life, and a New Perspective. *SUNY Digital Repository.* http://hdl.handle.net/1951/71867

Smith, K. M. (2010–2011). Female voice and female text: Testimonio as a form of resistance in Latin America. *Florida Atlantic Comparative Studies Journal, 12,* 21–38.

Umaña-Taylor A. J., & Updegraff, K. A. (2007). Latino adolescent's mental health: Exploring the interrelations among discrimination, ethnic identity, cultural orientation, self-esteem, and depressive symptoms. *Journal of Adolescence, 30,* 549–567. https://doi.org/10.1016/j.adolescence.2006.08.002

Weaver, G. R. (1994). Understanding and coping with cross-cultural adjustment and stress. In G. R. Weaver (Ed.), *Culture, communication and conflict: Readings in intercultural relations* (pp. 169–189). Ginn Press.

Chapter 5
Work

> "There are patterns in everything. The color in light, the reflections in water... in math, these patterns reveal themselves in the most incredible form. It's quite beautiful."
>
> Srinivasa Ramanujan, an Indian mathematician portrayed in the film *The Man Who Knew Infinity*.

Questions to Consider While Watching
The Man Who Knew Infinity (2015)

- Ramanujan was in an arranged marriage, and he married his wife when she was 10 years old (eventually leaving her to go to Cambridge when she was 15). How old should a child be in order to marry? Should old men be allowed to marry young girls, a common practice in many parts of the world? Where does culture end and child rights begin?

- Is the racism Ramanujan experienced at Cambridge exaggerated in the film?

- How is Ramanujan's culture heritage reflected in his diet? Did it contribute to his illness?

- Ramanujan is referred to derisively by some Cambridge faculty as "Gunga Din." What is the significance of Kipling's poem to the film?

- G. H. Hardy, a confirmed bachelor, refers to his work with Ramanujan as "the one romantic incident in my life." Does this comment carry sexual overtones?

- How did being raised in a caste society prepare Ramanujan for the racism he encountered at Cambridge?

- Ramanujan is reported not to have spoken until the age of three. How common are developmental delays in children who grow up to be brilliant? Can you give other examples?

- Ramanujan belonged to the Brahmin caste. Can you identify other castes?
- Mathematicians are often portrayed as odd and eccentric. Is there any evidence for this pervasive stereotype?
- Ramanujan is a Hindu, like 80% of India's population. What other major religions are practiced in India?
- Edna St. Vincent Millay wrote, "Euclid alone has looked on beauty bare." How does this line relate to *The Man Who Knew Infinity*?
- Ramanujan never finished his college education. Can you think of other examples of brilliant people who dropped out of college?
- Why are there many more eminent male mathematicians than female mathematicians?
- India currently has a population of approximately 1.5 billion people. Can you calculate how many people in a population this size have an IQ of 160 or greater (i.e., 4 standard deviations above the mean)?
- Psychologists, like mathematicians, often work collaboratively. How did Daniel Kahneman and Amos Tversky work as a team?
- What is the difference between an immigrant and an emigrant?

Work and Culture

Culture figures prominently in the workplace, and different cultural groups respond differently to workplace demands and job requirements. To cite one example, Europeans are accustomed to long vacations, and every country in the European Union (EU) is required to grant employees at least 4 weeks of paid vacation. By contrast, the average Japanese worker only takes seven vacation days each year (Renzulli, 2015).

Age is one cultural variable that figures prominently in workplace settings, and stereotypes are common. It is hard to imagine an old Silicon Valley start-up CEO or a young Walmart greeter. Older employees are more likely to have been in one job or work at one job site for their entire careers; by contrast, millennials (people reaching young adulthood in the early part of the 21st century) are likely to expect, and find themselves in, numerous different jobs in different locations over their working career.

Educational differences are obviously important in the workplace, and employers value employees with superior knowledge and tangible skills. One clear example is found in the military: Officers have almost always graduated from college; enlisted soldiers, sailors, and airmen typically have not. Nurses take orders from doctors – and get paid considerably less – in part because of an informal caste system operating in hospitals, but in part because of differences in education and training. However, **role strain** results when there is a disconnect between education and experience; many a young Lieutenant just out of college has been tutored by a crusty Senior Master Sergeant, and smart medical residents almost always defer to the judgment of senior ward nurses. There is also a clear and robust relationship between education and income. In general, people who have professional degrees make about six times as much as people who did not graduate from high school (Strauss, 2011).

Racism may be a factor in highly technical work settings in which there are many workers who have **guest worker (H1-B) visas**. Technology companies argue that they need these visas to fill critical company positions with highly skilled employees; however, many people believe the H1-B program has been exploited and the real motivation for offering work visas is to lower the company's cost for these highly paid employees. The H-1B system currently uses a lottery to determine which applicants will get a visa; in fiscal year 2024 the U.S. Citizenship and Immigration Services (USCIS) approved 110,791 H-1B visa applications out of a pool of 758,994 applicants. It appears likely that the Trump administration will radically restructure the H1-B visa program, quite possibly replacing the lottery system with a straightforward system based solely on talent and national needs.

A similar dynamic is found with farm workers, many of whom are undocumented workers who earn more working as laborers in the United States than they can make working in their home country. The fear of undocumented workers, labeled as "murders and rapists" by Donald Trump, played a key role in the 2016 and 2024 presidential elections.

Geography is a potent cultural variable with ramifications in the workplace. For example, Manhattan is known for the pace of work that occurs there: People move quickly, and business transactions are completed swiftly. This stands in marked contrast to the interactional style likely to be encountered in the Deep South, where casual conversation and friendly banter are often expected as prologue to any sort of business deal.

Work and *The Man Who Knew Infinity*

The Man Who Knew Infinity is a 2015 film directed by Matt Brown that stars Dev Patel (known best for his roles in *Slumdog Millionaire, The Best Exotic Marigold Hotel*, and *Monkey Man*) in the lead role as Srinivasa Ramanujan with support from Jeremy Irons, who plays mathematician and Cambridge professor G. H. Hardy. The film is based on a biography of Ramanujan, a brilliant autodidact from Madras, India.

One of Ramanujan's difficulties in being accepted at Cambridge, despite his obvious brilliance, involved his lack of formal academic credentials (he had focused on mathematics and never completed his university education). To his credit, Hardy was able to appreciate his creativity and his genius, and he wasn't concerned about his protégée's lack of a university degree.

The film illustrates the clash of cultures on many different levels. Ramanujan was poor; by contrast, Cambridge professors were comfortably affluent and often wealthy. Ramanujan was deeply religious, and he viewed his mathematical ability as a gift from God; by contrast, many of the professors (like G. H. Hardy and Bertrand Russell) were atheists. Ramanujan was a strict vegetarian, unlike his Cambridge colleagues who fancied meat pies and mutton. Ramanujan was an autodidact; everyone else at Cambridge has impressive academic pedigrees. Ramanujan believed his novel mathematical insights came from God ("An equation has no meaning for me unless it expresses a thought of God"); Cambridge intellectuals demanded rigorous and methodical proofs.

Figure 5.1.   *The Man Who Knew Infinity* (2016, Paramount Pictures). Produced by Edward R. Pressman Film and Animus Films. Directed by Matthew Brown. *The Man Who Knew Infinity* illustrates many of the cultural challenges associated with the transition from a life of poverty in a developing country to life in an elite, refined, and highly structured environment like Cambridge.

British racism is most apparent in the film when three WWI soldiers confront Ramanujan, calling him a "**Wog**" (a highly offensive racial slur applied to dark-skinned people) and "a freeloading little Blackie." The soldiers beat him senseless for no reason other than the color of his skin. The racism of the Cambridge faculty is just as real, but not as conspicuous. **Linguistic privilege** is clearly present when Hardy asks, "You don't expect me to talk in Tamil, do you?" Ramanujan replies: "No, but you expect me to talk in English." Perhaps it says something about our own cultural bias that almost every high school student can recognize the names and identify the work of Isaac Newton and Albert Einstein ... but almost no one knows the name of a mathematician of equal stature, Srinivasa Ramanujan.

Anyone who desires to know more about the lives of Hardy and Ramanujan can read R. S. Albert's chapter in *Genius and Mind: Studies of Creativity and Temperament* (Albert, 1998). Dean Simonton's (2016) review of *The Man Who Knew Infinity* in *PsycCRITIQUES* is also illuminating. Simonton notes:

> Although he was only 32 years old when he died, [Ramanujan] started to make major contributions to pure mathematics while still in his 20s. These contributions have secured him a permanent and prominent place in history. Indeed, mathematicians continue to develop his ideas to the present day. More than that, Ramanujan has been called not just a genius, but rather a "magical genius." Unlike an "ordinary genius," who comes up with ideas that colleagues believe they could also conceive were they only "100 times smarter," Ramanujan's theorems and conjectures would provoke others to say, "I have no idea where those results came from" (Kolata, 1987, p. 1519).

Prejudice, Discrimination, Oppression, Racism, and Ethnocentrism

Hidden Figures (2016) is a remarkable film based on the true story of three African American women who supplied much of the brainpower necessary for NASA to put astronaut John Glenn into space following the successful Russian launch of Sputnik 1. The three women, Dorothy Vaughan, Mary Jackson, and Katherine Johnson (played by Taraji P. Henson, Octavia Spencer, and Janelle Monáe, respectively), had to overcome both racist and sexist barriers to achieve success, and the film highlights the challenges they faced.

In an early scene, a racist cop stops the three women after their car breaks down as they are driving to their job at NASA's Langley Research Center. The policeman is initially incredulous that Black women could be working at the space center; after becoming convinced that they were telling the truth, he escorts them to work. The scene highlights the problem of **racial profiling** and the specific phenomenon of "**driving while Black**" (DWB). More information about this practice is available in a special issue of the *Journal of Contemporary Criminal Justice* (Novak, 2012).

It is somewhat shocking to realize that as late as 1961, employees were segregated by race, and there was a special division for 20 African American women working in the space program as "human computers" (before the introduction of real computers). Katherine Johnson breaks out of this special program because she is brilliant, and someone with her talents is needed to work with the White engineers.

Moving to an integrated team proved problematic for many reasons, not the least of which was the fact that the "Colored restrooms" and dining facilities for Black workers were housed in a separate building. When the head of the program, Al Harrison (played by Kevin Costner), chides Johnson for being away from her desk so often, she tears up and replies:

> There are no colored bathrooms in this building, or any building outside the West Campus, which is half a mile away. Did you know that? I have to walk to Timbuktu just to relieve myself! ... I work like a dog day and night, living on coffee from a pot none of you want to touch! So, excuse me if I have to go to the restroom a few times a day.

Harrison promptly marches to the Ladies room and tears down a "Whites Only" sign, commenting, "Here at NASA, we all pee the same color." Historically, marginalized groups have been stigmatized by the requirement that they use separate facilities for toileting (e.g., the military once had separate toilets for officers and enlisted personnel; Black and Whites once had sepa-

---

Karl Zielinski: Mary, a person with an engineer's mind should be an engineer. You can't be a computer the rest of your life.

Mary Jackson: Mr. Zielinski, I'm a Negro woman. I'm not gonna entertain the impossible.

Karl Zielinski: And I'm a Polish Jew whose parents died in a Nazi prison camp. Now I'm standing beneath a spaceship that's going to carry an astronaut to the stars. I think we can say we are living the impossible. Let me ask you, if you were a white male, would you wish to be an engineer?

Mary Jackson: I wouldn't have to. I'd already be one.

A Jewish engineer supports the dreams of an African American woman in *Hidden Figures*.

Figure 5.2.   *Hidden Figures* (2016, Fox 2000 Pictures, Chernin Entertainment, Levantine Films, TSG Entertainment). Produced by Peter Chernin, Jamal Daniel, Donna Gigliotti, Kevin Halloran, et al. Directed by Theodore Melfi. *Hidden Figures* has been criticized as a "White savior" film, in part because of an iconic scene in which Kevin Costner's character uses a sledgehammer to tear down a hated "colored bathroom" sign.

rate toilets and drinking fountains; and until the Americans With Disabilities Act, handicapped people were required to use separate restrooms). In the film, we see that the bathroom for White women is clearly cleaner, neater, and better maintained than the restroom for African American women – "**separate but equal**" is a comforting concept for many people, but it was never achieved, in restrooms or in education.

Fei Wang (2018), in an article titled "Hidden Figures and White Savior," criticized this part of the film, asking:

> What if instead of Al Harrison, the white boss, we let Katherine the black heroine smash the sign? And when security came to intervene, Harrison could back her up. Indeed, in a systematic racist society, any regulation changes must come from white people who set the rules. So there are many "good white people." But do they need to be shown actively "saving" the minorities? Couldn't they take a back seat, [letting] a minority be the hero ...?

We are currently seeing "bathroom politics" play out in the transgender community, with states like North Carolina passing laws requiring people to use the bathroom of the gender they were assigned at birth rather than the gender with which they identify.

Another powerful symbol of the racism inherent in the NASA workplace was Katherine Johnson's coworkers' insistence that she drink from a separate coffee pot, as they were uncomfortable sharing the communal coffee that was made each morning. This occurs despite the grudging acceptance of Katherine's brilliance and mathematical expertise.

In one scene, a supervisor remarks to Dorothy, "Despite what you think, I don't have anything against y'all," and the viewer realizes that this woman really believes what she says. Dorothy replies sympathetically, "I know *you* probably believe that." Psychologists John Dovidio and Samuel Gaertner (Dovidio & Gaertner, 2004; Gaertner & Dovidio, 2005) have proposed a theory of **aversive racism** in which overt expressions of racism decline over time, while subtle and sometimes unconscious manifestations of bias persist. The interaction between Dorothy and her supervisor nicely illustrates this theory.

Cultural Identity, Acculturation, Assimilation

Brooklyn (2015) is a charming film about a young Irish woman, Eilis Lacey (played by Saoirse Ronan), who immigrated to the United States via Ellis Island in 1951. She settles in Brooklyn, finds a boarding home, gets a job as a sales clerk, and before too long is romantically involved with Tony, her Italian plumber boyfriend (played by Emory Cohen). However, like many immigrants, she is homesick for her country of origin, and she misses her widowed mother and her sister (and she feels guilty about leaving them). Her homesickness is almost overwhelming when she hears a countryman singing an Irish ballad.

Brooklyn illustrates many of the challenges facing new immigrants, and one gets a sense for what it must be like to be vetted by an Ellis Island

Eilis: [*instructing a new immigrant*] You have to think like an American. You'll feel so homesick that you'll want to die, and there's nothing you can do about it apart from endure it. But you will, and it won't kill you. And one day the sun will come out – you might not even notice straight away, it'll be that faint. And then you'll catch yourself thinking about something or someone who has no connection with the past. Someone who's only yours. And you'll realize... that this is where your life is.

The protagonist in *Brooklyn* offers advice similar to the advice she received when first immigrating to the United States.

immigration official. Eilis, who has been quite sick on the ship coming over to the United States, is coached by her Irish roommate who has visited the United States and who knows what to do and say to convince the officials that she is "immigration worthy."

Tony invites Eilis to meet his parents, and she is anxious about the encounter. Other girls in the rooming house help prepare her, coaching her about what to say and demonstrating the proper way to eat spaghetti. One thing leads to another, and eventually Eilis and Tony acknowledge their love for one another. Eilis's life becomes complicated when her sister unexpectedly dies and she returns to Ireland to comfort her mother, but Tony talks her into marrying him before she leaves Brooklyn.

After returning home to southeast Ireland, Eilis is torn and conflicted about returning to the United States and Tony, and she is attracted to a new man who implores her to stay and marry him. She eventually decides to return to the United States to build a new identity and a new life with her Italian plumber husband.

Eilis had distinct advantages many immigrants don't have. She had a job and a sponsor waiting for her (an Irish priest played by Jim Broadbent), and she spoke English (although with a strong Irish brogue – which many people find attractive). Other immigrants aren't so lucky, and many arrive without basic language skills. This can be especially problematic for children who are taught in "English only" classes. Many arrive without any guarantee of a job, and they have little chance of finding work if they don't speak English. Affordable housing, transportation, and healthcare are also often out of reach.

Immigration policy was a major issue in the 2024 Presidential election, and President Trump has significantly limited the number of immigrants allowed into the United States since winning the election. He is infamous for his campaign assertion that many of the immigrants from Mexico were criminals: "When Mexico sends its people, they're not sending their best. ... They're sending people that have lots of problems, and they're bringing those problems with them. They're bringing drugs. They're bringing crime. They're rapists. And some, I assume, are good people" (Terkel & Liebowitz, 2024).

President Trump also signed an executive order on March 1, 2025, designating English as the **official language** of the United States. This order rescinds a 2000 directive by President Bill Clinton that required federal agencies to provide assistance to non-English speakers. The new policy allows agencies to decide whether to offer services in other languages.

Value Conflicts, Value Orientations

House of Sand and Fog (2003), directed by Vadim Perelman, uses the trope of a house to illustrate and underscore core conflicts in belief systems and values. Perelman is a Russian émigré, and the film vividly illustrates many of the challenges confronting people of power and influence who are forced to flee from their home country due to political upheaval like that which existed in Iran in 1979 when the Shah was deposed.

Massoud Amir Behrani, played by Ben Kingsley, is a formerly affluent Iranian Colonel who was closely connected to the Shah until a revolution occurred and he fled the country with his inner circle. Behrani immigrated to the United States, hoping to start a new life with the limited money he was able to bring with him. Although once wealthy, he is now obligated to support his family by working two menial jobs, paving highways during the day and working at a roadside convenience store in the evening. Despite being poor, Behrani continues to wear a suit when he is not working, cleaning himself up in the convenience store washroom before returning to his home. He also drives a Mercedes, the last symbol of the life he once lived.

Behrani has enough money to make a down payment to purchase a home that is being foreclosed because of the owner's failure to pay her taxes. The owner, Kathy Nicolo (played by Jennifer Connelly), is a depressed, recovering alcoholic who doesn't take time to open the mail, letting it pile up on the

Esmail: Why did that man say we would be deported?

Behrani: I do not know. But we are American citizens. We own this house. They can do nothing to us now.

Esmail: I feel bad for that lady, Baba-jan.

Behrani: The woman's house was taken from her because she did not pay her taxes. That happens when one is not responsible.

Esmail: But...

Behrani: Do you understand? Do not feel bad. Americans they do not deserve what they have. They have the eyes of small children who are forever looking for the next source of distraction, entertainment, sweet taste in the mouth. We are not like them. We know rich opportunities when we see them and do not throw away God's blessing.

> A former Iranian Colonel explains core cultural differences to his wife who is concerned about deportation in *House of Sand and Fog*.

floor. Her modest California home, which she had inherited from her father, is her best hope for pulling her life together.

Behrani's new life as an immigrant is much harder than the life he had in Iran, and the transition is hard for his wife and son as well. Kathy's husband has left her, and she also has a difficult life. The tension in the film results in part from the fact that we realize that both Behrani and Kathy have a legitimate claim on the home. Although the Behranis are new US citizens, Kathy tells Behrani's wife that she will have them deported if she doesn't get her house back.

The wife, Nadi (played by Shohreh Aghdashloo), shows genuine kindness when Kathy arrives at her former home, resumes drinking, and attempts suicide. Nadi is a powerful role model for her son. Behrani is also a kind man; he keeps Kathy from shooting herself, brings her into his home, and remarks to his son, "She is a bird, a broken one. Your grandfather used to say that a bird that flies into your house is an angel. You must look upon his presence as a blessing."

At one point in the film, Behrani implores God to save his son's life, promising to give *nazr*. **Nazr** is a Muslim word that is usually translated as "an offering" or "a vow." Behrani cries out in his grief, "I make *nazr* only for my son ... I will do whatever is your will ... I will let the birds cover me and peck out my eyes! Please, God, my *nazr* is in your hands!"

The film's ending is powerful and unforgettable, and watching the movie will help you understand cultural differences in family dynamics. It also will

Figure 5.3.   *House of Sand and Fog* (2003, DreamWorks Pictures, Cobalt Media Group, Bisgrove Entertainment, Miramax). Produced by Michael London, Shawn Lawrence Otto, Vadim Perelman, Nina R. Sadowsky, et al. Directed by Vadim Perelman. Ben Kingsley's character comforts Jennifer Connelly's suicidal character in *House of Sand and Fog* (2003).

make you appreciate what it must feel like to move from a very high-status social position to one considerably lower in the social pecking order. This is the position international physicians find themselves in when they immigrate to the United States and cannot get licenses, often working as nursing assistants or phlebotomists.

Social Norms and Norm Violations

Norm violations occur when somebody behaves in an unexpected and often uncomfortable way. For example, a man is likely to feel uncomfortable in a restroom with eight unused urinals if a stranger enters the room and selects an immediately adjacent urinal. No one is ever *taught* that it is important to leave empty urinals between you and someone urinating in the same room, if they are available, but it is something that *everyone just knows*. However, cultural differences often result in unwitting norm violations, and these are sometimes beautifully captured in films.

One of our greatest joys is introducing younger students to older films that shaped our own view of the world and our own values. *My Cousin Vinny* (1992) is one of those films. It beautifully captures two clashing cultures, and the habits, customs, accents, and mores of Manhattan are presented in bold relief from those of rural Alabama.

Two teenage boys from New York University are driving cross-country to UCLA, and they decide on impulse to visit the Deep South. After stopping at a convenience store, they are mistaken for murderers and arrested. Because they can't afford an attorney, they call on one of the boy's cousins, Vincent (Vinny) Laguardia Gambini, someone who graduated from law school but who has never tried an actual case. He did pass the bar exam – but only after six tries in 6 years. Vinny agrees to try to help, and he drives to Alabama with his fiancée, Mona Lisa Vito (played by Marisa Tomei). Much of the humor in

---

Vinny Gambini: [*Vinny and Lisa receive their breakfast orders, Vinny looks at his skeptically*] What's this over here?

Grits Cook: You never heard of grits?

Vinny Gambini: Sure, I've heard of grits. I've just never actually seen a grit before.

An inexperienced Manhattan attorney confronts Southern cooking for the first time in *My Cousin Vinny*.

the film derives from the dramatic contrast in style between Vinny and Lisa's New York style of interacting and the more laconic habits and mannerisms of the judge and opposing lawyer.

In the 2016 Republican primary, candidate Ted Cruz criticized Donald Trump for having "**New York values**." According to Cruz, "Everyone understands the values in New York City are socially liberal, pro-abortion, pro-gay marriage and focus around money and the media."

There is some evidence that violence in the United States is more common in Southern states. Richard Nisbett and Dov Cohen (1996) have attempted to account for this fact in terms of a "**culture of honor**," noting:

> [There] is something about white southern culture that causes the violence, [and this book explores] how the culture of honor, self-protection ethic, and a widespread presence of guns contribute to a cycle of violence in which arguments lead to deadly retribution; links southern white culture to urban ghetto culture, both of which encourage violent responses to a perceived affront; investigates how cultural ideas about gender and masculinity lead to the acceptance of violence to maintain a man's reputation as strong and powerful [and] uncovers the attitudes, beliefs, and behaviors concerning honor, self-protection, and violence.

There is substantial empirical support for the "culture of honor" concept (Cohen et al., 1996). For example, three experiments were conducted with University of Michigan students who had grown up in the North or the South:

> [Participants] were insulted by a confederate who bumped into the participant and called him an "asshole." Compared with northerners – who were relatively unaffected by the insult – southerners were (a) more likely to think their masculine reputation was threatened, (b) more upset (as shown by a rise in cortisol levels), (c) more physiologically primed for aggression (as shown by a rise in testosterone levels), (d) more cognitively primed for aggression, and (e) more likely to engage in aggressive and dominant behavior. Findings highlight the insult–aggression cycle in cultures of honor, in which insults diminish a man's reputation and he tries to restore his status by aggressive or violent behavior. (p. 945)

Stereotyping

Stereotypes, prejudice, and discrimination are related terms that refer to different domains: **Stereotypes** are generalizations about groups of people; they are primarily cognitive and are often unconscious. **Prejudice** is the affective dimension of a stereotype; we respond differently to members of different groups, in part based on how similar they are to the cultures with which we identify. **Discrimination** is the behavioral manifestation of prejudice;

Hilly Holbrook: They carry different diseases than we do. That's why I've drafted the Home Health Sanitation Initiative.

Eugenia 'Skeeter' Phelan: The what?

Hilly Holbrook: A disease-preventative bill that requires every white home to have a separate bathroom for the colored help. It's been endorsed by the White Citizen's Council.

Eugenia 'Skeeter' Phelan: Maybe we should just build you a bathroom outside, Hilly.

A young woman is insulted by a racist neighbor's insistence that Black people not use the same toilets as White people in *The Help*.

discrimination results in unjust treatment of people because of their age, race, gender, religion, or sexual orientation.

The Help (2011) is a movie that illustrates many of the stereotypes about, prejudice against, and discrimination toward Black people that existed in the Deep South in the early 1960s. The movie is set in Jackson, Mississippi; although it is a comedy, the film presents significant social commentary, and there are passing allusions to the **civil rights movement** that was contemporaneous with the film's time and place (e.g., civil rights leader Medgar Evers was murdered outside his Jackson, Mississippi home in 1963).

The story is told from the perspective of a young woman (Skeeter, played by Emma Stone) who has just graduated from Ole Miss and who aspires to be a writer. She decides to write about the Black women who served as maids and nannies, and who had raised Skeeter and so many of her White friends. At first, all the African American maids and housekeepers ("the help") are suspicious and distrustful; however, eventually two of the housekeepers agree to help, Aibileen Clark (Viola Davis) and Minny Jackson (Octavia Spencer), and eventually everyone wants in on the game, realizing that Skeeter is sympathetic to their situation. Spencer won an Oscar as Best Supporting Actress for her role.

Much of the humor in the film is scatological, and the movie gets laughs and provides a sense of justice when one particularly racist White woman enthusiastically but unknowingly eats a shit-filled pie. A large focus of the film relates to the stereotypical belief that the African American women who wash the family's clothes and bathe the family's children are somehow unclean. The White women in Jackson refuse to let their Black employees use indoor toilets, believing "they carry different diseases than we do." One of Skeeter's childhood friends drafts a "Home Health Sanitation Initiative" that would make it a crime for a Black employee to use a White employer's toilet. Another woman marks her toilet paper with a pencil so she can make sure her servant doesn't surreptitiously use the toilet when she is supposed to be cleaning the bathroom, but the employee (Aibileen) brings her own toilet paper from home to foil this heavy-handed attempt to regulate her behavior.

The maids are only allowed to shop in White groceries when wearing their uniforms. Racism is pervasive and persistent, and the inferiority of the Black employees is simply accepted as a matter of fact by the women who employee them, despite the fact that almost all of the White homeowners had been raised by Black nannies, and these same Black women were the ones providing love and care for the White children when some of the White mothers in the film neglected or abused their children.

Although the film serves our purposes as an illustration of stereotypes in the workplace, some reviewers have criticized the movie. For example, writing in *PsycCRITIQUES*, Jesse Valdez (2013) notes:

> The film fails to present certain aspects of oppression that were common in the lives of Black women. The historical facts about disrespect and verbal abuse by White adults and children, sexism, and rape are avoided. Skeeter's motivation may be interpreted as self-serving, and her actions may be seen as unrealistic and

Figure 5.4. *The Help* (2011, DreamWorks, DreamWorks Pictures, Reliance Film Entertainment, Participant). Produced by Mohamed K. Al-Mazrouei, Michael Barnathan, Nate Berkus, Jennifer Blum, et al. Directed by Tate Taylor. Octavia Spencer's character (Minnie Jackson) is befriended by Celia Foote (Jessica Chastain) in *The Help*.

unlikely to have occurred in real life. Also problematic is the fact that the maids' revealing stories are successfully published under the leadership of a White woman. Many may question such an event and its portrayal of Skeeter, a White woman, as the **savior of the oppressed**.

The film has generated controversy. It has been criticized, for example, by those in domestic service as a disservice to their occupation. The book's author has been accused of basing characters on real persons without appropriate acknowledgment.

A point made by James Meredith stands in contrast to the film's plot: he stated that he was "taught to believe that the most dishonorable thing that a Meredith [or any member of his family] could do was to work in a white woman's kitchen and take care of a white man's child" (1966, p. 19). Although the film parallels similar real-life events, those events may be a distortion of reality and a disservice to many who have been oppressed by a racist society.

Indigenous People

Hombre (1967) stars Paul Newman as John Russell, a White man who as a child had been captured and raised by Apaches. He then spent time with a White father but eventually ran away to return to his home with the Apaches. He is **bilingual** and **bicultural**, and not entirely comfortable with life in either world, but he has chosen to live his life as an Apache. However, when his White father dies Russell inherits a boarding house, and he cuts his hair and comes to town to claim his inheritance. He later endures a long stagecoach

---

Audra Favor: I can't imagine eating a dog and not thinking anything of it.

John Russell: You even been hungry, lady? Not just ready for supper. Hungry enough so that your belly swells?

Audra Favor: I wouldn't care how hungry I got. I know I wouldn't eat one of those camp dogs.

John Russell: You'd eat it. You'd fight for the bones, too.

Audra Favor: Have you ever eaten a dog, Mr. Russell?

John Russell: Eaten one and lived like one.

Audra Favor: Dear me.

Paul Newman's character explains what it feels like to be starving to another stagecoach passenger in the movie *Hombre*

ride with a racist couple, eventually moving up to the top of the coach to sit by the driver because a woman in the coach objected to sitting next to an Indian. (The stagecoach driver is a Mexican; while clearly inferior to the White people inside the coach, he has a higher status than his Indian passenger.) When bandits attack the stagecoach, it quickly becomes apparent that Russell is the only person with the talent and experience necessary to keep the group alive. Richard Boone plays Grimes, the bandit leader, who takes Ruth, the racist woman, hostage and threatens to let her die slowly from heat and thirst unless the woman's husband (played by Fredric March), a Bureau of Indian Affairs agent who has embezzled money meant for Indian relief, turns over the money he has stolen. Russell has the requisite skills needed to save himself; however, he sacrifices his own life to save the life of the woman who initially refused to ride with him in the stagecoach.

American Indians had historically been portrayed in films as savages, and alcohol has been a staple part of the Western genre (Wedding, 2000). Who can imagine a Western film without a saloon? *Hombre* was one of the first Westerns to portray Indians in a positive light, contrasting Russell's somber stoicism with the avarice and racism of his fellow passengers on the stage.

Other Movies About Work That Will Teach You About Culture

Communication styles differ across cultural groups, and some individuals may come from cultural traditions in which it is considered bad form to challenge authority or authority figures. Some employees may be servile to the point of being obsequious (we see this a bit in *The Man Who Knew Infinity*). Employees from individualistic cultures may want to work alone; by contrast, employees from collectivistic cultures often prefer working on teams. Cultural groups differ in their perspectives on time, and this can be problematic in a work environment in which schedules and deadlines are important. Tensions also can arise over holidays and holy days, or when addressing the need of a Muslim employee to take time to pray during the workday.

Harvard psychiatrist Chester Pierce coined the term **microaggression** in 1970 to describe subtle but real attempts to degrade members of marginalized groups. Microaggression is common in the workplace, where more blatant displays of racism might put someone's job at risk.

Numerous films illustrate multicultural issues in the workplace, either as a prominent theme or in passing, and it is a real issue that managers must cope with on a daily basis. Racism in its ugliest form is portrayed in films dealing with slavery (e.g., *12 Years a Slave* [2013]). Racism in the workplace also is seen in films like *Hidden Figures* (2016), *The Help* (2011), *The Butler* (2013), and *Driving Miss Daisy* (1989).

Sexism is a close cousin to racism, and sexism in the workplace is illustrated by films like *9 to 5* (1980), *In the Company of Men* (1997), *Fried Green Tomatoes* (1991), *A League of Their Own* (1992), and *Erin Brockovich* (2000). *The Invisible War* (2012) is a powerful film documenting the ubiquity of **rape culture** in military settings, and *G. I. Jane* (1997) illustrates some of the challenges confronting women trying to make their own way in a traditionally male workplace. We also highly recommend *North Country* (2005), a film about a woman working the mines who successfully files a sexual harassment suit.

The Magdalene Sisters (2002) is a powerful movie about young Irish women who are sent away to a Catholic home for "fallen" women where they are abused. Although dealing only tangentially with workplace issues, *Honor Diaries* (2013) is a film illustrating the challenges confronting women who live and work in patriarchal theocracies.

Critical Thinking Questions About Work and Culture

- How does culture affect organizational climate?
- Why are "female professions" (e.g., teaching, nursing, social work) typically undervalued in US society and their members underpaid?
- What is the etymology of the word "coolie," and why is it considered a pejorative term?
- What changes has the Trump administration proposed for the H-1B visa program?
- Should H-1B visas be awarded with a lottery system or solely based on merit?
- How would you describe the culture of Silicon Valley? Is it predominantly White centered?
- Would you try to change the organizational climate of a workplace if you noticed that all Black employees sat together at lunch, apparently deliberately avoiding interaction with White employees?
- Is the Protestant work ethic a bona fide feature of White culture?
- Do you boycott companies that may hold different values than your own (e.g., Coors Beer, Hobby Lobby, Chick-fil-A)?

- What are the North Carolina "bathroom wars?"
- Is domestic servitude sometimes the equivalent of slavery?
- How do you account for the recent and massive political backlash against DEI initiatives?

Further Exploration

If you only have time for one article, read:

Tizon, A. (2017, June). My family's slave. *The Atlantic*. https://www.theatlantic.com/magazine/archive/2017/06/lolas-story/524490/

If you only have time to read one chapter about work and culture, make it:

Wedding, D. (2013). Improving international multicultural competence by working and studying abroad. In R. L. Lowman (Ed.), *Internationalizing multiculturalism: Expanding professional competencies in a globalized world* (pp. 289–300). American Psychological Association.

If you have time to read an entire book, we recommend:

Ellis, B. H., Abdi, S. M., & Winer, J. P. (2020). *Mental health practice with immigrant and refugee youth: A socioecological framework*. American Psychological Association.

References

Albert, R. S. (1998). Mathematical giftedness and mathematical genius: A comparison of G. H. Hardy and Srinivasa Ramanujan. In A. Steptoe (Ed.), *Genius and mind: Studies of creativity and temperament* (pp. 111–138).

Cohen, D., Nisbett, R. E., Bowdle, B. F., & Schwarz, N. (1996). Insult, aggression, and the southern culture of honor: An "experimental ethnography." *Journal of Personality and Social Psychology, 70*(5), 945–960. https://doi.org/10.1037/0022-3514.70.5.945

Dovidio, J. F., & Gaertner, S. L. (2004). Aversive racism. In M. P. Zanna (Ed.), *Advances in experimental social psychology* (Vol. 36, pp. 1–52). Elsevier. https://doi.org/10.1016/S0065-2601(04)36001-6

Gaertner, S. L., & Dovidio, J. F. (2005). Understanding and addressing contemporary racism: From aversive racism to the common ingroup identity model. *Journal of Social Issues, 61*(3), 615–639. https://doi.org/10.1111/j.1540-4560.2005.00424.x

Kolata, G. (1987, June 19). Remembering a "Magical Genius": Ramanujan was born 100 years ago and grew up poor and uneducated, but his work continues to draw and inspire mathematicians. *Science, 236*, 1519–1521. https://doi.org/10.1126/science.236.4808.1519

Meredith, J. H. (1966). *Three years in Mississippi*. Indiana University Press.

Nisbett, R. E., & Cohen, D. (1996). *New directions in social psychology. Culture of honor: The psychology of violence in the South*. Westview Press.

Novak, K. J. (2012). Editor's introduction: Special issue on racial profiling. *Journal of Contemporary Criminal Justice, 28*(2), 120–121. https://doi.org/10.1177/1043986212446871

Renzulli, K. A. (2015, February 6). Why America should follow Japan's lead on forcing workers to take vacation. *Money.* http://time.com/money/3698791/japan-workers-vacation/

Simonton, D. K. (2016). When Hardy met Ramanujan [Review of the media The Man Who Knew Infinity, by M. Brown]. *PsycCRITIQUES, 61*(42).

Strauss, S. (2011, November 2). The connection between education, income inequality, and unemployment. *Huffington Post.* http://www.huffingtonpost.com/steven-strauss/the-connection-between-ed_b_1066401.html

Terkel, A. & Liebowitz, M. (2024, September 19). From "rapists" to "eating the pets": Trump has long used degrading language toward immigrants. *NBC News.* https://www.nbcnews.com/politics/donald-trump/trump-degrading-language-immigrants-rcna171120

Valdez, J. N. (2013). The power of the oppressed [Review of the media The Help, by T. Taylor]. *PsycCRITIQUES, 58*(2).

Wang, F. (2018, January 28). *Hidden figures and white savior.* https://medium.com/colored-lenses/hidden-figures-and-white-savior-771c49abbcd2

Wedding, D. (2000). Alcoholism in the Western genre: The portrayal of alcohol and alcoholism in the Western genre. *Journal of Alcohol and Drug Education, 46*(2), 3–11.

Chapter 6
Politics

"Yes, I live in a castle, Tony! Alone. And rich White people pay me to play piano for them because it makes them feel cultured. But as soon as I step off that stage, I go right back to being just another nigger to them. Because that is their true culture. And I suffer that slight alone, because I'm not accepted by my own people 'cause I'm not like them, either. So, if I'm not Black enough and if I'm not White enough and if I'm not man enough, then tell me, Tony, what am I?"

Don Shirley, an African American classical music pianist, to Tony Vallelonga, his Italian American driver and bodyguard, in *Green Book*.

Questions to Consider While Watching *Green Book* (2018)

- How did the history of slavery in the United States affect the relationship between African Americans and Whites in the Deep South?
- What is your racial image of classical musicians?
- Why do you think there are significantly more White American classical musicians compared to African American classical musicians?
- Why is it hard to associate African Americans with classical music?
- How many African American classical musicians can you name?
- What do you think about the relationship between Italian Americans and African Americans during the 1960s in New York?
- Are there differences in racial politics across diverse geographical areas of the United States? If yes, can you explain?

- How do you think Don Shirley's intersectional identities with regard to race, sexual orientation, gender, education, and high socioeconomic class affected him?
- What does the phrase "driving while Black" conjure up for you?
- Why do you think Tony Vallelonga got angry and hit a southern policeman when the policeman accused him of being part Black?

Politics and Culture

Politics and culture are inextricably linked, and they have a reciprocal relationship. In other words, politics informs culture, and culture informs politics. Politicians need to respond to the needs of their communities, otherwise, they do not get elected or re-elected. However, historically, the needs of multicultural communities and people of color have not been well represented in US politics. Let us take a brief look at the history of the country's politics with people of color.

US national politics have been ambivalent, and at times, conflictive regarding the needs of **people of color and indigenous individuals** (POCI; Comas-Díaz et al., 2019). Early on, the US governmental political position toward the indigenous populations resulted in war against them, genocidal attacks, and displacement (making indigenous people immigrants in their own country). The history of slavery in the United States accentuated racism toward African Americans. Moreover, belief in **US Manifest Destiny** – the 19th century belief that US settlers were destined to expand across the continent – fostered the Mexican American War, and the annexation of Texas, California, and other Mexican lands. Additionally, the Spanish American War in 1898 ended with the US annexation of Cuba, Puerto Rico, the Philippines, and Guam. In effect, the United States colonized the Philippines, Guam, and Puerto Rico (Comas-Díaz, 2007). Even more, the history of US immigration laws shows evidence of the racial exclusion of Chinese, Japanese, Mexicans, Haitians, and other people of color (Johnson, 1998). Consequently, the political relationship between the US government and people of color has been complicated and conflicted.

Politics and *Green Book*

Green Book (2018) is a movie about Donald Shirley (played by Mahershala Ali), an African American classical and jazz virtuoso pianist and composer, who hires Frank (Tony the Lip) Vallelonga (played by Viggo Mortensen), a working-class Italian American, as his driver and bodyguard during his concert tour through the Midwest and the Deep South in 1962. Directed by Peter Farrelly and written by Nick Vallelonga (Tony Vallelonga's son), Peter Farrelly, and Brian Hayes Currie, *Green Book* is a film inspired by a true story. Indeed, Nick Vallelonga based his writing on interviews between Shirley and his father and on letters his father wrote to his mother during the trip. *Green Book* won the Oscar for Best Picture, Best Original Screenplay, and Best Supporting Actor (Mahershala Ali) during the 91st Academy Awards.

The title of the movie is based on a book, *The Negro Motorist Green Book*, written by African American travel writer Victor Hugo Green, as a mid-20th century guide for African Americans traveling in the United States. During that historical–political era, African Americans were racially segregated due to state laws in the South that required separate facilities such as hotels, restaurants, bathrooms, and gasoline stations, among other sites. These racial segregation laws are examples of the **Jim Crow laws** that emerged after the Civil War in the southern states. Even though northern states did not have these laws, African Americans also faced discrimination in areas such as work, housing, and education in the North. Accordingly, Victor Hugo Green wrote his book to help African American travelers find suitable accommodations during those racial and politically restrictive times. In real life, Donald (Don) Shirley, a child musical prodigy, studied classical music, but due to the limited opportunities for African American classical musicians, he left his music career. He had two honorary doctorates, and he was known as Doc Don Shirley. Indeed, Donald Shirley had studied psychology at the University of Chicago and worked as a psychologist. He returned to music after he obtained a grant to study the relationship between music and juvenile crime. Don Shirley is portrayed as a virtuoso and erudite pianist and composer, combining classical music with jazz and other forms of American music (Weber, 2013).

Green Book shows the prejudice, racism, and discrimination toward African Americans prevalent not only in the Deep South, but also among some northeast areas. Donald Shirley is a successful African American classical and jazz pianist and composer living in an elegant apartment above Carnegie Hall in New York. He needs to hire a driver to accompany him during an 8-week concert tour through the Midwest and Deep South. Don interviews Frank (Tony the Lip) Vallelonga, a bouncer at the Copacabana Club, who is temporarily unemployed because the club is closed due to renovations. The amusing job interview scene highlights the dramatic differences between Don and Tony. Based on Tony's work references and with the consent of Dolores, Tony's wife (played by Linda Cardellini), Don offers Tony the job and he accepts. Both men expect to be back in New York by Christmas Eve. The differences between Don and Tony arise and worsen early in the journey. Don is disgusted with Tony's coarse behavior, and Tony resents Don's asking him to be more refined. However, as the trip progresses, the tension between them diminishes. Tony admires Don's musical genius and is outraged by the racial discrimination Don confronts on their journey.

There are several pivotal scenes in the movie. The first one occurs when Don goes solo to a bar and is threatened by racist White men. Tony is alerted, goes to the bar, and rescues Don. After this incident, Tony asks Don to not go out in public without him. A friendship flourishes and Don helps Tony to write his letters to Dolores. In addition to editing, correcting, and making suggestions, Don infuses a lyrical style into Tony's love letters, and Tony appreciates Don's help. The friendship between these two very different men strengthens.

The second central scene presents Don's police detention at a YMCA swimming pool due to a sexual encounter he had with a young White man. Tony arrives at the YMCA and manages the situation with the officers, keeping Don from being arrested.

A subsequent pivotal scene during the tour journey has significant political implications. A White policeman pulls over Tony and Don while driving late at night. The cop insults Tony by sarcastically asking him if he is part Black. This kind of behavior may relate to the racial discrimination that early **Italian immigrants**, especially those from southern Italy, experienced in the United States. Compared to northern Europeans, southern Italians had darker skin, were NOT considered White, and thus, were subjected to significant racial discrimination (Demetri, 2018). Additionally, being mostly Catholics, as opposed to the White Protestant Anglo Saxon majority, Italians and Italian

---

Tony Lip: Christ, I'm blacker than you are.

Dr. Don Shirley: Excuse me?

Tony Lip: You don't know shit about your own people. What they eat, how they talk, how they live. You don't even know who Little Richard is.

Dr. Don Shirley: Oh, so knowing who Little Richard is makes you blacker than me?

Tony Lip: [nods]

A gay, Black virtuoso musician is teased by his White driver, underscoring the differences between race and class, in *Green Book*.

Americans faced discrimination and were associated with marginalized groups, such as Mexicans (Demetri, 2018). Tony reacts to the insult by punching the policeman. His behavior may be consistent with a projected **internalized racism** (i.e., he was accused of being "part Black"). Indeed, an important scene at the beginning of the movie shows several Italian Americans engaging in racist behaviors toward an African American worker in Tony's home. This scene is relevant because social psychology research has demonstrated that African Americans and Asian Americans were less closely identified with being American than White Americans (Devos & Banaji, 2005). Based on these results, the researchers concluded that to be American is implicitly associated with being White. These studies raise the question what does it mean to be an American (Li & Brewer, (2004).

Tony and Don are incarcerated after Tony attacks the police officer. While in jail, Don asks to talk with his lawyer, but instead, he calls the US Attorney General Robert (Bobby) E. Kennedy, who intervenes with the governor, resulting in Don's and Tony's release from jail. Don's access to Robert (Bobby)

Figure 6.1. *Green Book* (2018, Participant Media, DreamWorks Pictures, Innisfree Pictures, Louisiana Entertainment, Wessler Entertainment). Produced by Jim Burke, Brian Currie, Steven Farneth, Peter Farrelly, et al. Directed by Peter Farrelly. *Green Book* illustrates the racism in the Deep South and the unlikely connection between a highly educated virtuoso African American musician and a working-class Italian American bouncer.

E. Kennedy, the brother of President John F. Kennedy, reflects the political privilege resulting from his musical success, in contrast to his racial oppressive status. The concept of **intersectionality** – the effect of overlapping multiple sources of oppression such as race, gender, socioeconomic class, sexual orientation, religion, and other identity markers (Crenshaw, 1989) – helps us to understand the conflict between Don's areas of oppression and privilege. He faced discrimination as an African American who was "not man enough." However, Don was also privileged as an educated and highly successful African American musician. Don is angry with Tony for losing his temper and forcing Don to disturb Bobby Kennedy, a political ally, who is busy working to improve the Civil Rights of African Americans.

A fourth impactful scene occurs during Don's last concert performance at a country club in Birmingham, Alabama. The night of the concert, Don is not allowed to eat in the Whites-only dining room. Angry, he threatens to cancel the concert. There is a confrontation between the country club manager and Tony. *Will Don be allowed to eat in the Whites-only dining room? Will he play his last concert in Alabama, or will he walk out of his contract?*

Don and Tony embark on their trip back to New York, hoping to make it by Christmas Eve. On their way there, a policeman stops them in Maryland. *What happens next? Do Don and Tony reach New York? Is Tony able to celebrate Christmas Eve with Dolores and his family? How does Don celebrate Christmas Eve?*

Green Book raises the question of how strong a friendship can be between a highly educated African American virtuoso musician and a working class Italian American bouncer with limited education, given the context of 1960s racism. Watch this riveting movie and go back in time to observe and understand the pervasive racism that existed in the South during the 1960s.

Prejudice, Discrimination, Oppression, Racism, and Ethnocentrism

In 1947 Seretse Khama, the heir to the Kingdom of Bechuanaland (now Botswana), falls in love with Ruth Williams, a White English office worker. The film *A United Kingdom* illustrates their true love story, which takes place within the context of a fading British colonial power. In this way, the movie interconnects global political events with a real personal story.

A United Kingdom was directed by Amma Asante, who won the 2018 Outstanding World Cinema Motion Picture (Black Reel) for directing this film. Guy Hibbert wrote the screenplay based on the book *Colour Bar* by Susan

Williams. Cinematographer Sam McCurdy and his crew shot the movie's exterior scenes in the village where Seretse and Ruth lived in Botswana. This beautiful cinematography imparts the movie with an outstanding realism (Turan, 2017).

No man is free who is not master of himself.

Seretse Khama in *A United Kingdom*

In *A United Kingdom*, Seretse Khama (played by David Oyelowo) is the heir to the Bechuanaland kingdom, and his uncle, Tshekedi Khama (played by Vusi Kunene), sends him to England to study law. Ruth Williams's (played by Rosamund Pike) sister, Muriel Williams (played by Laura Carmichael), invites Ruth to a Missionary Society Dance event. Seretse and Ruth meet at that event, and they discover they share similar interests, such as American jazz music and spirited swing dancing. They fall in love, and as a mixed-race couple are subjected to racial prejudice, discrimination, and aggression, including that of George Williams – Ruth's father – who tells her: "You disgust me."

Seretse and Ruth marry and travel to Bechuanaland to obtain Seretse's community ratification of his marriage. Tshekedi Khama, Seretse's uncle and regent, openly disapproves of the union, and demands that Seretse abdicate his royal position. You can observe the community's decision-making process in a culturally fascinating scene depicting the Kgotla: "Are you now to uphold the abomination that is Apartheid in our own Kgotla?"

As a **collectivistic society**, the whole Bechuanaland community is required to vote in a Kgotla. The term "Kgotla" refers to a traditional community council/court in Botswana villages, where decisions are made by consensus.

Seretse and Ruth's marriage creates international political problems. The government of South Africa, Bechuanaland's neighbor, has adopted a of policy **Apartheid**, and considers the royal interracial marriage an affront. Consequently, South Africa pressures Britain to change its policy toward Bechuanaland. A meeting between Seretse and the British Foreign Officer Sir Alistair Canning (played by Jack Davenport) shows the full power of the colonizing empire over its protectorates (colonies).

Now you'll see how an empire defends itself, Mr. Khama.

Sir Alistair Canning talking to Seretse Khama in *A United Kingdom*.

> Africa can never be free until those who live in her, White and Black, recognize that race has no bearing on equality and justice.
>
> Seretse Khama in *A United Kingdom*

The British government, in a covert alliance with apartheid South Africa, opposes the emergence of racial tolerance in Africa. A series of political events highlight the imposition of colonial power and capitalistic pressures. A special inquiry is established to decide if Seretse is fit to become King of Bechuanaland. As a result, Seretse is forcibly exiled from his country. He is separated from Ruth for several years, making him miss the birth of his first child, a daughter. Seretse's exile became a political *cause célèbre* at the national and international level. This film will allow you to witness the effects of colonization and understand the need for decolonization and liberation.

Ultimately, *A United Kingdom* is an engaging real-life story that defied one kingdom and united another.

Figure 6.2.   *A United Kingdom* (2016, Fox Searchlight Pictures, Pathe UK, BBC Film, Ingenious Media, British Film Institute, et al.). Produced by Theuns De Wet, Widens Pkolo Dorsainville, Brunson Green, Peter Heslop, et al. Directed by Amma Asante. *A United Kingdom* explores the intersection of colonization, imperialism, exploitation, and racism.

Cultural Identity, Acculturation, Assimilation

Malcolm X (1999) is a biographical movie about an African American Muslim human rights activist – Malcolm X. Spike Lee directed and co-produced the movie. The screenplay is by Spike Lee and Arnold Peri and is based on the book *The Autobiography of Malcolm X*, a Malcolm X and Alex Haley collaboration. Indeed, Alex Haley completed the book after Malcolm X's assassination. The film stars Denzel Washington (as Malcolm X), Angela Bassett (as Dr. Betty Shabazz, Malcolm X's wife), Albert Hall (as Baines), Al Freeman, Jr. (as Elijah Muhammad), and Delroy Lindo (as West Indian Archie). Spike Lee has a supporting role as Shorty. There are cameo appearances by Bobby Seale (Black Panther Party co-founder), the Reverend Al Sharpton, and future South Africa president Nelson Mandela.

The film follows Malcolm X's life, emerging from his traumatic childhood when members of the **Black Legion**, a White supremacist political movement that split off from the Ku Klux Klan and operated in the Midwestern United States during the 1930s, murdered his father, a preacher. Adding to this traumatic loss, Malcolm witnesses his mother's institutionalization due to mental illness. Later, he becomes a petty criminal and after a falling out with West Indian Archie, a gangster, he escapes Harlem and goes to Boston. Malcolm engages in burglary with his best friend Shorty, and both get arrested. Malcolm is sentenced to ten years in prison. There he meets Baines, a fellow inmate, who introduces him to the **Nation of Islam**. Malcolm X becomes a disciple of **Elijah Muhammad**, the leader of the Nation of Islam. The FBI targeted Muhammad for his social justice activism and he was incarcerated for sedition, due to instructing his followers to not serve in the armed forces (Colley, 2014). Malcolm X converted to Islam as did many incarcerated African American men at that time. Zoe Colley (2014), in her article "All America is a prison: The Nation of Islam and the Politicization of African Americans Prisoners, 1955–1965," identifies the reasons for this phenomenon. She argues that the Nation of Islam exposed **White privilege** and promoted racial justice. This political stand appealed to many African Americans who lived in terrible poverty, dilapidated housing, and crime-infested communities, and who routinely experienced police brutality.

With his conversion to Islam, Malcolm X rejects the White mainstream society's Black inferiority ideology and transforms his racial identity into one of racial pride and self-respect. As part of his spiritual rebirth, Malcolm rejects his slave heritage and changes his surname (a product of slave heritage) to X. He marries Dr. Betty Shabazz, an African American educator and civil rights advocate.

Malcolm X's identity transformation is consistent with the multicultural psychological concept of **racial/ethnic identity development**. In his original 1971 article, African American psychologist William E. Cross identifies Black racial identity developmental stages as (1) **pre-encounter** (person is unaware of being absorbed in White society values and wants to fit in); (2) **encounter** (as a result of racist events, the individual focuses on identity as a member of an oppressed group); (3) **immersion/emersion** (the person develops a simultaneous desire to identify with visible symbols of African American culture and actively avoids White society symbols; (4) **internalization** (the individual develops a solid sense of African American identity); and (5) **internalization-commitment** (the person feels comfortable with an African American racial identity and exhibits commitment to the African American community). There are several models of racial ethnic identity development according to the historical experiences of the specific minority group members (Phinney, & Ong, 2007) and the experiences during the lifespan (Yip, 2008). Racial ethnic identity is an important concept, since research showed that the resilience of ethnic minority adolescents to racial discrimination increased when they developed a positive ethnic/racial identity and learned about their racial/ethnic group's history (Romero et al., 2014).

> We declare our right on this earth, to be a human being, to be respected as a human being, to be given the rights of a human being, in this society, on earth, in this day, which we intend to bring into existence *by any means necessary*.
>
> Nelson Mandela quoting Malcolm X at the end of the movie *Malcolm X*, with Malcolm saying the last four words (in italics) in a film clip.

Malcolm X becomes the chief orator of the Nation of Islam and predicates African Americans' separation from White society. However, a defining event changes Malcolm X's racial and political perspective. He completes the **hajj,** a pilgrimage to Mecca – the holiest city in Islam – that is an obligation for every able-bodied Muslim. As a result of this journey, Malcolm X reevaluates his beliefs on race and recognizes that Muslims come in all colors, including White. With this awareness, Malcolm X begins to teach an inclusive racial and political perspective. Malcolm X was assassinated on February 21, 1965. His murder inspired many African Americans to declare: "I am Malcolm X."

Value Conflicts, Value Orientations

Blood Diamond (2006) is a political war movie directed and co-produced by Edward Zwick. Charles Leavitt wrote the story and the screenplay. The actors in the movie include Leonardo DiCaprio (as Danny Archer), Djimon Hounsou (as Solomon Vandy), and Jennifer Connelly (as Maddy Bowen). The movie is set in Sierra Leone during its Civil War (1991–2002) between government supporters and rebel factions. The title of the movie refers to diamonds mined in zones controlled by insurgent forces that oppose recognized governments. These rebels sell the conflict (blood) diamonds and use the money to subsidize their military actions. In addition to civil wars, blood diamonds result in human enslavement, environmental degradation, human rights abuses, and dreadful conditions for the mine workers (CBS News, 2001).

Blood Diamond begins with the Sierra Leone's rebels, the Revolutionary United Front's (RUF), raid of the village where fisherman Solomon Vandy lives. He is captured and is forced to work in the RUF diamond mines. Solomon's wife and daughter make it to a refugee camp in Guinea. Sadly, his son Dia Vandy (played by Kagiso Kuypers) is kidnapped and is sent to an RUF camp to be brainwashed to become a **child soldier.** Solomon finds a rare and valuable pink diamond at the mine and buries it for safekeeping. The Sierra Leone government army attacks the rebel zone where Solomon is working. As a result, he is arrested, and Solomon is placed in the same jail as Danny Archer.

Danny Archer is a White African mercenary. Robert Mugabe's rebels had killed Danny's parents, making him an orphan since childhood. To survive, Danny becomes a diamond smuggler. He transports smuggled diamonds to his ex-commander, South African mercenary Colonel Coetzee (played by Arnold Vosloo).

We meet Danny trying to cross Sierra Leone's border with a hidden supply of diamonds. The police catch Danny and imprison him. In jail, he hears the story of an exquisite pink diamond extracted by a fisherman. Guided by greed, Danny arranges for Solomon and himself to be released, planning to

Colonel Coetzee: This red earth, it's our skin. The Shona say the color comes from all the blood that's has been spilled fighting over the land. This is home. You'll never leave Africa.

A description of the violent effects of European colonization and exploitation on Africa and Africans in *Blood Diamond*.

get the priceless pink diamond in return for helping Solomon to be reunited with his family. Danny asks Maddy Bowen, an American journalist who is seeking information for a story about blood diamonds, to help Solomon. Danny promises Maddy to give her the information she needs, in exchange for her help in finding Solomon's family. This action-packed movie follows Solomon, Danny, and Maddy in numerous adventures.

Solomon and Danny, both African men – one Black, the other White – are diametrically opposite from each other. Danny's deceitful orientation is a stark contrast to Solomon's honesty. Similarly, Danny and Maddy, in spite of their common whiteness, differ greatly from each other. As an idealistic American woman, Maddy is unaware of the value conflict that many progressive Americans (including herself) have regarding blood diamond politics.

A poignant scene in the movie occurs when Dia Vandy, now a hardened killer, holds both Solomon and Danny at gunpoint. Solomon confronts his son Dia, but the child soldier refuses to recognize his father. *What happens next? Does Dia eventually recognize his father, or not? Are there long-term psychological effects for child soldiers?*

Child soldiers who are brainwashed suffer severe mental health effects. To illustrate, Betancourt et al. (2010) researched the effects of **stigma** on the psychosocial adjustment of former child soldiers in Sierra Leone. The researchers found that child soldiers who were stigmatized after returning to their community had poorer psychosocial adjustment (defined as symptoms of depression, anxiety, and hostility) than those child soldiers who received family and community support.

Blood Diamond presents conflict (blood) diamonds as an international political issue. Watch this movie and find out what the **Kimberley Process Certification Scheme** enacted in 2000 means for the diamond industry.

Danny Archer: Let me tell you something. You sell blood diamonds, too.

Maddy Bowen: Really?

Danny Archer: Yeah.

Maddy Bowen: Tell me, how is that?

Danny Archer: Who do you think buys the stones that I bring out? Dreamy American girls who all want a storybook wedding and a big, shiny rock like the ones in the advertisements of your politically correct magazines. So, please, don't come here and make judgments on me, all right?

A description of the devastating effects of diamond mining in
Africa in *Blood Diamond*.

Israelism (2023) is a powerful film that documents the transformations in belief and behavior that occur when two young American Jews visit Israel and see first-hand how the Israel Defense Force (IDF) treats Palestinians. The film illustrates and underscores tensions in the relationship between American Jews and Israel, as well as the difference between young and older Jews as they think about Israel's actions toward Palestinians. There is a deep and profound **generational divide**: Older Jews in the United States tend to focus on the horrors of October 7, 2023, and the Hamas attack on southern Israel that resulted in 1,139 deaths; over half of the deaths involved civilians, including 38 children. Around 250 Israeli civilians and soldiers were taken as hostages, and many of these individuals remain hostages at the time of this writing (Khatib et al., 2024).

By contrast, younger Jews – like many of those portrayed in *Israelism* – tend to focus on the ongoing destruction of Gaza and the deaths of thousands of Palestinian civilians and children and the context of the conflict, highlighting the role of the Nakba and harsh realities faced by Palestinians. Almost 50,000 Palestinians have been confirmed killed by the IDF, but experts estimate by July 2024 that the number of Palestinians killed exceeded 186,000. *Israelism* includes interviews with numerous Jews who believe this response to be disproportionate and unjustified and are now not affiliating their Jewish identity with the ethno-state of Israel. The film also illustrates how college life in the United States has been disrupted by campus protests over Israel's dramatic and sustained escalation of the war. Terms such as *ethnic cleansing* and *genocide* are also explored in this documentary. As a result of many young Jews' misalignment with the ethno-state of Israel, the documentary has been controversial, and prominent Jewish leaders have called on the US Jewish diaspora community to stop screening the documentary.

Social Norms and Norm Violations

Black Panther (2018), a Marvel fast-paced action movie, is more than a superhero film. It integrates Marvel superheroes with politics, world history, and the experience of African Americans (Brody, 2018). *Black Panther* celebrates the African and African American experience, generating a social and cultural movement. It depicts the African American reality as part of mainstream society, as opposed to showing whiteness as the default mainstream society (Smith, 2018). *Black Panther* also displays the diversity within the African American community (Katz, 2018), including social norms.

Wakanda will no longer watch from the shadows. We cannot. We must not. We will work to be an example of how we, as brothers and sisters on this earth, should treat each other.

T'Challa in *Black Panther*

The impact of *Black Panther* on the African American community is enormous. A huge commercial success, *Black Panther* shows the positive aspects of being Black in the United States, as well as being African in the world. Moreover, the movie is an example of **Afrofuturism** – a multi-genre perspective that blends the African diaspora with science, technology, and philosophy (Scott, 2019). Furthermore, *Black Panther* elevates the African American collective racial identity. As such, it promotes the African and African American cultural values of communalism, spirituality, strength, and power.

Black Panther has mostly Black actors, including Chadwick Boseman (as T'Challa/Black Panther), Michael E. Jordan (as Erik Killmonger), Lupita Nyong'o (as Nakia), Angela Bassett (as Ramonda), Forest Whitaker (as Zuri), Danai Gurira (as Okoye), Letitia Wright (as Shuri), Daniel Kaluuya (as Wa'Kabi), and Winston Duke (as M'Baku), among others. Based on writers Stan Lee and Jack Kirby's Marvel Comics, Director Ryan Coogler wrote *Black Panther* with Joe Robert Cole, and Kevin Feige produced the movie. *Black Panther* received numerous awards nominations during the 91st Academy Awards, winning Oscars for Best Original Score, Best Achievement in Production Design, and Best Costume Design.

According to Ryan Coogler, the film's director, *Black Panther* is a political movie (Katz, 2018). It is empowering, revolutionary, and feminist, and the film's title has historical and political roots. The **Black Panther** political movement began during the Civil Rights era and became a political party

T'Challa: We can still heal you....

Erik Killmonger: Why, so you can lock me up? Nah. Just bury me in the ocean with my ancestors who jumped from ships, 'cause they knew death was better than bondage.

A reference to Black Africans' suicide by jumping off the ships caring slaves. The decision to choose death over slavery is highlighted in *Black Panther.*

(https://en.wikipedia.org/wiki/Black_Panther_Party). Black Panther activists promoted social and racial justice for African American individuals and communities. Besides exhibiting innovation, the movie *Black Panther* conveys a strong feminist message. This is a film in which Black women do not need to dress in a suit to be fierce warriors. Women characters such as Nakia, Okoye, and the Dora Milaje all-women royal guard embody female strength. Additionally, Shuri (T'Challa's sister) is a technology genius. These Wakandan women are bright, assertive, brave, inspiring, and triumphant. The line of succession in Wakanda is male, and T'Challa accepts an offer to be king under the benevolent oversight of his mother, Queen Ramonda.

Wakanda, a utopian African nation untouched by slavery, stands in sharp contrast to African American communities. The wealthiest nation in resources and sophisticated advanced technology, Wakanda has never been colonized. This is important because **colonization** is a crucial element in the development of the Western World. Wakanda has the sole supply of *vibranium*, the world's strongest metal. However, to protect its vibranium, Wakanda isolates itself with the help of its advanced technology (posing as a developing country), in order to prevent being colonized and oppressed.

Black Panther's protagonist (T'Challa) and antagonist (Killmonger) have different value orientations. The movie presents T'Challa (Black Panther), a political leader and king of Wakanda, whose authority is challenged. According to Chadwick Boseman (quoted in Smith, 2018), T'Challa and Killmonger are mirror images, separated only by the accident of where they were born. The antagonist, Killmonger, is a sympathetic character because his father was killed when he was a boy in the United States and as a result, he grew up facing oppressive experiences predominant among many disadvantaged African American youth. Even though Killmonger has Wakandan ties, his violence and destructiveness may relate to a **posttraumatic slave syndrome** (PTSS). Joy DeGruy (2005) coined the term to explain African Americans' adaptive **survivalist reactions**, such as a propensity for anger and hostility, as the result of a multigenerational history of slavery and oppression. Killmonger struggles with his rage about how Black people around the world are oppressed, and he develops a sociopolitical goal of liberating Black people around the globe.

The wise build bridges, while the foolish build barriers.

T'Challa addressing the UN about Wakanda's plan to share its resources with the world, in *Black Panther.*

As political opposites T'Challa represents isolation, while Killmonger stands for inclusion. Watch this empowering movie and witness how T'Challa learns from Killmonger to challenge Wakanda's traditional social norms in order to help the world.

Stereotyping

The movie *BlacKkKlansman* (2018) follows the true story of Ron Stallworth, the first African American detective in the Colorado Springs Police Department. The film is based on Stallworth's memoir *Black Klansman* and focuses on Stallworth's penetration and exposure of the local Ku Klux Klan. Spike Lee directed and co-wrote the movie with Charlie Wachtel, David Rabinowitz, and Kevin Willmott. The actors in the film are John David Washington (as Ron Stallworth), Adam Driver (as Detective Phillip "Flip" Zimmerman), Laura Harrier (as Patrice Dumas), Alec Baldwin (as Dr. Kennebrew Beauregard), and Topher Grace (as David Duke). There is a cameo appearance by the venerable singer/actor/activist Harry Belafonte as Jerome Turner. The movie received numerous award nominations and won an Oscar for the Best Adapted Screenplay at the 91st Academy Awards.

BlacKkKlansman shows how an African American detective infiltrates the Ku Klux Klan, pretending to be White. Stallworth is hired as the first African

---

Ron Stallworth: Hello, this is Ron Stallworth calling. Who am I speaking with?

David Duke: This is David Duke.

Ron Stallworth: The Grand Wizard of the Ku Klux Klan, *that* David Duke?

David Duke: The last time I checked. What can I do for you?

Ron Stallworth: Well since you asked, I hate niggers, I hate Jews. Spics and micks. Italians and chinks. But my mouth to God's ears, I really hate those Black rats, and anyone else that doesn't have pure White Aryan blood running through their veins!

David Duke: I'm happy to be talking to a true White American.

Ron Stallworth: God bless White America.

A hilarious and conning exchange between Ron Stallworth, an African American man pretending to be a White racist during a conversation with David Duke (head of the Ku Klux Klan) in order to entrap Duke in the film *BlacKkKlansman.*

Flip Zimmerman: I'm Jewish, but I wasn't raised to be. It wasn't part of my life. I never thought much about being Jewish, nobody around me was Jewish. I wasn't going to a bunch of Bar Mitzvahs, I didn't have a Bar Mitzvah. I was just another White kid. And now, I'm in some basement denying it out loud. *chuckles* I never thought much about it, now I'm thinking about it all the time. About rituals and heritage. Is that passing? Well, then I have been passing.

A Jewish policeman who did not grow up in a religious home realizes that he has been passing as a White man his entire life in *BlacKkKlansman.*

American officer in Colorado Springs Police Department and is assigned to the records room. There he is subjected to racial **microaggressions** and insults by White officers. He requests a transfer, and he becomes an undercover officer. Stallworth is successful as an undercover officer during a local rally where a speech is to be given by civil rights leader Kwame Ture (Stokely Carmichael, a member of the Black Panther Party and spouse of singer Miriam Makeba), after which he is reassigned to the intelligence section.

Stallworth decides to approach the Ku Klux Klan after reading about the Klan in a local newspaper. He pretends to be a White racist who wants to

Figure 6.3.   *BlacKkKlansman* (2018, Focus Features, Legendary Entertainment, Perfect World Pictures, QC Entertainment, Blumhouse Productions). Produced by Jason Blum, Marcel Brown, Matthew Cherry, Edward Hamm, et al. Directed by Spike Lee. *BlacKkKlansman* is based on the true story of Ron Stallworth, the first African American detective to work in the Colorado Springs Police Department. The film concludes with footage from the 2017 Unite the Right rally in Charlottesville, Virginia.

become a member of the local Klan. Stallworth successfully deceives several Ku Klux Klan members by posing as a White supremacist and speaking in **Standard English** on the phone. He then develops a telephone relationship with David Duke, a White supremacist and former Grand Wizard of the Ku Klux Klan. David Duke is fooled by Stallworth's Standard English speech during a telephone call.

The movie shows how racial stereotypes are misleading. For instance, many White individuals associate African Americans' speech, such as **African American Vernacular English** (AAVE), with inferior intelligence. However, **Ebonics**, a form of AAVE, is rooted in West African languages with its own sophistical grammar and phonological structures (Ndemanu, 2015). Consequently, many African Americans are "bilingual," in the sense that they speak Standard English as well as African American Vernacular English.

Duke's stereotyping African Americans as inferior to White Americans prevents him from discovering Stallworth's clever strategy. Stallworth earns David Duke's trust and gets invited to become a member of the local Ku Klux Klan group. He asks his Jewish colleague, Flip Zimmerman, to go instead of him to impersonate him. Throughout this experience, Zimmerman questions himself about his ethnic identity.

Do you think Flip Zimmerman was successful at **passing** (as White)? What stage in his **ethnic identity development** is Zimmerman approaching when he says (about being Jewish): "I'm thinking about it all the time?

Ku Klux Klan member Felix Kendrickson (played by Jasper Paakkonen) suspects Flip Zimmerman of being Jewish and orders him – at gunpoint – to do a polygraph test. *What happens next?*

This powerful and entertaining political film shows the pervasive racism among some segments of the population during the 1970s. Eerily, it also provides a mirror that reflects our current racial climate.

Indigenous People

On December 29, 1890, United States soldiers killed several hundred Lakota Indians near Wounded Knee Creek. Most of the massacred people were children and women. The event was called the Wounded Knee Massacre. **Wounded Knee**, located on the Pine Ridge Indian Reservation, is in southwestern South Dakota.

Bury My Heart at Wounded Knee (2007) is a made for television film (HBO) that relates the Wounded Knee Massacre from the perspective of the Native American people. This historical and political drama is based on Dee Brown's book of the same title. Grounded by real events, the film was written by Daniel Giat and directed by Yves Simoneau. The main actors in the movie are Adam Beach (as Charles Eastman), Anna Paquin (as Elaine Goodale), August Schellenberg (as Sitting Bull), Aidan Quinn (as Henry L. Dawes), Colm Feore (as General William Tecumseh Sherman), and Fred Thompson (as President Ulysses S. Grant).

The film depicts a transition from Native Americans' traditional ways to living in reservations. As such, it highlights how the US government mistreated Native Americans. Although focused on the specific incident of Wounded Knee, the movie relates the account of the US expansion to the West, displacing Indigenous people of their lands, culture, identities, and lives. To contextualize the movie, we present a historical overview. According to history.com (https://www.history.com/topics/native-american-history/wounded-knee), the US government had serious concerns about the increased practice of an indigenous spiritual movement called the "**Ghost Dance.**" This practice taught Indians that they were restrained in reservations because they had angered their gods, and thus, needed to reject the ways of White men. On December 15, 1890, reservation police tried to arrest **Sitting Bull**, a Sioux Chief, falsely accusing him of being a Ghost Dancer, and killed him. This event triggered more conflicts in Wounded Knee and eventually led to the massacre.

The film *Bury My Heart at Wounded Knee* illustrates these historical events and centers on several characters. Charles Eastman, né Ohiyesa, is a mixed-race Sioux medical doctor, educated in US universities, and is shown to be responsible for the success of the cultural assimilation of Indians into mainstream US society. From 1790 to 1920, the US government enacted an

Charles Eastman: And now you speak of coercion. I don't understand.

Henry Dawes: If you don't put that land into the hands of individual Indians in 5 years – less – homesteaders and ranchers will demand it all...for nothing. The Indian must own his own piece of earth, Charles.

Charles Eastman: Do you know that there is no word in the Sioux language for that, sir?

Henry Dawes: For what?

Charles Eastman: To "own the earth." Not in any native language.

Henry Dawes: Well, then you should invent one.

An example of why and how the United States government justified taking land from Indigenous people in *Bury My Heart at Wounded Knee.*

Henry Dawes: I'm not defending their brutality, Mr. President. The Sioux resisted because by the '68 treaty this land is theirs, and we have no legal ...

General Sherman: That treaty was only support to feed them for 4 years. And yet, here we are, 8 years later, and you Senators are passing a million-a-year-appropriation to keep filling their bellies. Why?

Henry Dawes: To keep them from starving, General.

President Ulysses S. Grant: And that's all it's done. Made them beggars. Hasn't advanced them one bit. Those smart enough not to sign....

A capitalist and imperialist explanation for oppressing Indigenous people in the United States in *Bury My Heart at Wounded Knee*.

Americanization process to culturally change Indigenous people into Americans. Education and boarding schools were used as civilization tools (Adams, 1995). *What effect did Eastman's US education have on his cultural and racial, ethnic identity?* To answer this question, let us examine the following conversation between Eastman and Senator Henry Dawes.

Elaine Goodale, Eastman's future wife, is Superintendent of Indian schools in the Dakotas, and actively works to improve Indians' conditions on the reservation. Senator Henry Dawes advocates for humane treatment of the Indians to President Ulysses S. Grant. Moreover, he proposed a governmental policy (The **Dawes Commission**) to disperse Indian lands (the Great Sioux Reservation) to allow for American claims for land, and simultaneously, preserving enough land for the Sioux.

Senator Henry Dawes opposes William Tecumseh Sherman (General Sherman), who is antagonistic toward the Native Americans. As a historical point, General Sherman was responsible for the US engagement in the Indian Wars. *Do you know that General Sherman's father named him Tecumseh (as a middle name) after an Indian chief of the Shawnees the father admired* (Sherman, 1890)? *What effect do you think having an Indigenous middle name had on General Sherman's ethnic cultural identity?*

Bury My Heart at Wounded Knee received numerous nominations at the 59th Primetime Emmy Awards and won six Emmy Awards. Watch *Bury My Heart at Wounded Knee* and witness the heartbreaking history of how the US government's expansion policies displaced Native Americans and turned them into immigrants in their own land.

Other Movies About Politics That Will Teach You About Culture

Politics and culture are favorite themes in movies, and there are numerous movies that illustrate their close relationship. Movies like *Bury My Heart at Wounded Knee* illustrate the nefarious effects of capitalism, racism, and genocide against Indigenous people in the United States; by contrast, *Malcolm X* and *BlacKkKlansman* show how some African Americans have overcome racism. Likewise, the movie *Black Panther* demonstrates the contrast between the value orientations of a fictionalized African country and those of the United States.

The relationship between politics and racism are felt around the globe. Movies such as *A United Kingdom* and *Blood Diamond* depict the damaging connection between colonization, capitalism, and racism on people of color around the world. A sense for the politics of Rome can be found in *Gladiator* (2000) and *Gladiator II* (2024). *Oppenheimer* (2023) depicts Cold War politics, and *Braveheart* (1995) will introduce you to the courage of Scottish warriors fighting King Edward I of England. Classic films like *Casablanca* (1942) will help you learn about the Second World War, and *Don't Look Up* (2021) will teach you about the callous way politicians have responded to the climate crisis. *Lawrence of Arabia* (1962) illustrates the role of warring Arab tribes during the First World War, and *Gangs of New York* (2002) introduces Bill the Butcher and gives you a sense for life in the 1860s in the Five Points area of New York City. *All the King's Men* (2006) will introduce you to the corruption of Governor Huey Long of Louisiana. *Milk* (2008) stars Sean Penn as Harvey Milk, and the movie will leave you thinking about the relationship between sexuality and politics (Milk was the first openly gay man elected to public office in California). Films like *Lincoln* (2012) will teach you about politics as well as history, as will *Wag the Dog* (1997), *Mr. Smith Goes to Washington* (1939), *Dr. Strangelove or: How I Learned How to Stop Worrying and Love the Bomb* (1964), and *All the President's Men* (1976). In short, there are thousands of political films out there, and we believe you can learn a great deal about politics, history – and culture! – from watching them.

Critical Thinking Questions About Politics and Culture

- Even though racial segregation is outlawed in the United States, do you think there is de facto racial segregation in social norms in the United States?
- What is your racial identity?
- How do you feel about your racial ethnic identity?
- What developmental stage is your racial/ethnic identity?
- How can you know if a member of a minority group is passing?
- What do you think are the conditions under which members of racial and ethnic minority groups can pass?
- Do you have friends of different race/ethnicity than your own? If so, how many?
- Have you been (or are you now) in an interracial romantic relationship?
- Do you own diamonds? Do you know people who own diamonds? How do you know if these diamonds are blood (conflict) diamonds or not?
- What do you think is the responsibility, if any, of the diamond retailers to make sure that they are selling conflict-free diamonds?
- Do you think the United States has a history of genocide against Native Americans? Do you think genocide is still occurring? If yes, can you explain how?
- How do you feel about the current relationship between Native American Nations and the US government?
- Do you think the US government needs to make reparations to Native Americans? How about African Americans?

Further Exploration

If you only have time to read one article, make it:

Farrar, N., & Hanley, T. (2023). Where "culture wars" and therapy meet: Exploring the intersection between political issues and therapeutic practice. *Counselling & Psychotherapy Research, 23*(3), 593–597. https://doi.org/10.1002/capr.12623

If you only have time to read one chapter, make it:

Cross, W. E., Jr. & Fagen-Smith, P. I. (2001). Patterns of African American identity development: A life span perspective. In C. L. Wijeyesinghe, & B. W. Jackson (Eds.). *New perspectives on racial identity development: A theoretical and practical anthology* (pp. 243–270). New York University Press.

If you have time to read an entire book, make it:

Comas-Díaz, L., Adames, H. Y. & Chavez-Dueñas, N. I. (Eds.). (2024) *Decolonial psychology: Toward anticolonial theories, research, training, and practice*. American Psychological Association.

Additional Sources for Exploration

Learn more about intersectionality: Watch Kimberlé Crenshaw's (TED-WOMEN 2016)

TED Talk: The Urgency of Intersectionality at: https://www.ted.com/talks/kimberle_crenshaw_the_urgency_of_intersectionality

Watch Don Shirley perform *Blue Skies* on YouTube at:

https://www.youtube.com/watch?v=EQdUljb4tLc

References

Adams, D. W. (1995). *Education for extinction: American Indians and the boarding school experience, 1875–1928*. University of Kansas.

Betancourt, T. S., Agnew-Blais, J., Gilman, S.E., Williams, D. R., & Ellis, H. (2010). Past horrors, present struggles: The role of stigma in the association between war experiences and psychosocial adjustment among former child soldiers in Sierra Leone. *Social Science & Medicine, 70*(1), 17–26. https://doi.org/10.1016/j.socscimed.2009.09.038

Brody, R. (2018, February 16). The passionate politics of Black Panther. *The New Yorker*. https://www.newyorker.com/culture/richard-brody/the-passionate-politics-of-black-panther

CBS News. (2001, June 14). *Diamonds: A war's best friend*. https://www.cbsnews.com/news/diamonds-a-wars-best-friend/

Colley, Z. (2014). "All America is a prison:" The Nation of Islam and the politicization of African American Prisoners, 1955–1965. *Journal of American Studies, 48*(2), 393–415. https://doi.org/10.1017/S0021875813001308

Comas-Díaz, L. (2007). Ethnopolitical psychology: Healing and transformation. In E. Aldarondo (Ed). *Promoting social justice in mental health practice* (pp. 91–118). Lawrence Erlbaum Associates.

Comas-Díaz, L. Hall, G.N. & Neville, H. A. (2019). Racial trauma: Theory, research, and healing: An introduction to the special issue. *American Psychologist, 74*(1), 1–5. https://doi.org/10.1037/amp0000442

Crenshaw, K. (1989). Demarginalizing the intersection of sex and race: A Black feminist critique of antidiscrimination doctrines, feminist theory and antiracist policies. *University of Chicago Legal Forum, 1898*(1), 91–118.

DeGruy, J. (2005). *Post-traumatic Slave Syndrome: America's legacy of enduring injury and healing*. Uptone Press.

Demetri, J. (2018, April 26). *Italians in America: From discrimination to adoration (or almost)*. https://www.lifeinitaly.com/heritage/italian-discrimination

Devos, T., & Banaji, M. R. (2005). American = White? *Journal of Personality and Social Psychology, 88*(3), 447–466. https://doi.org/10.1037/0022-3514.88.3.447

Johnson, K. I. (1998). Race, the immigration laws, and domestic race relations: A magic mirror into the heart of darkness. *Indiana Law Journal, 73*(4), Article 2. http://www.repository.law.indiana.edu/ilj/vol73/iss4/2

Katz, B. (2018, January 19). Black Panther director Ryan Coogler on why his superhero movie is a political film first. *Observer*. https://observer.com/2018/12/black-panther-ryan-coogler-says-marvel-movie-is-political/

Khatib, R., McKee, M., & Yusuf, S. (2024). Counting the dead in Gaza: Difficult but essential. *The Lancet, 404*(10449), 237–238 https://www.thelancet.com/journals/lancet/article/PIIS0140-6736(24)01169-3/fulltext https://doi.org/10.1016/S0140-6736(24)01169-3

Li, Q., & Brewer, M. B. (2004). What does it mean to be an American? Patriotism, nationalism, and American identity after September 11. *Political Psychology, 25*, 727–739. https://doi.org/10.1111/j.1467-9221.2004.00395.x

Ndemanu, M. T. (2015). Ebonics, to be or not to be? A legacy of trans-Atlantic slave trade. *Journal of Black Studies, 56*(1), 23–43. https://doi.org/10.1177/0021934714555187

Phinney, J. S., & Ong, A. D. (2007). Conceptualization and measurement of ethnic identity: Current status and future directions. *Journal of Counseling Psychology, 54*, 271–281. https://doi.org/10.1037/0022-0167.54.3.271

Scott, S. (2019, January 12). A beginner's guide to Afrofuturism: Titles to watch and read. *Essence*. https://www.essence.com/entertainment/a-beginners-guide-afrofuturism/#408134

Sherman, W. T. (1890). *Personal memoirs of General W. T. Sherman*. Charles L. Webster & Co.

Smith, J. (2018, February 19). The revolutionary power of Black Panther: Marvel's new movie marks a major milestone. *Time Magazine*. https://time.com/black-panther/

Romero, A. J., Edwards, L. M. Fryberg, S. A., & Orduña, M. (2014). Resilience to discrimination stress across ethnic identity stages of development. *Journal of Applied Social Psychology, 44*, 1–11. https://doi.org/10.1111/jasp.12192

Turan, K. (2017, February 9). Review: David Oyelowo and Rosamund Pike breath life into the star-crossed lovers in the true story "A United Kingdom." *Los Angeles Times*. https://www.latimes.com/entertainment/movies/la-et-mn-united-kingdom-review-2017-story.html

Weber, B. (2013). Donald Shirley, a pianist with his own genre, dies at 86. *The New York Times*. https://www.nytimes.com/2013/04/29/arts/music/donald-shirley-pianist-and-composer-dies-at-86.html

Yip, T. (2008). Everyday experiences of ethnic and racial identity among adolescents and young adults. In S. M. Quintana & C. McKown (Eds.). *Handbook of race, racism, and the developing child* (pp. 182–202). Wiley.

Chapter 7
Immigration

> "You can live your whole life and never know who you are
> until you see the world through the eyes of others."
>
> From the theatrical trailer of *The Visitor*

Questions to Consider While Watching
The Visitor (2007)

- Do you have a history of immigration in your family?
- If so, what do you know about the culture of your immigrant ancestors?
- Have you encountered difficulties understanding and or communicating with immigrants (even if they speak English)?
- How do you feel about undocumented immigrants?
- What do you think about the current United States policy of immigration?
- Is there a difference between the experience of immigrants of color in the United States when compared to phenotypically White immigrants?
- How did some people's reaction to Muslim individuals change after 9/11?
- What are your thoughts about Islamophobia?
- Do you think Tarek was a victim of Islamophobia?
- Why do you think Zainab left the apartment after Tarek was arrested?
- What are some of the reasons immigrants and refugees leave their countries of origin?
- How does a nativist and/or xenophobic sociopolitical climate affect immigrants and refugees?
- What are some contributions of immigrants and refugees to the development of the United States?

Immigration and Culture

Immigration is as ancient as history. People of all colors, ages, genders, and nationalities have immigrated throughout the ages. Many individuals immigrate due to financial, political, religious, economic, or personal reasons, or due to a combination of these factors. In other words, people immigrate in search of a better life. Indeed, immigration may be part of humankind's collective unconsciousness.

Immigrants and refugees have contributed to the rebirth and transformation of the United States. An official motto of the United States, *E pluribus unum* ("From many, one") illustrates the historical relevance of immigration in the development of the country. Moreover, the United States is a nation of immigrants:

> Give me your tired, your poor
> Your huddled masses yearning to breathe free

These words are part of the poem "The New Colossus," written by Emma Lazarus as part of the fundraising for the pedestal of the Statue of Liberty (https://en.wikipedia.org/wiki/The_New_Colossus).

Notwithstanding immigration's historical role, many immigrants, especially immigrants of color and refugees, face serious difficulties when they encounter a sociopolitical climate of nativism, racism, xenophobia, and anti-immigration. There are numerous movies that address the experiences of immigrants and refugees.

Immigration and *The Visitor*

The Visitor (2007) was directed by Tom McCarthy, who won the 2008 Independent Spirit Award for Best Director. Richard Jenkins stars as Walter Vale, and he was nominated for Best Actor in the 2009 Academy Awards. *The Visitor* addresses issues of undocumented immigration, cross-cultural communication, and Islamophobia in New York City's post-9/11 era.

Walter Vale is a widowed college professor who pretends to be busy. He takes piano lessons, because his late wife was a classical concert pianist. However, he is not interested in piano lessons. Indeed, some individuals cope with grief through the "internalization" of the dead person's activities. Walter's life, on automatic pilot, gets interrupted when he is asked to present a paper, to which he marginally contributed, at a conference in New York City. He travels from Connecticut to Manhattan and is surprised when he finds an unmarried immigrant couple living in his apartment. Zainab, a young African woman from Senegal, and Tarek, a young Palestinian Syrian man, explain to Walter that they rented the apartment from a man who said he was the owner. As they prepare to leave the apartment, Walter invites them to stay.

Tarek is a *djembe* player (a drum originally from West Africa), and Walter shows interest in learning to play the *djembe*. Tarek teaches him, and they join a drum circle in Central Park. On their way to the apartment, two police officers erroneously charge Tarek for subway turnstile jumping. Tarek shows them his subway ticket, but the police officers arrest him anyway. Walter vouches for Tarek's innocence, but to no avail; Tarek is taken to a detention center. Because both Tarek and Zainab are undocumented, Walter hires an immigration lawyer to prevent Tarek from being deported. Zainab cannot visit Tarek due to her undocumented status and moves out of the apartment to live with friends.

Figure 7.1.   *The Visitor* (2007, Groundswell Productions, Next Wednesday Productions, Participant Media). Produced by Omar Amanat, Michael London, Patty Long, Chris Salvaterra, et al. Directed by Tom McCarthy. *The Visitor* is a beautiful film that shows how a widowed man came to change his views about immigrants – and life.

We wonder whether **Islamophobia** was a reason for Tarek's arrest. The fear, prejudice, and/or hatred against Islam and/or Muslims is a form of ethnic/racial and religious discrimination. Islamophobia is one of several reasons that Muslim immigrants are discriminated against and sometimes become victims of hate crimes (Haque et al., 2018; Moffic et al., 2019).

Mouna, Tarek's mother, has not heard from Tarek, and arrives at Walter's apartment. She worries about Tarek being deported because her journalist husband was assassinated years ago back in her country. Since Mouna is also undocumented, she cannot visit Tarek at the detention center. A budding romantic relationship emerges between Walter and Mouna. Within this context, Walter becomes a human connector between mother and son.

Will Tarek be deported? What will happen to Zainab? Does the relationship between Walter and Mouna have a future?

The Visitor raises important questions about immigration, undocumented immigrants, discrimination, and interethnic/interracial relationships. Specifically, it alludes to the nefarious effects of Islamophobia on Muslim immigrants. *The Visitor* illustrates ways of coping with grief – both dysfunctional and functional. More importantly, it places a mirror to the relationship between self and other, and raises the question: *Who is the Visitor?* In other words, when you intimately interact with immigrants, you visit their lives, just as they visit your life. Walter's life changes after meeting Tarek, Mouna, and Zainab. *How did Walter's life change? How did he cope with Tarek's absence?* To answer these questions, we invite you to find out the cultural meaning of the African word *djembe*.

Prejudice, Discrimination, Oppression, Racism, and Ethnocentrism

The Three Burials of Melquiades Estrada (2005) was written by Guillermo Arriaga and directed by Tommy Lee Jones. The film's stars include Tommy Lee Jones (as Pete Perkins), Barry Pepper (as Mike Norton), Julio Cedillo (as Melquiades Estrada), Melissa Leo (as Rachel), and January Jones (as Lou Ann Norton). The movie is inspired by the death of Ezequiel Hernandez, Jr., a Mexican adolescent killed during a United States Marines military exercise at the US/Mexico border. Tommy Lee Jones won the Best Actor Award at the 2005 Cannes Film Festival, and Guillermo Arriaga won the Best Screenplay Award at the 2005 Cannes Film Festival for this film.

The Three Burials of Melquiades Estrada is the story of an undocumented Mexican immigrant who lives in Texas and works as a cowboy. His best friend,

Figure 7.2.   *The Three Burials of Melquiades Estrada* (2005, Sony Pictures Classics, EuropaCorp Distribution, and Monopole-Pathé). Produced by Luc Besson, Michael Fitzgerald, Tommy Lee Jones, and Pierrel-Ange Le Pogam. Directed by Tommy Lee Jones. Tommy Lee Jones directs and stars in *The Three Burials of Melquiades Estrada*, a movie inspired by the real-life killing of a Texas teenager by Marines conducting military drills near the Texas/Mexico border.

Pete Perkins, is a White American rancher. Melquiades shoots a coyote that is threatening his goats. Nearby, Mike Norton, a United States border patrol officer, believes that he is being attacked, and shoots Melquiades, killing him. He buries Melquiades's body without reporting the death. Pete Perkins finds out that Norton killed his best friend. Since Pete has promised Melquiades to take his body to Mexico, he kidnaps Mike Norton. He then forces Norton to dig up Melquiades's body and take the body to Mexico. Both Pete and captive Mike travel on horseback to Melquiades's Mexican hometown with Melquiades's decomposing body tied to a mule.

The Three Burials of Melquiades Estrada illustrates how the human rights of undocumented migrants are not recognized – even in death. Many undocumented immigrants experience oppression, indignity, and disempowerment. Moreover, numerous immigrants of color, especially undocumented ones, serve as quintessential **scapegoats**. For example, in times of economic hardship, national insecurity, and limited resources, individuals increase their tendency to scapegoat (Dobbings & Skillings, 2000). In short, as undocumented immigrants become the other, they are dehumanized. The fact that Mike Norton, a US Border Patrol Officer, killed Melquiades and buried him without reporting the death robs Melquiades of his humanity. *The Three Burials of Melquiades Estrada* relates how Pete and Mike embark on a grueling physical and existential journey. *Will they reach their destination in Mexico? Will Pete Parker be able to find Melquiades's Mexican family? Will Melquiades be* *buried in his hometown? Does Mike Norton find redemption for killing Melquia-des?* Watch this heartbreaking movie to find the answers to these questions.

Cultural Identity, Acculturation, Assimilation

The film *Lion* (2016) introduces us to Saroo, an immigrant of color, who is searching for his cultural identity. *Lion* is a biographical drama directed by Garth Davis; the screenplay was written by Luke Davies. The film is based on Saroo Brierley's book *A Long Way Home.* Dev Patel (Saroo as a young adult) and Nicole Kidman (Saroo's adopted mother – Sue Brierley) are the stars of this remarkable movie. Immigration in this film is presented through the lens of cross-cultural adoption.

One day Saroo, a 5-year-old Indian boy, accompanies his older brother Guddu to a train station. Guddu works sweeping at the train station to help their mother after their father abandoned the family. Saroo is sleepy and takes a nap.

"Don't go anywhere, I will be right back," Guddu tells Saroo at the train station. When Saroo wakes up, he cannot find Guddu. He searches for Guddu and boards a train trying to find his way home. Saroo embarks on a journey that ends when an Australian couple from Tasmania adopts him. Twenty-five years later Saroo embarks on another journey – hoping to find his way home.

"I'm adopted, I am not really Indian," Saroo replies to an Indian college classmate when asked which part of India he was from.

Saroo's response to his classmate reflects a lack of cultural and ethnic identity. Raised by a White Australian couple, Saroo is acculturated to a White Australian culture. Cross-cultural and **interracial adoptions** are complex issues imbued with pros and cons. When adopted children look phenotypically different from their adopted parents, their adoptee identity is visibly evident and creates additional stress on the adoptee of color. A culture-blind and color-blind attitude is not helpful in these situations. Moreover, a belief that love conquers all in cross-cultural, interracial, and transracial adoption may also be unrealistic. Therefore, it is helpful to teach the adoptee about his or her original culture in order to develop an ethnic/racial identity. Indeed, developing a **racial/ethnic identity** is a crucial concept in multicultural psychology because racial socialization promotes healthy development of an ethnic/racial identity. Racial and ethnic socialization involves learning how race and ethnicity (and their intersection with other diversity variables) inform the lives of people of color (Neblett et al., 2012). Many White parents do not, and cannot, engage in racial socialization of their adopted children of color.

Given the prevalence of racial and ethnic discrimination, racial socialization is a protective factor against this type of discrimination (Harris-Britt et al., 2007). Without racial/ethnic socialization, many adopted children of color are unprepared to cope effectively with racism and racial discrimination throughout their lives.

Saroo wonders about his biological family when Sue Brierley, his adopted mother, becomes ill with cancer. Saroo feels that he needs to find his biological mother and family. The rest of the movie vividly documents Saroo's long way home. This film received six Oscar nominations and became one of the highest-grossing Australian movies. Watch this powerful movie and find out why it is titled *Lion*.

Value Conflicts, Value Orientations

Sin Nombre (Without a Name) (2009) is an engaging film depicting the harrowing journey that many Central American immigrants take to escape years of extreme violence, civil wars, mass killings, and other violent acts. As such, this movie is an excellent example of **peri-migration trauma**. *Sin Nombre* is written and directed by Cary Joji Fukunaga and produced by Mexican actors Gael Garcia Bernal and Diego Luna.

Sin Nombre relates the story of Sayra (played by Paulina Gaitan), a Honduran adolescent girl, and a gang member, Willy, nicknamed Casper (played by Edgar Flores), who travel to the United States border. The movie illustrates the dramatic difference in value orientations between these two incongruous characters.

Traveling on the top of a train, Sayra, her father, and uncle want to reach the Mexico/US border to start a new life with relatives in New Jersey. This journey is extremely dangerous as numerous Central Americans fall off the train. Moreover, immigrants are assaulted, robbed, abused, and sometimes killed by gang members during the train's regular stops. Casper is a member of the **Mara Salvatrucha** (aka **MS-13**), a violent transnational gang formed in Los Angeles by immigrants from El Salvador escaping the civil war. Currently, MS-13 has members in Central America as well as in the United States. The movie shows that Casper has a romantic relationship with his girlfriend Martha, but keeps it secret from the gang. One day Martha follows Casper to a gang meeting, and Lil Mago, the gang leader, walks her out. He tries to rape Martha and accidentally kills her. Afterwards, Mago casually tells Casper that he will find another girl. Unfortunately, this way of treating women is a common occurrence. Ramirez and Ream (2014) reported that **sexual abuse** is

A psychic once told me: You will reach the United States, not in God's hands, but in the hands of the devil.

Sayra tells Casper in *Sin Nombre*

the major reason why young Central Americans leave their countries. Indeed, Latin America and the Caribbean have the highest violence against females and the highest incidences of femicide in the world (United Nations Women, 2017).

After Martha's murder, Casper is consumed with grief. He struggles with a conflict regarding Martha's death and his anger towards Lil Mago versus his commitment to the Mara Salvatrucha's cultural values. Casper, Smiley (a young boy whom Casper mentored into the gang), and Lil Mago go to a location along the train tracks to rob the traveling immigrants during the train stop. They climb on the train and begin to rob the immigrants. When Lil Mago sees Sayra, he picks her up and tries to rape her. Casper kills Mago and tells Smiley to leave the train. Casper knows that he broke a Mara Salvatrucha code of honor and stays on the train. Since Smiley will tell the gang members what

Figure 7.3. *Sin Nombre* (2009, Scion Films, Canana Films, Creando Films, and Primary Productions). Produced by Gerardo Barrera, Pablo Cruz, Gael García Bernal, Amy Kaufman, and Diego Luna. Directed by Cary Joji Fukunaga. A young girl from Honduras and a gangster from Mexico unite to illegally cross the US/Mexican border in *Sin Nombre*.

happened, Casper knows that they will try to kill him for breaking the Mara Salvatrucha's cultural code. Indeed, when Smiley reports to the gang members what happened on the train, they assign him the task of killing Casper. Back on the top of the train, some of the immigrants try to attack Casper, but Sayra interferes on his behalf. After she loses her father and uncle, Sayra decides to travel with Casper toward the Mexico/US border.

The rest of *Sin Nombre* shows Sayra and Casper being chased by the gang members.

Central American immigrants' journey is paved with trauma. *Sin Nombre* examines their traumatic immigration, focusing on the peri-migration journey. *Will Sayra and Casper reach the border? Will Smiley find Casper? Will Smiley kill his mentor? Does the psychic's prophecy about Sayra come true, or not?* To answer these questions, watch *Sin Nombre*, a film that movie critic Roger Ebert (2009) described as "riveting from start to finish."

Social Norms and Norms Violations

A Better Life (2011), directed by Chris Weitz and written by Eric Eason, is a dramatic film based on a story by Roger L. Simon. The movie is about an undocumented Mexican, Carlos Galindo (played by Demián Bichir), and his son Luis (played by Jose Julian). Mexican actor Demián Bichir was nominated for an Academy Award for Best Actor in this movie.

Carlos works as a gardener in Los Angeles. His 14-year-old son, Luis, is in high school, but cuts classes, and eventually is suspended for assaulting another student. Carlos worries about Luis's potential involvement in a gang because Luis's girlfriend associates with gang members. Moreover, Luis considers his father to be a loser. When he asks Carlos for money, and Carlos does not have it, Luis replies: "I'll jack a little old lady."

Carlos works for Blasco, who owns a landscaping business and a truck. Blasco's business is profitable, and he decides to return to Mexico. Carlos offers to buy Blasco's business.

Carlos asks Anita, his sister, for a loan to buy Blasco's truck. She is ambivalent because as an undocumented man, Carlos cannot get a driver's license,

This country is a land of dreams. It can be a hard place, a cruel place. But it's where I work, where I dream of a better life for my son.

Carlos Galindo in *A Better Life*

and he will be deported if the police stop him. Nonetheless, Anita gives him the money. Carlos buys the truck and hires Santiago, an undocumented Salvadoran immigrant, to help him in his gardening business. On their first workday, Santiago steals Carlos's truck. The next day Carlos and Luis go to an apartment complex known for housing undocumented migrant workers. There they are told that Santiago works at a nightclub as a dishwasher. On their way to the nightclub, Carlos and Luis attend a Mexican event and Carlos confides to Luis that their mother abandoned them. Luis tells Carlos that he doesn't like Mexican culture or music. This scene is relevant in multicultural psychology because many children of immigrants of color defend themselves against racial and ethnic discrimination by rejecting their parents' original cultures. Moreover, to assimilate and become "Americans," most second-generation Latinx speak English as their preferred language, and many do not speak Spanish (Lutz, 2006).

Carlos and Luis find Santiago at the nightclub's parking lot and demand that he returns the truck. Santiago replies that he sold the truck and sent the money to his family in El Salvador. Carlos is sympathetic to Santiago's plight. Luis gets angry with Carlos for defending Santiago and leaves. The next day Luis agrees to accompany Carlos to the establishment where Santiago sold the truck.

To get back on track, Carlos breaks the law and steals his truck (which now belongs to someone else). What kind of message does Carlos give Luis by breaking the law? *Multicultural psychologists examine context in order to understand behavior.* If you use a contextual lens to examine Carlos' behavior, what do you conclude? In assessing this question, consider psychologist Dan Ariely's empirical studies of dishonesty. Ariely holds two PhDs, one in cognitive psychology and the other in business administration. In his Corruption Experiment (Dis)Honesty Project, Dr. Ariely found that normalizing corruption leads people to be dishonest (Ariely, 2017).

Do you think Carlos violated societal rules by stealing his stolen truck? Does the issue of context inform your answer? Given Carlos's behavior, do you think Luis will break the law in the future?

The police stop Carlos after he takes his truck out of the establishment that bought it from Santiago. Carlos is sent to prison, and later on, he is deported. *How will Luis fare without his father? Will Luis stay in school or join a gang? Will Carlos try to return illegally to the United States in search of a better life?* Watch this emotive movie about the love of a father for his son, and witness how far a father will go to better the life of his son.

Stereotyping

Being an immigrant can be painful and isolating. The movie *In America* (2002) is a beautiful rendition of the experience of an immigrant Irish family in New York City. The film is based on a semi-autobiographical screenplay by Jim Sheridan and his daughters (Naomi and Kirsten) who were nominated for an Academy Award (Best Original Screenplay). The stars of the film are Samantha Morton (as Sarah), Paddy Considine (as Johnny), and Djimon Hounsou (as Mateo). Samantha Morton was nominated for an Academy Award for Best Actress, and Djimon Hounsou was nominated for an Academy Award for Best Supporting Actor in 2003.

Johnny Sullivan, his wife Sarah, and their daughters, 10-year-old Christy and 5-year-old Ariel, arrive in the United States with an Irish tourist visa. They enter the country illegally via Canada, where Johnny was working as an actor. Johnny and Sarah are coping with the death of their 5-year-old son Frankie, who died of a brain tumor. Specifically, Johnny has been unable to cry and mourn Frankie's death. This evocative film is presented through the eyes of Christy, the older daughter. She records their life in the new country with a camcorder.

When some immigrants confront oppression, ethnocentrism, and stereotyping, many develop empathy for individuals who, like them, are considered **"the Other."** *In America* illustrates the development of this process. Due to limited funds, the Sullivan family settles in a dilapidated building inhabited by drug addicts, transvestites, and an African (Nigerian) photographer named Mateo, known as the "man who screams."

Sarah finds a job in an ice cream parlor. Johnny goes to auditions but has no success. When Sarah discovers she is pregnant, Johnny finds a job as a taxi driver. Since they are Catholic, they enroll the girls in a Catholic school. For Halloween, Sarah makes costumes for Christy and Ariel. However, their classmates make fun of the girls' homemade costumes. Christy is upset with her classmates' discrimination toward her. She and Ariel are stereotyped as poor immigrants. Back in their apartment, Christy and Ariel ask their mother for permission to go trick-or-treating. Sarah agreed, but only in the building. After unsuccessfully knocking on several doors, they knock at Mateo's apartment, and he opens the door after a long time. Unable to give them candy, Mateo gives them a glass bottle filled with change. In gratitude, Sarah invites Mateo for a meal at their apartment, and they become friends. However, Johnny is concerned about Mateo.

The Sullivan family learns that Mateo is not an immigrant. Mateo is an African American man dying of AIDS. Due to his illness, Mateo has been a reclusive and lonely man. Until now Mateo enjoys his friendship with Christy, Ariel, and Sarah. Later, he falls down the building stairs and is knocked unconscious. Christy tries to help him, but residents of the building prevent her from helping because Mateo is HIV positive. As a Black male with AIDS, Mateo is stereotyped by many residents in the building.

As immigrants, Christy, Ariel, Sarah, and Johnny are the Other within a WASP (White Anglo Saxon Protestant) population. The Sullivan's poverty, and their being subjected to stereotypes, seems to nurture their development of empathy toward Mateo.

As Sarah's pregnancy progresses, Mateo's health deteriorates. When Sarah goes to the hospital to give birth, Mateo is taken to the hospital to die. The doctor announces that Sarah's pregnancy is in danger. The Sullivans don't have the money to pay the hospital bills. Sarah's baby girl is born prematurely and is in poor health. Sarah responds to the stress of hospitalization and suffers an emotional breakdown in which she blames Johnny for their son's death.

Will the baby girl recover? How are Johnny and Sarah going to pay the hospital bills? Who really is Mateo? Will Johnny be able to grieve the death of his 5-year-old son Frankie? Watch this poignant movie to see how immigration, grief, and otherhood intersect in people's lives.

Indigenous People

Directed by Gregory Nava, *El Norte* (1983) is an independent film in Spanish and Mayan languages. Gregory Nava and Anna Thomas wrote the screenplay based on Nava's story. They were nominated for an Academy Award for Best Original Screenplay in 1985.

El Norte is a powerful story about siblings Rosa Xuncar (played by Zaide Silvia Gutiérrez) and Enrique Xuncax (played by David Villapando), two Mayan peasants who survive a massacre in their native Guatemala during a civil war. Arturo Xuncar, their father, is a coffee picker who organizes a labor union among other coffee pickers. A coworker betrays him, and the

To the rich, the peasant is just a pair of strong arms.

Arturo Xuncar describes the plight of the Indio to his son Enrique in *El Norte*.

Figure 7.4. *El Norte* (1983, American Playhouse, Channel Four Films, Independent Productions, Island Alive, Public Broadcasting Service). Produced by Anna Thomas. Directed by Gregory Nava. A brother and sister flee Guatemala to make a harrowing journey to Los Angeles.

Guatemalan army kills Arturo and the other peasants who cooperated. *El Norte* is a film with magical realism features, and it is infused with Mayan spirituality.

The government soldiers destroy Rosa and Enrique's Mayan village. Moreover, they abduct the siblings' mother, who is presumed to be *desaparecida* (missing). Consequently, Rosa Xuncar and Enrique Xuncar decide to seek refuge in "el Norte." The siblings engage in a difficult and terrifying journey to the United States via Mexico.

The siblings settle in Los Angeles, find a place to live, learn English, and get jobs. They also encounter a series of distressing experiences.

El Norte shows the racist and genocidal acts performed against the indigenous peoples of Guatemala. In fact, government-sponsored agents did

I don't know. They are not speaking Spanish. They must be speaking some kind of Indian language.

A Latinx US border patrol officer talking about Rosa and Enrique in *El Norte*.

In our land, we have no home. They want to kill us … In Mexico, there is only poverty. We can't make a home there either. And here in the north, we aren't accepted. When will we find a home, Enrique? Maybe when we die, we'll find a home.

Rosa speaking to Enrique in *El Norte*.

commit horrific crimes against the Mayas in Guatemala, and José Efraín Ríos Montt, a former president of Guatemala, was indicted for genocide and crimes against humanity in 2012. Discrimination against indigenous people permeates Guatemalan society. Sadly, many *ladinos*, the *mestizos* in Guatemala, discriminate against the Mayan people as an expression of their **internalized colonization** and racism.

Rigoberta Menchú, an indigenous Guatemalan activist, was awarded the Nobel Peace Prize Award in 1992. You can learn more about her activist work in her autobiography, *I, Rigoberta Menchú* (Menchú, 2009).

El Norte is a lyrical film that portrays the plight of Central American political refugees. At the same time, the movie illustrates the beauty and spirituality of Mayan culture. As such, *El Norte* is an ode to the resilience of the human spirit.

Other Movies About Immigration That Will Teach You About Culture

Many immigrants go through a series of stages in their journey, including pre-migration, peri-migration (in-transit), arrival, and post-migration stages. Some immigrants, like Central Americans, may face a traumatic pre-migration journey due to the extreme violence in countries of the **Northern Triangle** (El Salvador, Guatemala, and Honduras). The illegal drug trade and extreme poverty have increased the violence in these countries, forcing many Central Americans to immigrate for survival reasons. During arrival, most immigrants cope with cultural, linguistic, and financial difficulties, in addition to acculturation stress. While disadvantaged immigrants cope with socioeconomic pressures, immigrants of color are exposed to racism, colorism, xenophobia, ethnocentrism, and other intersecting types of discrimination.

Sadly, undocumented immigrants can become the focus of prejudice and discrimination, and even health providers may develop a **political**

countertransference (a belief that all undocumented immigrants are criminals) when interacting with undocumented immigrants (Chung, 2005). Moreover, some immigrants of color face hate crimes and even death. On the other hand, many Latino immigrants are resilient (Bermudez & Mancini, 2013). **Immigrant resilience** refers to a group of qualities that characterize people who decide to leave their country for a better life (Estrada-Moreno et al., 2025).

Fortunately, many resilient immigrants engage in positive psychology (Cobb et al., 2018). A self-selected group, many Latinx, Asian, and Caribbean immigrants in the United States, as well as immigrants in other countries, have displayed resilience (American Psychological Association, 2012). For example, numerous Latinx immigrants exhibit the **Hispanic paradox**, a research-based phenomenon showing that Latinx immigrants have better health compared to US born and raised Latinxs (Morales et al., 2002). Sadly, children of immigrants of color do not necessarily inherit the immigrant paradox. Their health status is not the same as their immigrant parents due the prejudice and racial discrimination against Americans of color.

There are several movies that illustrate the experiences of immigrants, both documented and undocumented. Some films you might want to watch to learn more about immigration include *Gangs of New York* (2002), *America Unfiltered: Portraits and Voices of a Nation* (2024), *Scarface* (1983), *The Terminal* (2004), *Brooklyn* (2015), *The Goat Life* (2024), *A Separation* (2011), *Spanglish* (2004), *The Old Oak* (2023), *Angela's Ashes (1999)*, *In America* (2002), *A Better Life* (2011), *Human Flow* (2017), *Which Way Home* (2009), *Icebox* (2018), *Entre Nos* (2009), *Minari* (2020), *The Joy Luck Club* (1993), *Gran Torino* (2008), and *Green Card* (1990).

Critical Thinking Questions About Immigration and Culture

- Do you know the difference between emigrants, immigrants, refugees, and transnationals?
- From which countries do most immigrants come when moving to the United States?
- Do you think context matters in assessing criminal behavior? Why?
- What is the relationship between nativism and immigration?
- Can you compare Canada's immigration policy with the current US immigration policy?

- How do you feel about Carlos Galindo stealing what was stolen from him?
- What do you think the role of spirituality is in the lives of immigrants?
- How do you think immigrants of color are treated in comparison with White immigrants?
- How do you think the United States government has treated Native Americans?
- Do you think the United States has a history of genocide against Native Americans?
- Has Donald Trump influenced how most American citizens feel about immigrants? How do feel you about Trump's anti-immigration agenda?
- Does it seem inherently racist for the US to admit White Afrikaners from South Africa while refusing immigration to Black and Brown refuges from Central America?

Further Exploration

If you have time to read one article about immigrants and culture, read:

Viruell-Fuentes, E. A., Miranda, P. Y., & Abdulrahim, S. (2012). More than culture: Structural racism, intersectionality theory, and immigrant health. *Social Science & Medicine,* 75(12), 2099–2106. https://doi.org/10.1016/j.socscimed.2011.12.037

If you only have time to read one chapter, read:

Hays, P. A. (2022). Making a culturally responsive diagnosis. In P. A. Hays (Ed.), *Addressing cultural complexities in counseling and clinical practice: An intersectional approach* (4th ed., pp. 207–230). American Psychological Association. https://doi.org/10.1037/0000277-010

If you have time to read a book, go to:

Rothe, E. M., & Pumariega, A. J. (2020). *Immigration, cultural identity, and mental health: Psycho-social implications of the reshaping of America.* Oxford University Press. https://doi.org/10.1093/med/9780190661700.001.0001

To witness the experience of real undocumented immigrants in the United States, you can watch this documentary:

Igual Que Tú (The Same As You). https://vimeo.com/121426324

To read about the experience of a transracial adoption on a woman's racial identity, see Melissa Guida-Richards' story in the *Huffington Post:*

"My Adoptive Parents Hid My Racial Identity from Me for 19 Years." https://www.huffpost.com/entry/transracial-adoption-racial-identity_n_5c94f7eae4b01ebeef0e76e6

References

American Psychological Association Task Force on Immigration (2012). *Crossroads: The psychology of immigration in the new century.* American Psychological Association.

Ariely, D. (2017). *The Corruption Experiment (aka The Dis)Honesty Project.* YouTube. https://www.youtube.com/watch?v=2KyavuKmdNE

Bermudez, J. M., & Mancini, J. A. (2013). Familias fuertes: Family resilience among Latinos. In D. S. Becvar (Ed.), *Handbook of family resilience* (pp. 215–227). Springer Science + Business Media. https://doi.org/10.1007/978-1-4614-3917-2_13

Chung, R. C.-Y. (2005). Women, human rights, and counseling: Crossing international boundaries. *Journal of Counseling and Development, 83,* 262–268. https://doi.org/10.1002/j.1556-6678.2005.tb00341.x

Cobb, C. I., Branscombe, N. R., Meca, A., Schwartz, S. J., Xie, D., Zea, M.C., Molina, L. E., & Martinez, C. R. (2018). Toward a positive psychology of immigrants. *Perspectives on Psychological Science, 14*(4), 619–632. https://doi.org/10.1177/1745691619825848

Dobbins, J. E., & Skillings, J. (2000). Racism as a clinical syndrome. *American Journal of Orthopsychiatry, 70*(1), 14–27. https://doi.org/10.1037/h0087702

Ebert, R. (2009, April 1). *A long journey to El Norte though the forges of hell.* https://www.rogerebert.com/reviews/sin-nombre-2009

Estrada-Moreno, I. S., Palma-Garcia, M. D., Gomez Jacinto, L. & Hombrado-Mendieta. M. I. (2025). Resilience in immigrants: A facilitating resource for their social integration. *Journal of Ethnic and Cultural Diversity in Social Work.* https://doi.org/10.1080/15313204.2024.2447274

Haque, A., Tubbs, C. Y., Kahumoku-Fessler, E. P., & Brown, M. D. (2018). Microaggressions and islamophobia: Experiences of Muslims across the United States and clinical implications. *Journal of Marital and Family Therapy, 45*(1), 76–91. https://doi.org/10.1111/jmft.12339

Harris-Britt, A., Valrie, C. R., Kurtz-Costes, B., & Rowley, S. J. (2007). Perceived racial discrimination and self-esteem in African American youth: Racial socialization as a protective factor. *Journal of Research on Adolescence, 17*(4), 669–682. https://doi.org/10.1111/j.1532-7795.2007.00540.x

Menchú, R. (2009). *I, Rigoberta Menchú* [I, Rigoberta Menchú]. Verso Books.

Moffic, S., Peteet, J., Hankir, A. Z., & Awaad, R. (Eds.). (2019). *Islamophobia and psychiatry: Recognition, prevention, and treatment.* Springer. https://doi.org/10.1007/978-3-030-00512-2

Morales, L. S., Lara, M., Kingston, R. S., Valdez, R. O., & Escarge, J. (2002). Socioeconomic, cultural, and behavioral factors affecting Hispanic health outcomes. *Journal of Health Care for the Poor and Underserved, 13*(4), 477–503. https://doi.org/10.1353/hpu.2010.0630

Neblett, E. W. J., Rivas-Drake, D., & Umaña-Taylor, A. J. (2012). The promise of racial and ethnic protective factors in promoting ethnic minority youth development. *Child Development Perspectives, 6*(3), 295–303. https://doi.org/10.1111/j.1750-8606.2012.00239.x

Ramirez, M., & Ream, A. K. (2014, July 24). Migrant children are fleeing a region rife with sexual violence. *The New Republic.* https://newrepublic.com/article/118820/sexual-violence-major-cause-immigration-us

United Nations Women. (2017, February 15). *Take five: Fighting femicide in Latin America.* http://www.unwomen.org/en/news/stories/2017/2/take-five-adriana-quinones-femicide-in-latin-america

Chapter 8
Horror and Fantasy

Alithea: I cannot, for the life of me, summon up one
eligible wish. And you're asking me for three?
Jinn: Is there any life in you? Are you even alive?
Alithea: You know, in some cultures, abstinence from
desire means enlightenment!
Jinn: Then you are a pious fool!
Alithea: If I'm content, why tempt fate?
Jinn: And you're a coward!

A contented woman frustrates a jinn
by refusing to make a wish in
Three Thousand Years of Longing.

Questions to Consider While Watching
Three Thousand Years of Longing (2016)

- This movie and book were based on a lore of the jinn that was told by Arabs, Muslims, and other people of the Global South. Do they belong to everyone to tell, particularly those from colonizing cultures?
- Do people from outside a culture understand that culture's folklore as well as those who are from it? Does it limit their story telling capacity?
- Are jinn stories horror if they are considered real by some cultures?
- Why, in Istanbul, a city of millions surrounded by many who believe in the jinn, does a White woman, who does not believe in the jinn, find the jinn's bottle?
- Is colonial White supremacy frightening to the jinn? Why?
- Is the love between Alithea and the jinn real, or is it a consequence of her desire to be loved by the jinn? Is this real love or slavery?

- Why does Sheba give up the jinn (represented by a dark-skinned man), who provides her with everything, to be with a mortal man who can control the jinn (and who is represented by a light-skinned man)?
- If you were given three wishes by the jinn, what would your wishes be?

Horror and Fantasy

In a world where we witness horrors on the daily news and uncensored hate on our social media feeds, do traditional horror films fade into the realm of fantasy? Over time, ghost stories have become softer and have been integrated more into suspense or even family genres. Think of the recent series *Wednesday* (a remake of *The Addams Family*) or the films *Hocus Pocus* and *Harry Potter*. Vampires are now symbols of lifelong love and erotica (*Interview With the Vampire, Twilight*, etc.) and a way to escape the mundane realities of everyday life. And movies related to gore are now categorized as horror, reflecting the horror of human atrocities, alleged genocides in many parts of the world, and the very bloody nature of the evening news.

In many cultures outside our modern Western culture, stories of ghosts and fairies were always blended in with culture (e.g., the *Wendigo* in Indigenous culture, or the Headless Horseman in historical American culture, and the jinn in many Arab and Muslim cultures). Although the supernatural always produced wonder, it was by the standards of many cultures not a reflection of what we consider horror. Some of these folk tales may have inspired fear, but they also inspired faith, wonder, life lessons, and in some cases, love. For example, in Abdulrehman's book *Jinn in The Family* (2025), a fictional story grounded in the real cultural and familial folklore of Zanzibar, the jinn are accepted as everyday characters that play a part in love, death, politics and even the development of culture and identity in an ordinary Zanzibari family. The story follows historical and modern characters, all of who engage with the jinn and magic as a part of their common everyday experience, where the supernatural is considered an expected and normal part of Zanzibari, Arab, and African cultures. And in turn, many modern movies and television miniseries that are truly frightening are less focused on the supernatural and more on what humans can do to each other. Where in some cases the stories of jinn are mythology and fictional (e.g., Aladdin), for many in cultural communities of the **Global Majority**, they are literal stories about actual beings, actual characters, and real-life situations. Although many readers may believe the spiritual world does not exist, for others it is very real, and culture and life engage directly with that spiritual world, the way many in the White

Figure 8.1.   *Three Thousand Years of Longing* (2022, Kennedy Miller Mitchell, Metro-Goldwyn-Mayer, FilmNation Entertainment, and CAA Media Finance). Produced by Ali Akdeniz, Rachael Gill, Dean Hood, Craig McMahon et al. Directed by George Miller. The jinn, the central character in *Three Thousand Years of Longing*, is amazed to discover Tilda Swinton's character doesn't want anything!

Western world deal with work and politics and life's challenges. In other situations, for people of color and those from cultural communities of the Global South, and those of us living in Western worlds, the harsh truths of racism are more prevalent and frightening than jinn, ghosts, or spirits.

Three Thousand Years of Longing (2022) is a fantasy genre film directed by George Miller (who also directed the *Mad Max* series) based on the book of the same title by A. S. Byatt (also known as Dame Antonia Susan Duffy), an acclaimed British novelist, poet, and short story writer. The screenplay was cowritten by George Miller, A. S. Byatt, and Augusta Gore. On the surface, the film is a modern take on the genie in a bottle trope and the story of the conundrum involved in picking three wishes. And though it crosses the two genres of horror (through the coverage of jinn) and fantasy (a genie in a bottle), it is also a romance. What is new to many Western audiences is a standard cultural mythology about the jinn in numerous cultures around the world. In fact, stories on the involvement of the jinn in the romantic lives of humans, among many other aspects of life, are addressed in Abdulrehman's *Jinn in the Family* (2025), a book in which the lore of Jinn in Zanzibar is told through family stories that combine fear, longing, love, and everyday life with the supernatural.

The movie *Three Thousand Years of Longing* follows a literary scholar, Dr. Alithea Binnie, who arrives to give a scholarly presentation in Istanbul. As she begins her visit, she has several supernatural experiences, which she disregards, focusing instead on her narrative that stories (and the supernatural) are meant to provide humanity with context. As one character, Professor Gunhan, says about Alithea's work in her introduction, "Jinn, ghosts, aliens, whatever helps, there are those that need to believe in them." Alithea explains, "Stories were once the only way to make our bewildering existence coherent." And she remarks, "Sooner or later our creation stories are replaced by the narratives of science. And all gods and monsters outlive their original purpose and are reduced to metaphor."

At this point a jinn in the audience charges at Alithea aggressively and she passes out, but she ignores the event when she awakes. Following her talk, while exploring the markets of Istanbul, she is drawn to a glass bottle – a genie's bottle –amid hundreds in an antique shop in a city of millions who are more familiar with the stories of the jinn than Alithea could ever be. And yet, she is the one to find it. When she buys and uncorks this bottle in the privacy of her hotel room, she is surprised to see a jinn escape, filling her room. Alithea previously believed stories of folklore to be a means for humanity to cope; however, she is now challenged with the presence of a jinn from the mythology she trivialized in her scholarly writing. But rather than be angry or frightening, the jinn is accommodating and understanding, attempting to meet Alithea's needs, and he encourages her to make three wishes so he might be free from the bondage of the bottle.

Alithea believes the wishes are a trap. However, the jinn describes how he was imprisoned in the bottle, several times over thousands of years, all due to his affection for women who enslaved him through love (or, in Alithea's eventual case, her wish for him to love her). Since the jinn is a character portrayed by a Black man from an Arab/Muslim culture, being bound by the wish of a White woman, Alithea, the film presents an interesting parallel to slavery. It soon becomes clear that attraction does not prevent racism, entitlement, and **White supremacy**. And one must question whether the relationship between Alithea and the jinn is one of love or more the consequence of Alithea's first wish, that is, for the jinn to love her completely. Also, it is unclear whether this relationship reflects an intercultural and interracial relationship or the bonds of slavery in all its forms, including sexual (e.g., Alithea expects "love craft" from the jinn). But this theme of interracial, intercultural, and interspecies relationships is repeated in the film, beyond the relationship Alithea has with the jinn. Two characters in the film are the children of humans and jinn: Sheba and one of the princes of the Ottoman Empire.

The jinn's first story to Alithea, describing how he was imprisoned in a bottle, is an ancient one. He relates his counsel to Queen Sheba, and her love with King Suleiman; a story described in the 1,400-year-old text of the Quran but also in Jewish folklore. In this story the jinn describes the Islamic folklore of the jinns, including how Suleiman (Solomon) wooed Sheba. Though the jinns are described in the Quran in an entire chapter entitled "Surah Jinn," including the stories of love between Queen Sheba and King Suleiman, the movie takes some liberties to adjust aspects of these characters' stories but also pulls in folklore not described in the Quran. For example, according to the Quran, Sheba is not a jinn, but in the movie is described as half-jinn, a result of love between a human and a jinn. As a result, her legs are covered in long thick black hair.

Folklore from cultures across the Middle East, South Asia, and Africa commonly speak about love and mixed species children between humans and jinn (Lebling, 2011) and these creatures are commonly referenced in stories from the region, as noted in *Jinn in the Family* (2025). Furthermore, the movie pulls in descriptions not outlined in the Quran but in cultural stories from different parts of the world, often describing the feet and legs of the jinn as different. In some cases, the feet are backwards, and in others, they are hairy. Although some of these stories are written by White people outside of the cultures from which this mythology originated, the writer of this book and movie clearly did her research to confirm these little details often omitted from Western stories. Regardless of this variation in Sheba's appearance, she is described by the jinn as "not beautiful" but "beauty itself." And counter to beauty standards in the Western world, and some say globally due to the impact of **colonialist standards of beauty** on colorism in communities of color, Sheba is portrayed by Aamito Lagum, a Ugandan actress and model, who is, by all standards, both a beautiful woman and one of the darkest-skinned models. This presentation of "beauty itself" as a Black woman breaks with the racist standards of beauty typically represented in Western film. Breaking from this norm where White or light-skinned women are seen as the most beautiful, based on racism and colorism in our society, may reflect a subtle theme of antiracism by the director.

The film, particularly the story of Sheba, also brings up the issue of **internalized racism**. Though the jinn was Sheba's lover (and she had all the power and privilege that came with having a jinn as a lover), she was, instead, enchanted by the light-skinned Arab Suleiman, allowing him to vanquish the jinn in a bottle without Sheba protesting. The jinn feels betrayed, but given that both Sheba and the jinn are played by Black actors (and Suleiman by a light-skinned White passing man), we see the theme of interracial relationships appear in the film again: Sheba is enchanted by a lighter-skinned man and prefers him to a darker-skinned one with far greater abilities. Or is it,

> Did you have any trouble … with your foreign friends? Because we often ask ourselves, why would Dr. Binnie spend her time and intelligence studying the ways of others instead of upholding our own? …. Embarrassed by our British culture, are we? … You must understand dear, it's not how they look dear, it's about how they live, what they believe. What they eat. Everywhere we go now, there are ethnics. We are being overwhelmed, and we are inviting our doom. … It's not natural. Birds belong in the air and fish in the sea. And that is how the good lord meant us to be. It's science, it's a scientific fact!

> The main character, Alithea, a White woman, is challenged by her racist neighbors, two older White women who disapprove of her friendship with the jinn who is Black in *Three Thousand Years of Longing*.

again, due to the control of one species or race of a person over another? Sulieman, according to Islamic theology, had control over all jinns. With Sheba being half-jinn, did he control her too and did that reflect the concept of slavery?

Eventually the jinn travels to London with Alithea to live with her. He picks up on radio and television signals (news broadcasters) in London; these disturbing signals ultimately begin to affect his health and almost lead to his demise. What he picks up as electromagnetic frequency (disturbing his nature) from the news broadcasts is quickly paralleled by the racist older women who are Alithea's neighbors in the film. Clementine and Fanny, played by Melissa Jaffer and Anne Charleston, epitomize many racist and ignorant thoughts that encapsulate **colonial White supremacy** when talking to Alithea about her travels to Istanbul to study other cultural stories and about her relationship with a Black man (the jinn).

The jinn, like many people of color, is only welcome when sexually fetishized or when serving those who are White (there are similar themes in Jordan Peele's *Get Out*). When Alithea brings her neighbors the food of the jinn, they are accepting and appreciative of the food, but not of people of color and immigrants themselves. Alithea never asks the jinn about his name, so he remains simply a Black man providing sexual favors and "love craft" to a White woman who claims to be the authority on the cultural folklore of people of color. When the jinn shows up behind her and is introduced to the two old women, they are aroused by his physical appearance, and they each raise an eyebrow in a sign of interest. This is not uncommon in situations in which people of color are exoticized and fetishized for their looks (e.g., Asian women, Black men) but never fully given equal rights. And the same is the case for Alithea. She appreciates the jinn, but not well enough to let him be free; to the point where at the end the jinn almost dies, fading into literal dreams. Only when it is almost too late does Alithea accept the relationship with the jinn on the jinn's terms, where he can leave and live where it is comfortable and return to see her when he wishes. This is a rare outcome for people of color, and we were gratified by the jinn's release from his shackles in *Three Thousand Years of Longing*.

Movies That Explore Cultural Elements of Horror and Fantasy

An increasing number of films, and more recently, television series, have addressed culture and the experiences of people of color in the realm of fantasy and horror and specifically the more frightening element of trauma and racial trauma. Mike Flanagan, director of series such as *The Haunting of Hill House* and *The Fall of the House of Usher,* does this exceptionally well, and his annual Halloween releases were chilling. Yet it was never the ghosts that were frightening, but the people involved, their difficulties, and sometimes the secrets they kept.

Prejudice, Discrimination, Oppression, Racism, and Ethnocentrism

Midnight Mass (2021) is one of Mike Flanagan's annual Halloween miniseries in which religious fanaticism, racism, and Islamophobia are powerfully addressed through the genre of horror. In a series seemingly focused on the supernatural and the preying of a vampire on a small local isolated community, Flanagan's message is clear: The fervor and religious intolerance of the small Christian community toward the local sheriff and his son, who are Muslims, are truly the most frightening element of the show. The show covers a series of characters in this small, isolated community where, with the return of a mysterious priest, miraculous activities begin to occur; ultimately, we learn these are the work of a vampire.

Though the entire series is an allegory for consequences of hate and supremacy, key episodes to watch that demonstrate the horror of religious supremacy and Islamophobia are Episodes 3 and 6, entitled "Book III: Proverbs" and "Book VI: Acts of the Apostle." Episode 3, "Book III: Proverbs," lays a foundation of the experiences of the Sheriff (Hasan) and his son (Ali), Muslim minorities in a Christian fundamentalist community. The fear in this episode lingers around the microaggressions and Islamophobia they face, and the push Ali feels to leave his faith to adopt Christian fundamentalism to fit in – common fears in many cultural and religious minorities who live in Western countries (van Beurden & da Haan, 2020). Episode 6, "Book VI: Acts of the Apostles," shows the deepening of the racial and religious tensions, where microaggressions move to dangerous harm led by a fundamentalist leader, Bev Keene (played by Samantha Soyan), within the church community. The episode also shows how Bev's need for sustaining religious supremacy and power places the entire community at risk by allowing the vampire to gain more power and control. Metaphors are abundant and plentiful, and Flanagan's sharp wit and his feelings of supremacy become clear. Though Flanagan himself is an atheist and a sharp critic of fundamentalist religiosity, his ability to portray the experiences of religious minorities, such as Muslims, as ones of horror suggest that his proximity to the experiences of a community he is not a part of has allowed him to relay their concerns accurately as those of horror and fear.

Cultural Identity, Acculturation, Assimilation

His House (2020) is a haunting and unforgettable film directed by Remi Weekes, starring Sope Dirisu (Bol), Wunmi Mosaku (Sial), Malaika Wakoli-Abigaba (Nyagak), and well-known *House of the Dragon*'s star Mark Essworth (Matt). The film follows Bol, Sial, and Nyagak escaping war-torn South Sudan via boat to a new life of apparent prosperity and freedom in the United Kingdom. As they arrive, they find that what they fled from has followed them, both with the death of the young girl Nyagak and also the racism they face from case workers such as Matt and the entire system. The film is especially cogent at relaying the deeper horror of lost cultural identity and assimilation through internalized racism. Abdulrehman (2024) talks about the impact of racism and cultural and ethnic identity development in his book *Developing Anti-Racist Cultural Competence*. This impact is translated into film as we watch one character (Sial) develop insight as she sees the harm of colonialism when Black youth taunt and ridicule her for her accent, telling her to "go back to fuckin' Africa." At the same time her husband, Bol, realizes his survival in this new country is based on self-degradation and assimilation, and he quickly casts aside his cultural identity to adopt a British one. As discussed by Abdulrehman (2024), sometimes one's cultural identity can be linked to

Rial: My mother used to tell me a story.

[*pause*]

Rial: In our village, there was once an honorable but poor man who wanted a home of his own. He wanted it so badly, he began to steal from others. One day... he stole from an old man who lived by the river. He didn't know that this man was an apeth. A night witch. And so the thief could not know that when he built his home... the apeth, too, would live there. So, before long, the walls would whisper the spells of the apeth. From the shadows... the dead would come. The apeth would not stop... until he had consumed the man entirely.

[*pause*]

Rial: An apeth has arisen from the ocean. It has followed us here. It spoke to me.

> Rial, a refugee from South Sudan, shares a fable from her culture that illustrates how the need to fit in can be all consuming in *His House*.

trauma experienced in that culture, and people cast out the identity with the need to free themselves from the trauma, as Bol tries to do in this film. In one scene in which Sial prepares a beautiful meal for both of them in their new dilapidated government housing, with a blanket on the floor and in proper Sudanese fashion to be eaten by hand, Bol mocks her by getting a fork and a knife and saying, "Wonderful! Wonderful! But maybe next time we can use a table." Sial comments about the cutlery, "All I can taste is metal!" To which Bol replies, "You'll get used to it." And their conversation about getting used to the taste of metal in the cutlery reflects how many people of color must get used to White supremacy in the casting out of their own identity to survive. This internalized racism in which people of color, and in this case family, can harm and police each other into adopting White culture is the real horror, but it comes at a cost as they work hard to become people they are not. This is encapsulated in the exchange between Sial and Bol, when she says to him, "We are not like them!" and he replies, "we can be."

Sial once says to Bol, "After all we have endured, after what we have seen, what men can do. You think it is bumps in the night that frighten me? You think I can be afraid of ghosts?" When Bol resists, he is haunted by the ghost of Nyagak, who helps him recognize his wrongs. For him to eventually realize, "Your ghosts follow you. They never leave. They live with you. It's when I let them in, I could start to face myself." His realization of his **internalized**

Figure 8.2.   *His House* (2020, Regency Enterprises, BBC Film, New Regency Productions, Vertigo Entertainment, and Starchild Pictures). Produced by Alden Dalia, Aidan Elliott, Martin Gentles, Mark Huffam, et al. Directed by Remi Weekes. The ghost of the little girl, Nyagak, who drowned while fleeing Sudan with her parents, returns to haunt them in their government housing in London.

racism, the internalized colonial supremacy of British and White culture, allowed him to come to a balanced sense of self necessary for a healthy ethnic and cultural identity, as described by Abdulrehman (2024).

Value Conflicts, Value Orientations

Get Out (2017), directed by the comedic genius Jordan Peele, is a horror film that follows a young Black man who visits the family estate of his White girlfriend's parents and family. Like in the movies discussed earlier, the real horror is about the harm of racism, as discovered by the main character Chris, played by Daniel Kaluuya, when he realizes his White girlfriend, Rose, played by Allison Williams, is out to steal Black people's bodies for the eventual pleasure of her White family and friends. Inherent in the film is the **value conflict** between White people and Black people and other people of color. As noted by Rosenblum et al. (2022), White people's expressed egalitarianism (like Rose's family claims to practice) often reveals inegalitarian tendencies and sows a sense of distrust in Black people and those from communities of color. The film, through in the horror genre, helps us viscerally feel the sense of distrust and tension many people of color experience due to previous and numerous encounters with racism in our everyday lives (Abdulrehman, 2024), even when it comes to trusting healthcare providers (Corbie-Smith et al., 2002). Themes of mistrust and the differences in perceptions between the Black and White characters in the film reflect differing views of what each community feels, and this is perfectly encapsulated in the quote by Chris's friend, Rod (played by Lil Rel Howery), when he says, "I told you not to go in that house!" and also, "I'm telling you, they're going to make you a slave."

Furthermore, Rose's parents, a psychiatrist and a neurosurgeon, reflect **power and privilege**, especially in one scene in which the mother, a psychiatrist, hypnotizes Chris and controls him. This is an excellent allegory of concerns that White people and White culture take over and control people of culture, at minimum through **cultural appropriation** and **fetishization**. As one of the family's guests says to Chris, "Black is in fashion," while another feels his body and yet another says, "I just want to see what it feels like to be in your skin." And this fetishization explores the difference in how race and culture are experienced by White communities and by communities of color. At the end of the movie, although Rose's White family claims to have no prejudice against Black people and uses Black people to implant their brains into White people, those bodies lose all essence of being Black, as race is rarely tied to only ethnicity but also includes culture (Abdulrehman, 2024). This fear of a lack of understanding between racialized and non-racialized people that breeds a disease, portrayed in *Get Out*, is also reflected in the Swahili song at the beginning and end of the film, *Sikiliza* (Listen), the lyrics of which are translated as, "Brother, listen to the ancestors, run! You need to run far! Listen to the truth. Brother, listen to the ancestors, run, run!"

Social Norms and Norm Violations

Interview With the Vampire (2022) is the miniseries remake of the original 1994 gothic horror film and book of the same name by the late author Anne Rice. The series explores the making of vampire Louis de Pointe du Lac (played by Jacob Anderson) by ancient and charismatic vampire Lestat de Lioncourt (played by Sam Reid). The initial film and book were a metaphor for a long-term gay relationship between two men, and it focused exclusively on White people, with the film having an almost exclusively White cast. The newer 2022 series, by contrast, intersects the reality of history and portrays Louis as a Black man, showing the intersectionality of being both Black and in a same-sex relationship with a White man who has all the privilege and power associated both with whiteness and with who he (Lestat) considers himself to be, that is, better than "mere mortals." The new 2022 series is an excellent way to explore the concepts of intersectional social norms in society, both historically and at present, as the show changes time periods. The first three episodes of Season 1 are helpful in exploring the relevant concepts of social norms and their violations when it comes to issues of an intercultural relationship.

Episode 1, "In Throes of Increasing Wonder," begins the story in early 20th-century New Orleans, where segregation is prominent and racial tensions are high. Though Louis is from a wealthy Black family, his wealth does not shield him from racism. In this episode, he meets Lestat with whom he develops an intense and complicated relationship, and by the end of the episode Lestat offers Louis the "dark gift" of vampirism, a clear symbol of privilege. By entering this relationship with a White man, Louis, a man of color, increases his **privilege**. This is noted in the literature (Abdulrehman, 2024; Walton, 2021) where the greater the proximity to whiteness people of color have, the safer they are and more privilege they have. As the show progresses into Episode 2, "After the Phantoms of Your Former Self," Louis gains the privilege and power associated with being a vampire, but it does not prevent

Figure 8.3.   *Interview With the Vampire*, Episode 1, "In Throes of Increasing Wonder" (2022, Gran Via Productions). Produced by Rolin Jones and Mark Johnson. Directed by Levan Akin. *Interview With the Vampire* tells a story of love, lust, blood, and the confusing complexities that come with immortality.

him from being discriminated against by humans, a lower life form to him, simply because he is still Black. In one scene with business partners and clients, they see him as beneath them and less deserving of wealth due to race, which demonstrates how racism supersedes any other form of privilege. But to sustain this privilege and power, Louis must kill humans, which in Episode 3, "Is My Very Nature That of the Devil," presents a challenge. *Is privilege worth the cost of evil*, when racism is so clearly documented in the first three episodes? Across all three episodes, the power differential between Lestat (White) and Louis (Black) is always apparent. And the gift of darkness Lestat gives Louis is consistently thrown in his face, portraying Lestat as someone who revels in his being a White savior to Louis. The dynamics of power differences and the implications of White privilege and power in such relationships are more clearly explored in this series than in *Three Thousand Years of Longing,* discussed at the beginning of this chapter. If you continue to watch the series, themes of children and the **triangulation** between their child of color (Claudia) and Louis are explored in depth.

Stereotyping

The Boys (2020) is an explicit and rule-breaking fantasy TV series on Amazon Prime that highlights stereotypes and how they are used harmfully to manipulate the public in the most extreme of ways. A show that does not shy away from gore, nudity, or difficult conversations, *The Boys* addresses the stereotypes of superheroes as all good, when in fact they are often problematic, flawed, and in some cases evil and harmful despite marketing to the contrary. Season 2, specifically in Episodes 1 and 5, "The Big Ride" and "We Gotta Go Now," addresses stereotypes of what we expect from certain people of color, but also what we expect of White people. Episode 1 introduces the character Naqib, played by Samer Salem. Naqib is a Syrian "super terrorist" created by the same corporation that created the super heroes, known as "supes," who uses his powers to create a staged terrorist act on an American military base in the Middle East (Syria). Though Naqib's role is brief, it is quintessential in demonstrating how stereotypes of Arabs and Muslims as terrorists are used to manipulate the American public and politics to benefit the corporation that created both. The corporation then plays puppet master, encouraging the militarization of superheroes to address terrorist threats. Interestingly, the stereotype most focused on in this season is that of White people, particularly the White blonde-haired blue-eyed superhero Homelander (played by Antony Starr), who is supposed to be the opposite of Naqib: benevolent, heroic, and altruistic. In fact, it becomes clear that he is nothing more than shallow and narcissistic. This stereotype or **halo effect** for White people is further explored and challenged in Episode 5, where Homelander aligns himself and becomes romantically involved with a superhero named Stormfront (played by Aya Cash), who despite appearing to be young, was born in 1919 in Germany and was a Nazi. Further challenging the stereotypes of White supremacy, the show reveals that Stormfront was also married to Frederick Vought, the Nazi scientist who founded the corporation Vought Industries that created all supes including the super terrorist Naqib. This show is shocking and is explicit in its graphic nature and in the concepts it explores.

Indigenous People

True Detective: Night Country (2024) is a powerful and haunting HBO series that explores the eerie disappearance of eight men in the remote Arctic and their connection to unresolved issues of missing and murdered Indigenous women in the community. This is the fourth season of the *True Detective* franchise created by Issa Lopez and Nic Pizzolatto and can be watched separately as each season is a different story. It stars Jody Foster and Kali Reis as detectives Liz Danvers and Evangeline Navarro. Although *Night Country* is framed as a mystery/detective show, it fits within both the cultural Indigenous perspective and the supernatural. Ghosts and spirits are often referenced and are helpful in resolving the mystery. The show explores elements of multigenerational trauma and the impact of colonialism and industry on the Indigenous way of life and shows how they reflect sustained trauma against Indigenous people. As is the case in all shows and films reviewed in this chapter, the supernatural is not the frightening thing in the show, but rather the horror that is committed because of **colonial White supremacy**. There are only six episodes in this miniseries, and the entire show is worth watching. But if you need to focus on a limited number of episodes, Episodes 2–4 show Navarro, an Indigenous woman, working hard to advocate for the continued investigation and justice for the brutal death of an Inupiat woman, where her case along with the cases of many other missing and murdered Indigenous women is largely ignored in comparison with cases involving White people. This is a common phenomenon termed "**missing White woman syndrome**," a situation in which missing White women and girls are responded to far more swiftly than in the case of women of color (Skaloff & Fradella, 2019). In this process the team of Navarro and Danvers discovers the naked and frozen remains of several White scientists who were

Figure 8.4. *True Detective: Night Country* (2024, HBO Entertainment, Neon Black, Pastel, Parliament of Owls et al.). Produced by Layla Blackman, Sam Breckman, Blake Brown, Richard Brown, et al. Directed by Issa López. Kali Reis and Jodie Foster are magnificent as Officer Evangeline Navdarro and Police Chief Elizabeth Danvers in the HBO crime drama.

working in the remote community, one of whom has a spiral symbol carved into his forehead. Several issues including those of land rights, environmental exploitation, colonialism, and the strength of survival of Indigenous women in the community are raised. The horror or fantasy elements is once again tied not to the spirits that Navarro sees through visions, with an uncertainty of whether they are real or in her mind, but to the trauma of the murder and further lack of justice for Indigenous women and the community in Western society, even in remote land and country meant to be theirs. The directors do an excellent job of balancing the issue of disempowered murdered Indigenous women with a strong female cast, both of whom are leaders in this show. It should also be noted that between Danvers and Navarro the power dynamic between a White woman not taking an Indigenous woman seriously is played out, as experts on White feminism often point out in their work (Hamad, 2020). But the supernatural, used by the creator of this and the other seasons in this series, does what Alithea Binnie, from *Three Thousand Years of Longing*, says; they use "gods and monsters" to create meaning out of the real horrors faced by marginalized people of color.

Additional Films and Miniseries About Horror and Fantasy

The number of horror and fantasy movies and miniseries that reflect culture, diversity, and social justice is growing. There are times when the themes are directly reflected in the plot, and other times when they are indirect. Some of our favorite horror movies and miniseries include *Blood Quantum* (2019), *Ravenous* (2017) (both Canadian films), *Lovecraft Country* (2020), *The Babadook* (2014), *Candyman* (1992 and 2021), *Djinn* (2019) (by Toby Hooper, who directed *Poltergeist*), *Under the Shadows* (2016), *The Host* (2006), *Parasite* (2019), *Tigers Are Not Afraid* (2017), *Beloved* (1998), *The Vigil* (2019), *A Girl Walks Home Alone at Night* (2019), *Stigmata* (1999), *The Angry Black Girl and Her Monster* (2023), *The Orphanage* (2007), and *Sinners* (2025), a recent film that uses the vampire narrative as a metaphor for Jim Crow racism.

Some of our favorite movies and television shows that are focused on fantasy include *American Gods* (2017), *Ms. Marvel* (2022), *Moon Knight* (2022), *Black Panther* (2018), *Black Panther: Wakanda Forever* (2022), *Pachinko* (2022), *The Shape of Water* (2017), *Moana* (2016), *Avatar: The Last Airbender* (2024, live action), and *Wicked* (2024).

Critical Thinking Questions About Horror, Fantasy, and Culture

- In the presence of real-life global crises and human rights violations broadcast 24 hours a day on social media, are ghost stories an out-of-touch form of horror stories?
- When the true crime genre is gaining popularity, are we more entertained by the real-life terrors than mythology?
- Has our social media access to horrific war crimes and mass human suffering numbed us to the point that we must turn to fantasy and old-fashioned ghost stories to detach from the actual horrors of the real world?
- Have you ever heard of any ghost or jinn stories from cultures outside of North America? How are they different and are they more frightening? Why or why not?
- Is it essential to incorporate different cultural lore and tradition into television and movies to ensure greater representation?
- Are we so challenged to incorporate the culture of racialized people that we can only do so when viewing films about horror or fantasy?

- Is ensuring the supernatural elements of non-White cultures into film an essential way of shifting culture to be more inclusive?
- What is the most memorable supernatural or ghost story you've heard from different cultural communities?
- Do we need to bring back the art of ghost stories?

Further Exploration

If you only have time to read one article on the importance of representation in fantasy and superhero films, read:

Tyree, T. C. M., & Jacobs, L. J. (2014). Can you save me? Black male superheroes in Hollywood film. *Spectrum: A Journal on Black Men, 3*(1), 1–24. https://doi.org/10.2979/spectrum.3.1.1

If you only have time to read one chapter on the concept of culture, evil, and horror, we suggest you read:

Wester, M. (2019). The Gothic in and as race theory. In J. E. Hogle & R. Miles (Eds.), *The Gothic and theory: An Edinburgh companion* (pp. 53–70). Edinburgh University Press. https://doi.org/10.1515/9781474427791-004

If you have time to read one book about different cultural perspectives on ghosts or jinn, read:

Lebling, R. (2010). *Legends of the fire spirits: Jinn and genies from Arabia to Zanzibar.* I. B. Tauris.

References

Abdulrehman, R. (2024). *Developing anti-racist cultural competence.* Hogrefe.

Abdulrehman, R. (2025). *Jinn in the family.* Lead With Diversity Press.

Corbie-Smith, G., Thomas, S. B., & St. George, D. M. (2002). Distrust, race, and research. *Archives of Internal Medicine, 162*(21), 2458–2463.

Hamad, R. (2020). *White tears, brown scars: How white feminism betrays women of color.* Catapult.

Lebling, R. (2011). *Legends of the fire spirits: Jinn and genies from Arabia to Zanzibar.* Bloomsbury.

Rosenblum, M., Jacoby-Senghor, D. S., & Brown, N. D. (2022). Detecting prejudice from egalitarianism: Why Black Americans don't trust White egalitarians' claims. *Psychological Science, 33*(6), 889–905.

Skaloff, D., & Fradella H. (2019). Media messages surrounding missing women and girls: The "missing white woman syndrome" and other factors that influence newsworthiness. *Criminology, Criminal Justice, Law & Society, 20* (3), 80–102. file:///Users/papa/ Downloads/slakoff_20_3_final_draft_.pdf

van Beurden, S. L., & de Haan, M. (2020). 'I want good children, also for this country': How Dutch minority Muslim parents' experience and negotiate parenting, parenthood and citizenship. *Journal of Intercultural Studies, 41*(5), 574–590.

Walton, E. (2021). Habits of whiteness: How racial domination persists in multiethnic neighborhoods. *Sociology of Race and Ethnicity, 7*(1), 71–85.

Chapter 9
Star Wars and Social Justice

> **Indara: We are concerned that you are training children, which is against Republic law. Aniseya: Brendok is not part of the Republic.**
>
> Indara, a Jedi Master visiting the planet Brendok without permission of it's inhabitants, questions Aniseya, a local mother and head of a coven, about training children against the Republic Law in *The Acolyte*.

Questions to Consider While Watching *The Acolyte* (2024)

- Is it a wise decision to change the lore of a well-established series, such as *Star Wars*, to ensure it is more culturally relevant and appropriate? Or does this give in to cancel culture?
- Was the old *Star Wars* trilogy racist? Why or why not?
- Does addressing issues of social justice indirectly through fantasy and science fiction minimize or water down the issues?
- Are the Jedi good or are they supremacist colonial powers infringing on Indigenous people's right for self-determination?
- What are the parallels between the witches and Indigenous populations around the world?
- Is the Jedi Order that removes children from their families to train them as Jedis and protectors of the galaxy a form of colonial residential schooling? Why or why not?

In many films and television programs, issues related to culture, ethnicity, race, and social justice are approached directly; however, some genres, such as science fiction, can address these issues indirectly. For example, *Dune: Part Two* (2024) is based firmly on the culture and heritage of Arabs and Muslims and reflects cultures and social issues for those groups, but it has also been criticized for omitting these cultural groups as clear references (Shah, 2024). *Star Wars* has long been hailed for addressing critical issues indirectly such as fatherhood or men and masculinity, and there have even been claims that it promotes international harmony. But the original trilogy had few people of color, and concepts of international alliances largely involved White humans interacting with alien species. Though a Black actor, James Earl Jones, was used as the voice of quintessential villain Darth Vader, and Billy Dee Williams played the role of Lando Calrissian, representation of diverse people was largely missing. This criticism is widely referenced and has been noted by writers and producers of color in Hollywood. Award-winning writer and producer Anthony Q. Farrell (President and CEO of Canfro Productions), a Black Canadian of Caribbean descent with writing credits for shows such as *The Office* and *Little Mosque on the Prairie*, he had this to say about *Star Wars* (personal communication, November 20, 2024):

> I see through the code that the film used to have the masses understand its world with ruthless efficiency. Stereotypes. Good versus Evil. Light versus Dark. ... White versus Black. Luke, the blond-haired, blue-eyed, White-boy hero versus the gigantic, scary, all-Black villain. A villain who also had the Blackest voice known to mankind. Right from the jump, you know who to root for.

With the resurgence of *Star Wars* as a television series – allowing the stories to be told in greater depth and over time – diversity, culture, and aspects of social justice have been far more present. Farrell feels the new series is far grayer (personal communication, November 20, 2024):

> We dealt with black and white for so long because it was easier. Now that we're getting into the gray, we can have more difficult conversations about the good and the bad of both sides. The Jedi taking children for their own good. The Empire created apparent stability in certain corners of the galaxy. No one is completely good or completely bad.

But that has come at a cost and to the discontent of many fans used to **white-washed intergalactic stories** excluding people of color not just as heroes but as villains too. Nerd culture is well known to be racist, and research confirms this to be true (Jenkins, 2020); it even predicts why newer characters of color are disliked by nerd culture (Reysen et al., 2023). Whenever we have had actors of color represented in *Star Wars* films and miniseries, there has been an escalation of racist attacks against actors. This has included attacks on actors, writers, and the entire *Star Wars* franchise. One such example is the attack on actor Ahmed Best, who played Jar Binks, who some argue to be an animated racist trope of Black Caribbean people (Adamczak, 2023); he was harassed online to the point of poor mental health and suicidality (BBC News, 2018). Only recently was Ahmed Best vindicated in the role he was given as Kellaran Beq, the Jedi who saved Grogu (Baby Yoda) from the Order 66 Purge (where the colonial ruler, Emperor Palpatine, orders a genocide of all Jedi, executed by the Clone army). More recently, Moses Ingram as Third Sister, who plays a Force-user double agent aiming to get revenge by attempting to kill Darth Vader, was criticized by fans online with a variety of racist slurs (including the N-word; Breznican, 2022). When Disney attempted to address diversity with the characters Rey and Finn, they were again criticized. In that movie, though there was value for having people of color (Finn) seen as heroes (Abdulrehman & Graves 2017), it should be noted that rather than having a woman of color as the main heroine, the directors chose instead a White woman; but they did have other actors of color in supporting roles. As the *Star Wars* franchise has matured over time, we now see an increasingly diverse set of actors and characters reflecting cultures and people in our diverse global society. This has been limited to main characters such as Ezra Bridger (played by Eman Esfandi) reflecting Arabs and Muslims, Fennec Shand (played by Ming-Na Wen) reflecting East Asian people, Ahsoka Tano (played by Rosario Dawson) representing African-Caribbean and Puerto Rican people, and perhaps the most popular of all, Din Djarin or the Mandalorian (played by Pedro Pascal) representing Latino people. As the diversity of roles and actors has matured, so have the story lines. Whereas diversity was previously reflected in negative stereotypes, such as Watto (voiced by non-Arab Welsh actor Andy Secombe) as a cheap and unethical slave-owning savage Arab (Williams, 1999), we now see more accurate views of colonialism and cultural supremacy working their way into *Star Wars* lore, in series such as *The Acolyte* (2024). This inclusion of social issues related to cultural divides, colonialism, and supremacy has come at a cost. *The Acolyte* was harshly criticized by nerd/fan culture for straying too far from original lore (which centered Whiteness) and redefining the origin and use of the elusive concept of "the Force," an energy field created by all living things that holds the universe together, which is the concept behind the entire *Star Wars* saga and the power to wield that Force turns common men into both Jedi and Sith (both light- and dark-side users of the Force). *The Acolyte* (2024) and other earlier *Star Wars* miniseries muddy the traditional concept of light and dark sides and recognize that any Force-user can have access to light and dark, showing that polarizing views of the Force being good or bad can be problematic for the universe.

When watching the suggested series episodes described in the next sections, it will be important to pay attention to the recaps provided at the beginning of each episode. Given the series has a cumulative narrative, with greater depth and meaning offered the more shows you've watched, being aware of the small gaps that may occur provides the context to the episode and helps new viewers to the show better understand what is happening in that episode.

Social Justice and *The Acolyte*

In the history of *Star Wars*, Jedi have been considered users of the light side of the Force, good guys, and supporters of the rebellion against the colonial Empire led by users of the dark side of the Force (Sith). But they were also typically portrayed as White. Ironically, in the real world, those fighting in rebellions against colonial powers are typically people of color and a part of the **global majority**. Star Wars had these roles reversed. But what *The Acolyte* makes clear in its series is that the history of the galaxy was most likely written by the actual colonial power – the Jedi. The Jedi had a privileged and self-righteous belief they could enter any world, intrude on a civilization, and impose their beliefs and understanding of "the Force" upon those people. They believed that children who were Force sensitive needed to be taken away from the families and raised by the Jedi Order, preventing any emotional connection, and being trained to use the Force the way the Jedi felt it was appropriate (Trivedi, 2019). If we remove the context of *Star Wars* and all we thought we knew about the Jedi, this situation sounds very much like the **Sixties Scoop** in Canada and the forcing of Indigenous children into residential school systems in the Americas because European Christians believed Indigenous people, their culture, and their spirituality were savage and their children needed to be saved. *The Acolyte*, in particular Episode 3, "Destiny," and Episode 7, "Choice," challenges viewers, especially fans of *Star Wars*, about who the Jedi really are, and who and what are good, bad, and everything in between.

Episode 3: "Destiny"

This episode focuses on a group of witches on the planet Brendok, from a collectivist culture, who have a strong ancestral connection to the planet. In their chants in the episode we can hear them say, "the power of one; the power of two; the power of many!" They have a strong connection to the Force, but it is ancient and mystical, distinct from the Force used by Jedi or Sith not tied to concepts of good or evil. The episode shows how the coven of witches sees the Force as a living entity and tap into it for different rituals for their culture, including a rite of passage they are preparing for their children, a set of twins (Mae and Osha). When the Jedi arrive on Brendok investigating what they believe to be a divergence from the Force, they find the twins in the woods practicing using what they believe to be magic but is their own use of the Force. Claiming to uphold Republic law, intruding in their home and sanctuary, the Jedi then insist on taking the children away from their family. And they fear leaving the children with the witches will only expose them to danger and harm. When the Jedi first enter the witches' home, the leader, Indara (played by Carrie-Anne Moss) says to the leader of the coven and mother of the children, "Mother Aniseya, you cannot deny the right the Jedi have to test potential children. With your permission of course." This is double speak, violent **colonial language**, where it is demanding and entitled, and yet appears to offer the false impression of permission. Indara also sees the witches' rejection of the Jedi taking the children as a bizarre quality of their culture when she says, "The coven, they will never let her leave. They are so insular. So strange." The conversation between the Jedi about taking the children and the judgment of the witches' culture is rife with **microaggressions** and **patriarchal colonial racism**. The young Padawan Jedi Torbin (played by Dean-Charles Chapman) says, "There's something dangerous about those women!" And they together pontificate on the culture of the witches, as if the witches were people in a zoo. This method of understanding culture as referenced by Abdulrehman (2024) only promotes hierarchy and thus supremacy. But there is a glimmer of wisdom when Indara says to Sol, "Do not confuse what Osha wants with what you want." And Sol replies, "I want to do what is best for Osha." Indara finally responds, "You don't get to decide that." While the values of communities from the Global South are often seen as barbaric and in negative contrast to the values of Western culture, the opposite is often true (Abdulrehman, 2024; Abdulrehman & Clara, 2023), and the culture of communities of the Global South is often far more egalitarian when compared with Western ones. In the case of the culture of the witches, Mother Aniseya is willing to honor Osha's choice to leave with the Jedi (despite her own desire to keep her daughter close), and Sol is insistent on believing he knows what is best for children who are not even his.

The twins, Mae and Osha (played by Lauren and Leah Brady as children and Amandla Stenberg as adults), have differing views; Mae is bound tightly to her culture while Osha does not want to be a witch and wants to become a Jedi. According to the show, Mae and Osha, as the Jedi discover in their testing of them, are the same person split into two using the Force (as revealed in Episode 7). And their different views reflect how people of the Global South react to colonial White supremacy: some hold strong to their own identity and others want desperately to fit in and adopt the culture of colonial powers due to internalized racism. This is outlined in a model of cultural and ethnic identity development by Abdulrehman (2024). In Episode 3, the Jedi reinforce the internalized inferiority of Osha, who wants to be a Jedi, and tell her how special it is to be a Jedi, glamorizing it and further stoking the flames of division between her and her sister, Mae, but also within the coven of witches who are working hard to protect their children and ensure their culture is maintained. But as Mae and the rest of the coven begin to push back, the Jedi see this as violence and perceive it as an increased risk to the children, only further strengthening their resolve to take the children and undermining the culture of the witches as barbaric and savage.

Episode 7: "Choice"

The Acolyte Season 1, Episode 7, is titled "Choice" for good reason. It demonstrates the impact each of our decisions has not just on ourselves, but as the broader butterfly impact on society, culture, and people around us. For this episode, although many characters make pivotal decisions, it is the decisions

Figure 9.1.   *The Acolyte*, Season 1, Episode 7, "Choice" (2024, Lucas Film, Disney). Produced by Kor Adana, Damian Anderson, Jocelyn Bioh, Rob Bredow, et al. Directed by Kogonada. Sol makes a fateful decision to try to save the children in Brendok.

of the Jedi, particularly Sol (played by Lee Jung-jae), that are important. Sol's clouded colonial view of the witches, and his belief they and their culture were a danger to the child twins Mae and Osha, led to a self-fulfilling prophecy. He says judgmentally with only a single observation about the twins, "They do not treat them like children" and "I fear for the girls' safety." There are numerous choices made: intruding on their home, taking the girls (at least Osha) to the Jedi Order for training, fighting the witches because they saw them as a threat when they were only defending themselves, and the ultimate choice between Mae and Osha.

In this episode we see a conflict between the two parents of Mae and Osha, Mother Aniseya (the leader of the coven, played by Jodie Turner-Smith) and Mother Koril (played by Margarita Levieva), one attempting to honor Osha's choice to go with the Jedi and the other, Mother Koril, in full disagreement. This disagreement is common in immigrant families to Western countries where children will want to let go of their cultural values and practices for the dominant culture and feel like they fit in more (Abdulrehman, 2024). And although the decision is made to let Osha go with the Jedi, to never see her again, before Mother Aniseya can carry out her plan, the family home is invaded by the Jedi and an altercation leads to Mother Aniseya being killed by Sol. In a different part of the home, Mae and Osha have a conflict about Osha wanting to leave; Mae tries to subdue Osha and locks her in a room to prevent her from leaving with the Jedi. In our real world, attempts to protect culture and what can appear to be a controlling means to keep family members tied to culture can be perceived by many in White Western communities as enmeshment or families from non-White communities being controlling (Abdulrehman, 2024). But as shown in *The Acolyte*, it is a literal means of a fight for survival, working to protect and sustain identity from the strong grip of the influence of colonial White culture. In the episode, this struggle leads Mae to accidentally ignite a fire, leading to the collapse of the coven's home. Osha escapes and meets Mae and Sol on a bridge on the verge of collapse due to the spreading fire. As both children are at risk of plummeting to their doom, Sol makes a choice in needing to save one of the children; he chooses Osha, who had internalized racism, rejected her culture, and wanted to adopt the colonial Jedi way of life. The most striking part of the show is when Osha awakes on the Jedi ship, with her family and community now all presumed dead. She is unsure what happened to Mae, and Sol and the Jedi agree to lie to her. They spin the myth that Mae was evil (implying because she rejected the Jedi way and their insistence on stealing her sister) and she set a fire intentionally that burnt the whole home and their community to the ground. This sort of **gaslighting** is not uncommon by colonial powers, blaming occupied and colonial communities and people for their downfall and even for any harsh and violent response colonial powers take against them, such as with Palestinians (Buttu, 2014) and other occupied and colonized people in current society.

Prejudice, Discrimination, Oppression, Racism, and Ethnocentrism

Andor and Systemic Oppression and Class Struggle

Andor, Season 1, Episode 3: "Reckoning"

While the original *Star Wars* trilogy has been accused of being overly sanitized, ignoring the complexity that could have been possible, including its whitewashed cast and pristine galactic scenes appearing like sanitized

> **Cassian Andor:** Look, you got the money. I got the box. What else is there to talk about?
> **Luthen Rael:** I'll give you another thousand credits to tell me how you got it.
> **Cassian Andor:** [*chuckles*] Another thousand?
> **Luthen Rael:** Done. How?
> **Cassian Andor:** You just walk in like you belong.
> **Luthen Rael:** Takes more than that, doesn't it?
> **Cassian Andor:** What? To steal from the Empire? What do you need? A uniform, some dirty hands, and an Imperial tool kit. They're so proud of themselves, they don't even care. They're so fat and satisfied, they can't imagine it.
> **Luthen Rael:** Can't imagine what?
> **Cassian Andor:** That someone like me would ever get inside their house, walk their floors, spit in their food, take their gear.
> **Luthen Rael:** The arrogance is remarkable, isn't it? They don't even think about us.
>
> > Underscoring central themes of the series (the Empire's arrogance and the potential for ordinary individuals to exploit its blind spots), Cassian Andor meets Luthen Rael to sell a valuable Imperial Starpath device in *Andor*. Luthen, intrigued by Cassian's audacity and skill, offers him additional credits to explain how he managed to steal the device.

hospitals, *Andor* (2022) swings fully in the opposite direction and is one of the grittiest *Star Wars* series yet. *Andor* is the prequel to the film *Rogue One* (2016), about a band of rebels trying to steal the plans for the Death Star (an intergalactic weapon of mass destruction), which probably had the most diverse cast in *Star Wars* films at that time and reflected people of color as heroes (Abdulrehman & Graves, 2017). *Andor* goes further, demonstrating how gritty and challenging a rebellion against a colonial power (the Empire) can be. The miniseries addresses how the Empire as a colonial power occupies Indigenous planets abuses them for their resources and furthermore punishes the "rebel scum" who resist, defy, and fight back against colonial powers. Though the series is set on the fictional worlds of Ferrix and Kenari, the parallel for an armed resistance against racist and colonial powers in our own society's history is clear. Be it the armed resistance of Jews in the Warsaw ghetto of the Second World War, that of the Indigenous and Métis people against European settlers, the Zapatista uprising in Mexico, Black South Africans and the African National Congress, or Palestinians in Gaza and the West Bank, *Andor* reflects the struggles of many colonized and occupied people around the world. And as is suggested by the title of Episode 3 in Season 1, "Reckoning" (2022) demonstrates how a colonial power's systemic oppression and occupation of other worlds and cultures are bound to lead to resistance. The episode begins with a young Cassian Andor (subsequently named "Kassa" in Kenari culture and language), in the world of Kenari (an isolated planet long abused and now abandoned by the Empire after mining its resources for its own purposes), entering an abandoned imperial structure. Here, he is overwhelmed and taken home by an apparently well-meaning couple, Maarva and Clem Andor, who are scavengers surviving the rebellion by collecting scrap; they become involved part time in the rebellion against the Empire. They take Kassa, who they believe is the sole survivor of his people and likely to be subject to torture or worse by the Empire if they leave him there in Kenari. After having taken them with him to raise as their own son, the episode goes back and forth between when Cassion was a child (Kassa) and his life as an adult under the thumb of the occupation of the Empire. In searching for his sister in a brothel, he runs into two Imperial security officers who are corrupt and drunk. After attempting to extort him, a struggle breaks out and he accidentally kills one of them, leaving him on the run from The Empire. Trying to flee the planet by selling a rare piece of equipment, his buyer turns out to be a member of the Rebel Alliance, whose actual interest is in Cassian himself and in recruiting him to the Rebel Alliance. Being a child who survived occupation and what appears to be an ethnic cleansing of the Kenari people, Cassian is a cynical character focused on his own survival and

Figure 9.2.   *Andor* (2022, Lucasfilm, Marzano Films). Produced by John Gilroy, Tony Gilroy, John Hampian, Toby Haynes, et al. Directed by Toby Haynes. *Andor* is a *Star Wars* prequel television series that stars Diego Luna in the role of Cassian Andor.

financial gain. But his vulnerabilities and history make him a prime target for an idealistic group like the Rebel Alliance. Though the show is fiction, the concept of how oppression can often lead marginalized people to be recruited by resistance fighters is not an uncommon phenomenon and an expected consequence of oppression. Themes related to oppression include a lack of trust, poverty, and class struggles, which are all present in *Andor*, and notably present in Episode 3 of this single-season miniseries.

Cultural Identity, Acculturation, Assimilation

The Mandalorian (Season 1, Chapter 1): "The Mandalorian"

The Mandalorian (2019) was a significant milestone in the *Star Wars* franchise, as it was the first live action miniseries that brought *Star Wars* to television. Although there were several essential *Star Wars* miniseries prior to this that built up the foundation of the lore and canon necessary for the current run of live action miniseries reviewed in this chapter, including *Rebels* (2014–2018; which could be argued to have been the foundation of greater inclusion and multiculturalism in *Star Wars*), *The Mandalorian* brought *Star Wars* back to the general public consciousness making it popular yet again. One of the critical ways in which *The Mandalorian* did this, be it conscious or not to the viewer, was by integrating numerous cultural references in modern society into the cultural groups and main characters of the show. Not only was ethnic and racial diversity represented, but so was cultural diversity. In fact, the very first episode of Season 1 (2019) introduces us to Din Djarin (played by Pedro Pascal), who is a Mandalorian, and the character who the entire series was named after. Hinted at through this first episode, Mandalore was a world and people who resisted the colonial Empire and suffered heavily in what has been dubbed "the great purge," eventually leaving the planet uninhabitable. The remaining Mandalorians are therefore few and dispersed across the universe. The great purge is akin to many cultural experiences that have affected various people in the history of humanity (e.g., the Biblical exodus of the Jews from Egypt) and even more recent history (e.g., the first and second *Nakba*, or Catastrophe, of the Palestinian people). But over the course of the episode, we learn about the history of Mandalore, but also about the culture and how because of politics and catastrophes, that culture changed (Abdulrehman, 2024). For example, in the very beginning of the first episode where the Mandalorian is bounty hunting someone (a fish humanoid), he is asked by the character, "Is it true you guys never take off your helmet?"; and we learn that for the tribe Din Djarin belongs to, it is forbidden to ever remove one's helmet. Though not completely identical, we see similarities in cultural groups in our modern world, be it the Sikhs and their **turbans**, Muslim women and their **hijabs**, or orthodox Jews and their **kippahs**. As we follow the Mandalorian (Din Djarin, whose name is revealed later in the series) in his work as a bounty hunter, we also learn to survive following the Great Purge, he and others have had to take up being bounty hunters. And as discussed by Abdulrehman (2024) in understanding the fluidity and intersectional nature of culture, we see the Mandalorians also adopting what is known as the Bounty Hunters' Code; it is an intersecting identity with that of the Mandalorian culture. And though being a bounty hunter was an identity that came after the Great Purge for Din Djarin, the code and rules by which he must abide were strong enough to cause him to pause before he broke that code to return and save the baby (Grogu) who had been his bounty.

We follow the Mandalorian (Din) in this episode as he obtains information about this bounty of a 50-year-old, who pays in copious amounts of *beskar* (a highly sought after metal from Mandalore that is resistant to even light sabers), which he uses to rebuild his current armor. But as he gets to the bounty target, he finds a droid has also been enlisted to find the same bounty. When they both arrive, the Mandalorian finds a baby pram, and in it a young child. The droid informs him that some species age very slowly, and that even at 50 years, this species is still a child. While the droid was instructed to kill the bounty and bring in the body, the Mandalorian refuses to do so and instead breaks Bounty Hunter Code and shoots the droid to give this bounty, the child, an extended chance at life. Upon delivering the child to those seeking him, he is given his *beskar*, and has his new armor made; but he is obsessed by the thought of leaving the child behind, and the risk the child faces from those who want to harm him. It is clear they have sinister purposes (we find out later that they work for the Empire), and the Mandalorian begins to have flashbacks of himself as a child, having survived an attack from the Empire, losing both parents as a result. He remembers how he was taken in by Mandalorians, and how he adopted their culture as his own. Thrice now, we see the Mandalorian, Din, assimilate into a new culture or influence his identity, adopting each as his own or letting a meaningful experience influence who he is – first when he was adopted into a Mandalorian tribe after his parents were killed; second when he becomes a bounty hunter and adopts their code as his own; and last, where he feels deeply for the child, breaks the Bounty Hunter Code, and accepts responsibility for the child and returns freshly armored to the site where he dropped him off to fight those who meant to harm him and adopts the child as his own (this last part occurs in Episode 3, but is essential to the concept of **identity shift**). It is clear for the Mandalorian that critical life events caused his identity, values, and even his culture to be changed, in the same way it occurs for us all. This episode demonstrates that at times we have less control over our assimilation into groups or even the adjustment of our identity. This episode, "The Mandalorian," also makes it clear that assimilation into other cultures is sometimes a survival mechanism for us and sometimes for others. As the Mandalorian reminds himself, "I was once a foundling." Though implicit and less aware, it is also important to be mindful that the character of Din, the Mandalorian, has also shifted the culture or viewpoint of many viewers. Whereas men of color are typically seen as aggressive and domestically challenged, the Mandalorian's warmth, empathy, and connection to the child (baby Grogu) challenge these stereotypes, to the point that the actor who plays the Mandalorian, Pedro Pascal (a Latino man) is now colloquially known as "Internet daddy," causing many to swoon over his paternal charm (Sarner, 2023).

Social Norms and Norm Violations

The Mandalorian (Season 1, Chapter 3): "The Sin"

This episode continues to demonstrate the importance of Mandalorian culture and the Bounty Hunter Code in creating social norms by which Mandalorians and bounty hunters live and work. We see in this episode how Din Djarin adheres strictly to these rules and norms. Violation of the Bounty Hunter Code could mean the end of his means of obtaining a living, further marginalizing him and his people. But keeping to that code and his beliefs (e.g., not removing his helmet) is his strength. In many parts of the world, sustaining culture and not assimilating is a **norm violation**, but Din turns not assimilating into a character strength. As the matriarch of his community, the Armorer (played by Emily Swallow) says to Din, "How can one be a coward if one chooses this way of life?" And the Mandalorian armor appears also as a symbol of protection from the outside world, as many people from Muslim, Jewish, and Sikh communities will testify to as well with regard their religious clothing.

As Din considers his childhood, we see flashbacks of the trauma he survived that causes him to relate to the child he just handed over as a bounty. This builds an emotional attachment, which causes him to sin, as the title implies, by breaking his Bounty Hunter Code, and to return and fight to take back this child due to the emotional attachment and his own personal ethics and experiences. Where typically the need to **code switch**, or adjust cultural representation, has been vital for the safety of many marginalized cultural communities (Abdulrehman, 2024), Din otherwise took pride and built a reputation for being a rigid adherer to Bounty Hunter Code, securing an elite reputation. But this is also not uncommon in the professional world, where we use our professional boundaries and expectations as excuses to prevent opportunities to build empathy, understand responsibility, and sometimes advocate for those in need, such as marginalized communities (Abdulrehman, 2024). Instead, we obtain our privilege and our safety, and we do not challenge norms. Din, on the other hand, uses his privilege to help one of most marginalized, a child. And to do so, he needs to break with professional protocol, because a child's life depends on his ability to prioritize his moral compass over his professional obligations. Din, the Mandalorian, is an excellent example for how many professionals, especially psychologists, must use their privilege to benefit the most marginalized, instead of sustaining their privilege and safety and remaining silent on issues of human rights. This issue was seen in high relief when the American Psychological Association was shown to be complicit in the torture of detainees in Guantanamo Bay (Goodman, 2023) and recently in a response that justified mass killings of Palestinians in Gaza (Eidelson, 2024). This episode and the sin of the Mandalorian emphasize to us that some sins are necessary and must be accepted as the lesser of two evils, but also that we must value **cognitive flexibility**. It is important to also understand that for Din, the Bounty Hunter Code is an essential set of guidelines necessary for a professional reputation that is required for his survival. The code demonstrates the culture of his work. But he places his humanity before that and reflects a well-known saying by Abdul Sattar Edhi, a Pakistani philanthropist: "There is no religion higher than humanity" (Hussain, 2020).

Value Conflicts, Value Orientations

The Bad Batch (Season 1, Episode 1): "Aftermath"

Although much of the initial Star Wars movies and animated series revolved around the general premise of a rebellion against the colonial Empire, a newer animated series, *The Bad Batch*, focuses on the perspective of a Clone army used by the Empire to fight rebels and at one point also used by a larger Galactic Republic lead by Jedi generals who led Clone armies to fight the Empire (until one important twist that will be noted below). Clone armies were created from a single genetic template of Jango Fett, a Mandalorian bounty hunter, in exchange for the Clone creators (the Kaminoans, an advanced alien species specializing in cloning technology) creating a Clone for him to raise as a son (Boba Fett). In this sense, not only were the Clones created to look alike and have similar abilities but also to think alike and follow orders. This series focuses on, and in this episode introduces us to, a group of genetically enhanced Clones, Clone Force 99, also known as the Bad Batch. They are a special group of operatives with genetic mutations to offer not only slightly different physical appearances but also specific unique skills and abilities, and, as it becomes clear in the episode, to think independently.

The Bad Batch is initially sent on a mission on the side of the Galactic Republic, alongside the boy Jedi Padawan Caleb Dume (voiced by actor Freddie Prinze Jr.). At that time, the Empire (due to an evil Darth Sidious having funded the creation of the Clone Army and placing inhibitor chips in the brain of all Clones) triggers the infamous Order 66, causing the chip to override all programming to follow the Jedi generals, and instead turn on their generals and carry out the Empire's orders to kill all Jedi. But because the Bad Batch were genetic mutations, their chips were either absent or defective and they did not kill their Jedi, Caleb Dume. The ability or choice of the Bad Batch members to defy Order 66 and not betray the people they worked for so closely for so long embodies the tension between their ingrained loyalty to the Republic and their desire for personal freedom, representing a broader conflict of values within the Clone army. And this act of defiance sets them apart from other Clones but also sets up the conflict they now have from an army who are technically family (by way of being Clones) because they followed values they believe in. But this is not a unanimous decision. As they are introduced to a new Clone, Omega (voiced by actress Michelle Ang) – who is different in that she ages normally, is not a soldier, and is female – there is dissent among their ranks, particularly between squad leader Hunter (voiced by actor Dee Bradley Baker) and Crosshair (also voiced by actor Dee Bradley Baker). "You should've killed that Jedi. You disobeyed orders," says Crosshair (who remains loyal to the Empire out of habit) to Hunter about Caleb Dume. Hunter responds, "I did what I thought was right," reflecting a necessary review of personal ethics compared to blind loyalty because of cultural, ethnic, or even political alliance.

This episode raises a question: What happens when the rules set by your community, your cultural or ethnic group, or even your political party conflict with your own beliefs and values? Do we take time to consider whether our personal values align with those of a broader cultural or political group, perhaps doing the more difficult task required by **allyship** to stand against our broader community if it means harming those outside our group? Or do we do the easier thing and simply go along with the **group think** of the broader community or group we belong to? We see examples of this often tied to cultural and political differences, often reflected by ethnicity and faith, commonly seen in the world today. For example, when the group who called themselves the Islamic State of Iraq and al-Sham, more commonly known as ISIS, claimed to be an **Islamic caliphate** and to speak on behalf of all Muslims, the global Muslim community rejected ISIS and their violence (Sandberg & Colvin, 2020). Similarly, there are many Israelis who have over many years and more recently in the war against Palestinians in Gaza refused to serve in the **Israel Defense Force** because they too do not hold values of violence (Ziv, 2024). Exceptions like these force us to challenge stereotypes, aiming instead to understand individuals based on their values, not on broad sweeping generalizations of what we believe their values are. In this episode, as with many of the recent *Star Wars* series, we are beginning to see values of the characters that are not always consistent with those of their teams.

Stereotyping

Obi-Wan Kenobi (Season 1, Part 5)

This miniseries picks up on the life of the well-known *Star Wars* character Obi-Wan Kenobi (played by Ewan McGregor), who was Anakin Skywalker's (later in life and in this show Darth Vader) from the original trilogy. Where the original trilogy failed on representation, this miniseries has done a bit better, which is important because the old stories focused heavily on White men. Characters played by people of color included Tala Durith (played by Indira Varma), Fifth Brother (played by Sun Kang), Senator Bail (played by Jimmy Smits), Haja Estree (played by Kumail Nanjiani), Darth Vader (voiced by James Earl Jones), but most importantly, the critical figure of Reva Sevander or Third Sister (played by Moses Ingram). The character Reva is a critical departure from past series and is a greater step toward improved inclusion as it places a Black woman (a demographic of people who are often the most marginalized in our society) and places her in a bad-ass leading role of Reva Sevander – one of the only people who has ever had the strength and capability to try and take down the infamous Darth Vader.

After a quick flashback to Obi-Wan training his Padawan apprentice Anakin (prior to him becoming Darth Vader), we see Reva, who has worked hard to climb the ranks of the Empire as an Inquisitor (Force-sensitive assassins working for Darth Vader). Where in the old series we had stereotypes of who was good and bad (often tied to race), having a Black woman play a villain would continue to fit old stereotypes as well. We see her diligence pay off when Darth Vader knights her as the Grand Inquisitor, leading all other Inquisitors. Part 5 details her chasing Obi-Wan Kenobi on Vader's instruction with a small army of Stormtroopers with her. She finds Obi-Wan, who is working to bring the child Princess Leia (played by Vivien Lyra Blair) back to her adoptive father, Senator Bail. But Reva had taken over Leia's droid and had it control the functions of the structure they were in so Obi-Wan and those with him were trapped and could not leave. As Obi-Wan aims to reason with her through a massive fortress door, he realizes through his own intuition and logic that Reva is aware that Darth Vader is none other than Anakin Skywalker – a fact few know. From what he deduces and through the Force, he and Reva share a vision of her memory when she was a child Force user who survived the Order 66 Purge (Jedi genocide). The scene shows Anakin (who had eventually fallen to the dark side and joined the Empire) walk into a room of Force-using children in the Jedi temple only to slaughter them all. Reva survives by hiding among the dead bodies of her friends, swearing revenge.

She expresses anger for the absence of Obi-Wan at the time, as she reveals her plan was not to aid Vader, but to gradually gain his trust over years of work and eventually kill him. She expresses loneliness in her journey and refuses Obi-Wan's offer to help. Reva's strength and courage remain unmet by most characters in *Star Wars*. Where Obi-Wan fled to protect Anakin's children (Leia and Luke), Reva gives up her life and safety with the eventual aim to bring down Vader. Reva's character reflects strength, but it also challenges stereotypes of good versus evil and presents her as someone who has had to be evil (being an assassin) to achieve a greater good or at least meet her personal goal of revenge. The casting of the character also challenges not just typical *Star Wars* casting but that of broader Hollywood. Even when women of color are included, they tend to have lighter skin. Moses, who plays Reva, is a darker-skinned woman and the focus is on who she is versus her skin color. Ironically, this puts Moses in a position where she faced ongoing racist harassment and bullying online. And sadly, her character, in an even-footed battle between her and Vader, dies by lightsaber at the end of the episode.

Reva's character delves into the stereotypes of the typical **angry Black woman**. She is portrayed as a fierce, determined Inquisitor seeking power and revenge, but this subverts the stereotype through the complexity of her character. She is driven by trauma and survival instead of the typical and oversimplified thirst for power. Having been one of the few who survived the fall of the Jedi, her motivations are deeply rooted in the trauma of betrayal and oppression. This psychological profile provides depth to her behavior,

Figure 9.3.   *Star Wars: Obi-Wan Kenobi*, Season 1, Episode 5 (2022, Lucas Film). Produced by Candice Campos, Doug Chiang, Deborah Chow, Stephen Daldry, et al. Directed by Deborah Chow. Moses Ingram as Inquisitor Reva Sevandar and her Sith lightsaber. It wouldn't be a *Star Wars* film without a lightsaber battle!

avoiding the tropes of a one-dimensional villain, showing Black characters with greater nuance than is typically seen on television.

Reva's ambition to rise within the ranks of the Empire also reflects a struggle for acceptance and recognition, common to many women, but especially Black women (Billups et al., 2022). This can be seen as an allegory for marginalized groups striving for power within oppressive structures including the colonial empire. Lastly, Reva's struggle to reconcile her past as a Jedi with her current role in the Empire leads to her developing a unique identity as both Jedi and Sith. This is a wonderful metaphor of ethnic and cultural identity development in which many must find a balance between the **colonial culture** that is now a part of who they are (having lived within it for so long) and maintaining **roots** of who they really were, confirming a new distinct identity that is neither fully from one culture nor another.

Indigenous People

The Book of Boba Fett (Season 1, Episode 2): "The Tribes of Tatooine"

Although the *Star Wars* franchise addresses the issues of oppressed indigenous populations by the colonial empire, some characters were clearly meant to reflect stereotypes more than others. For example, the Tusken Raiders, also known as Sand People, made their debut in *Star Wars: Episode IV – A New Hope* (1977). Represented as a nomadic indigenous people to the planet Tatooine (Liptak, 2022), the Tusken Raiders appeared in the scene in which Luke Skywalker encounters them while searching for R2-D2 on Tatooine. They attack Luke, showcasing **stereotypes of indigenous people**, aggressive and territorial in nature, before being scared off by Obi-Wan Kenobi's timely arrival, again promoting the stereotype of cowardice and weakness in the face of a superior White man. And with *The Book of Boba Fett* being the space version of a Western movie, it would have been unwise for the writers and directors of this series to perpetuate the old cowboys and Indians genre that perpetuated **racist tropes** about Indigenous people. Thankfully the directors, including Canadian Deborah Chow, took a more nuanced and informed approach.

In their original portrayal, the Tuskens embody the mysterious, dangerous, and misunderstood "natives" commonly found in Western films, which can also be applied to indigenous people in the Middle East and reflect tropes of orientalism. This trope draws parallels to historical depictions of Indigenous peoples during colonial expansion. But in *The Book of Boba Fett*, the

Tusken Raiders are reframed to demonstrate characters of greater depth and cultural nuance.

Much like *Obi-Wan Kenobi*, *The Book of Boba Fett* brings back or alludes to many old characters from the original Star Wars trilogy. In Episode 2 of *The Book of Boba Fett*, titled "The Tribes of Tatooine," Boba, settling into the city of Mos Espa on Tatooine, takes over the role of Jabba the Hutt, who was the crime lord who originally kept control over Mos Espa and the planet. Boba continues his struggle to solidify his rule in Mos Espa while flashbacks reveal his time with the Tusken Raiders. These scenes are particularly important to understanding how this episode attempts to move away from old tropes about Indigenous people. In the present day, Boba interrogates a captured assassin, who reveals a conspiracy involving the Mayor of Mos Espa and the Hutt Twins, Jabba's cousins, who lay claim to Boba's new territory. In the flashbacks, we see Boba earning the respect of the Tusken Raiders by proving his worth through combat and helping them fight off a group of Pike Syndicate enforcers who are running spice (i.e., drugs) through their land. Boba teaches the Tuskens to use advanced combat techniques and helps them seize control of a train used by the Pikes. The way Boba teaches the Tusken Raiders could be interpreted as **patronizing and patriarchal**, but the fact that Boba is not White helps soften this potential misinterpretation. In fact, Temuera Morrison, who plays Boba, is Māori, an Indigenous people in New Zealand who are struggling with ongoing issues of systemic inequality, loss of land and cultural heritage, and efforts to reclaim sovereignty and ensure the preservation of their language and traditions. It could be said this episode may reflect Indigenous people helping other Indigenous people, a pattern we now see across the world today in situations in which Indigenous people are standing up for the rights of one another (Assaly, 2023; Te Pāti Māori, 2024).

Several scenes in this episode emphasize the value of Indigenous culture through the portrayal of the Tusken Raiders. For example, after Boba helps the Tusken Raiders defeat the spice (drugs) train, they formally integrate him into their community through **ritual**, as a sign of honor and respect versus the colonial entitlement to own and force themselves on Indigenous populations and land. There's also a scene in which the Tuskens send Boba on a vision quest, facilitated by a hallucinogenic lizard that guides him to a symbolic tree, reflecting **self-discovery** and **connection to their culture**. And in modern psychology we are also now turning to Indigenous healing through psychedelics (La Torre et al., 2024). Following this vision quest, Boba returns with a branch from the tree, which the Tuskens help him carve into a personalized staff (a *Gaffi* stick), symbolizing the transmission of traditional knowledge and the significance of hand carving tools as a **rite of passage**. This Gaffi

Figure 9.4.   *The Book of Boba Fett*, "The Tribes of Tatooine" (2022, Lucasfilm). Produced by Robert Rodriguez, Kathleen Kennedy, Colin Wilson, Dave Filoni, et al. Directed by Robert Rodriguez, Jon Favreau, Bryce Dallas Howard, and Dav Filoni. *The Book of Boba Fett* brings back Temuera Morrison as the iconic Boba Fett and introduces us to Ming-Na Wen as the dangerous assassin Fennec Shand.

stick is now a part of Boba's weaponry and is even sold as his primary accessory with some toy replicas of this updated character. These moments collectively reframe the Tusken Raiders from being portrayed as "savages" to a nuanced depiction of a proud, resourceful, and deeply spiritual Indigenous culture. This episode significantly deepens the portrayal of the Tusken Raiders, presenting them as a proud and resourceful community with rich traditions, rather than the violent caricatures of earlier depictions in the franchise. Their partnership with Boba symbolizes mutual respect and cultural exchange, shaping Boba into a more honorable and strategic leader.

Additional Movies and Miniseries About *Star Wars*

The original trilogy of the Star Wars movies comprised *Star Wars: Episode IV – A New Hope* (1977), *Star Wars: Episode V – The Empire Strikes Back* (1980), *and Star Wars: Episode VI – Return of the Jedi* (1983). These early films lacked representation, and many would argue they **culturally appropriated** many elements from Asian culture. But they can be helpful for understanding *Star Wars* lore as well as the newer prequel trilogy: *Star Wars: Episode I – The Phantom Menace* (1999), *Star Wars: Episode II – Attack of the Clones* (2002), and *Star Wars: Episode III – Revenge of the Sith* (2005). These films faced criticism, including of the racist connotations of the character Jar Jar Binks. But along with the new films, they too contribute to *Star Wars* lore. The most recent films focusing on the Skywalker family are *Star Wars: Episode VII – The Force Awakens* (2015), *Star Wars: Episode VIII – The Last Jedi* (2017), and *Star Wars: Episode IX – The Rise of Skywalker* (2019).

Many will argue that the most relevant, inclusive, and interesting *Star Wars* movies and television miniseries have focused on the broader *Star Wars* universe, not those focusing on the Skywalker family. The miniseries are good examples of this, but if you have the time, more important than the films outlined in the previous paragraph are the animated series by creator Dave Filoni, who has done an incredible job in expanding the *Star Wars* universe and the diverse characters in it. The involvement of people of color, such as Chilean-born and Winnipeg-raised Pablo Hidalgo as a writer, producer, and creative executive on Lucasfilm, and Toronto born writer, director and producer, Deborah Chow has also led to more diverse representation and perspectives that are reflected in the nuanced stories of the series. Animated shows in which both were involved include *Star Wars: The Clone Wars* (2008–2020), *Star Wars Rebels* (2014–2018), *Star Wars: The Bad Batch* (2021–present). There is also *Star Wars: Visions* (2021), which is a series of unrelated shorts created by independent filmmakers about the *Star Wars* universe, bringing in greater cultural influence to these short films. Finally, see the series *Ahsoka* (2023), which is a continuation of the very popular *Star Wars Rebels* with one of the most diverse casts of *Star Wars* to date.

Critical Thinking Questions About *Star Wars* and Social Justice

- Does addressing serious topics such as social justice, war, and genocide through fictional universes like *Star Wars* help people address these issues in real life?
- Do you believe that the public even recognizes the representation of serious social justice issues in our world in the narrative of the *Star Wars* universe?
- What social justice issues, if any, do you see reflected in the *Star Wars* stories?
- Do you believe hiding social justice issues in science fiction like *Star Wars* does injustice to the real issues?
- What influence, if any, do you believe greater representation of more diverse characters in *Star Wars* has on the psychological well-being of racialized and non-racialized viewers?

Further Exploration

If you only have time to read one academic article about *Star Wars* and social justice, read:

Harrison, R. (2019). Gender, race, and representation in the *Star Wars* franchise: An introduction. *Media Education Journal, 56*(2), 16–19. http://eprints.gla.ac.uk/195627/1/195627.pdf

If you have time to read a chapter, go to:

Loehr, G. T., Shackleford, L., Dill-Shackleford, K. E., & Metcalf, M. (2020). Sci-fi fandoms in the digital age: Star Trek, Star Wars, and Doctor Who fandoms and social media. In C. L. Wang (Ed.), *Handbook of research on the impact of fandom in society and consumerism* (pp. 305–322). Business Science Reference/IGI Global. https://doi.org/10.4018/978-1-7998-1048-3.ch015

If you only have time to read one editorial about *The Mandalorian* and its association with anti-colonialism, read this:

Shakibnia, M. (2021, January 11). *This is the way: Anti-war and anti-colonial lessons to learn from The Mandalorian.* Eleven-ThirtyEight. http://eleven-thirtyeight.com/author/mohammed-shakibnia/

References

Abdulrehman, R. (2024). *Developing anti-racist cultural competence.* Hogrefe. https://doi.org/10.1027/00515-000

Abdulrehman, R. Y., & Clara, I. (2023, February 3). *Testing bias: How the bias outside the box tool challenges the common conceptions of bias, and who carries them* [Conference session]. Society for Consulting Psychology Mid-Winter Conference, Manhattan Beach, CA.

Abdulrehman, R. Y., & Graves, C. (2017). The rogue idea of people of color as heroes: A review of why Rogue One: A Star Wars Story helps fight racism [Review of the film Rogue One: A Star Wars Story, by G. Edwards, Dir.]. *PsycCRITIQUES, 62*(30).

Adamczak, D. (2023, August 21). The Phantom Menace was racist and here is why that matters. *Contemporary Racism.* https://contemporaryracism.org/27658/the-phantom-menace-was-racist-and-here-is-why-that-matters/

Assaly, R. (2023, November 17). Why some Indigenous advocates and Palestinians feel they're natural allies. *The Toronto Star.* https://www.thestar.com/news/canada/why-some-indigenous-advocates-and-palestinians-feel-they-re-natural-allies/article_685ba94d-336e-512e-8126-06d40abd509e.html

BBC News. (2018, July 4). Star Wars: Last Jedi actress deletes Instagram photos after abuse. *BBC News.* https://www.bbc.com/news/entertainment-arts-44708983

Breznican, A. (2022, May 31). Moses Ingram shares racist messages from Star Wars haters. *Vanity Fair.* https://www.vanityfair.com/hollywood/2022/05/moses-ingram-racist-star-wars-comments

Billups, S., Thelamour, B., Thibodeau, P., & Durgin, F. H. (2022). On intersectionality: Visualizing the invisibility of Black women. *Cognitive Research: Principles and Implications, 7,* Article 100.

Buttu, D. (2014). Blaming the victims. *Journal of Palestine Studies, 44*(1), 91–96. https://doi.org/10.1525/jps.2014.44.1.91

Eidelson, R. (2024, November 13). *The American Psychological Association is abandoning its commitment to human rights by refusing to speak out on Palestine.* https://royeidelson.com/the-american-psychological-association-is-abandoning-its-commitment-to-human-rights-by-refusing-to-speak-out-on-palestine/.

Goodman, A. (2023, September 5). Doing harm: Roy J. Eidelson on how psychology undermines democracy. *Democracy Now!* https://www.democracynow.org/2023/9/5/doing_harm_roy_j_eidelson_psychology.

Hussain, A. (2020). No religion is higher than humanity: Abdul Sattar Edhi. *Medium.* https://medium.com/@ayesha.hussain156/no-religion-is-higher-than-humanity-abdul-sattar-edhi-dfe8da3cad9d

Jenkins, B. (2020). Marginalization within nerd culture: Racism and sexism within cosplay. *The Popular Culture Studies Journal, 8*(1). https://www.mpcaaca.org/_files/ugd/5a6d69_7ae86740cc574bd3991fb5435db0d8ad.pdf?index=true

La Torre, J., Gallo, J., Mahammadli, M., Zalewa, D., & Williams, M. (2024). Experiences of psychedelic drug use among people with psychotic symptoms and disorders: Personal growth and mystical experiences. *Journal of Psychedelic Studies, 8*(3), 357–367. https://doi.org/10.1556/2054.2024.00348

Liptak, A. (2022, January 14). How *The Book of Boba Fett* handles the Tusken Raiders and Indigenous tropes. *Transfer Orbit.* https://transfer-orbit.ghost.io/star-wars-tusken-raiders-book-of-boba-fett-indigenous-tribes-tropes/

Reysen, S., Packard, G. A., & Plante, C. (2023). Sexism and racism negatively predict preference for diverse characters in Star Wars fans. *Psychology of Popular Media, 13*(2), 256–261. https://doi.org/10.1037/ppm0000462

Sandberg, S., & Colvin, S. (2020). 'ISIS is not Islam': Epistemic injustice, everyday religion, and young Muslims' narrative resistance. *The British Journal of Criminology, 60*(6), 1585–1605. https://doi.org/10.1093/bjc/azaa035

Sarner, L. (2023, May 24). Pedro Pascal: I am having fun with being the internet's daddy. *New York Post.* https://nypost.com/2023/05/24/pedro-pascal-i-am-having-fun-with-being-the-internets-daddy/

Shah, F., (2024, June 26). Dune 2: Middle East and Muslim influence erasure. *Cosmopolitan UK.* https://www.cosmopolitan.com/uk/entertainment/a60007426/dune-2-middle-east-north-africa-muslim-influence-erasure/

Te Pāti Māori. (2024, November 30). *Te Pāti Māori statement on Gaza.* https://www.maoriparty.org.nz/te_p_ti_m_ori_statement_on_gaza

Trivedi, S. (2019). The harm of child removal. *New York University Review of Law & Social Change, 43*(523), 523–578. https://scholarworks.law.ubalt.edu/all_fac/1085

Williams, P. J. (1999, June 17). Racial ventriloquism. *The Nation.* https://www.thenation.com/article/archive/racial-ventriloquism/

Ziv, O. (2024, August 7). Three Israeli army refusers: 'We will not participate in genocide'. *+972 Magazine.* https://www.972mag.com/israeli-army-refuseniks-moav-mueller-greenberg/

Chapter 10
Genocide, Apartheid, Civil Rights, and Colonialism

"Need I remind you that you now reside in OUR house!"

Hedwig Höss in *The Zone of Interest*

Questions to Consider While Watching
The Zone of Interest (2023)

- Why does this film evoke intense emotion even though it does not show the graphic physical violence committed by the Nazis?
- How did you feel watching the normal lives of the Nazi family while knowing genocide was being committed on the other side of the family house?
- Many of the everyday problems and stressors of the Höss family are relatable. Did you relate to their everyday challenges or have empathy for them? Why or why not?
- Why do you think that the family, particularly the adults, had such little empathy for the people in the concentration camp so close to them even though they could see and hear the atrocities being committed?
- Is there a common thread between the Höss family or the average German citizen complicit in ethnic cleansing? Are people today in the Western world complicit and quiet in the many situations of ethnic cleansing and human rights violations against marginalized groups of people?
- What do we have to learn from *The Zone of Interest* about complicity in genocide and ethnic cleansing today, particularly when it comes to the complicity of non-racialized and non-marginalized people and the suffering of racialized and marginalized communities?
- Is there a connection between the experiences of the Jews in the Holocaust the Indigenous people in the Americas or Palestinians? How and why?

- Donald Trump and other politicians such as Netanyahu and Biden (nicknamed "Genocide Joe") are often compared to Hitler. How is the comparison justified? How is it unfair?
- Richard Brody, a reviewer for *The New Yorker*, argued that Jonathan Glazer's film is an extreme example of "Holokitsch." Is this criticism justified?
- Rudolf Höss accepted responsibility for the deaths of over two million people at Auschwitz, in what has been called "the most appalling genocide in history." He was hanged for his crimes along with 11 other Nazis. Were the hangings after the Nuremberg trials justified? Is murder ever justified?
- During a tour of Dachau, a guide told Danny Wedding that *The Zone of Interest* was the most accurate film ever made about the holocaust. Do you agree?

Culture does not exist in a bubble. It is influenced by many environmental factors, including time, politics, and immigration, but also world events and catastrophes (Abdulrehman, 2024). When marginalized groups are targeted by world events, it is important to consider the impact of those events on the culture of the marginalized group, as well as how it influences the broader culture of the majority and the perpetrating community. Salient political events also shape and define culture. For example, we cannot talk about the

Figure 10.1.   *The Zone of Interest* (2023, A24, Access Entertainment, Film4, JW Films, Extreme Emotions). Produced by James Wilson, Ewa Puszczyńska, and Jim Wilson. Directed by Jonathan Glazer. The family of a concentration camp commandant lives happily just feet from the buildings in which Jews and other "undesirables" were murdered daily.

culture of South Africans without addressing **apartheid**; the culture of either Israel or Palestine without addressing the **Nakba** and the occupation of Palestine; the culture of Black Americans and America without discussing **slavery, racism**, and the **civil rights movement**; Muslims without discussing **Islamophobia**; or Jews without addressing the holocaust or **antisemitism**. Films and media can help us understand both the experiences of the marginalized community and their culture, but also the shift in the culture of those who were complicit or actively engaged in harm against such marginalized communities. They help with two critical elements to cultural competence: developing **proximity** and understanding our own **biases** (Abdulrehman, 2024). *The Zone of Interest* is such a film: It helps us understand the culture of Nazi Germany, which normalized the dehumanization and extermination of Jews to support luxury and comfort for the lives of everyday German families. The perspective of the aggressor's culture in this film is far more informative about how and why one group of people can so easily harm another, normalizing violence and dehumanization.

The Zone of Interest (2023)

The Zone of Interest is directed by Jonathan Glazer, based upon a book by the same name by Martin Amis. The film is set in German-occupied Poland and follows the everyday life of a Nazi family, Commandant Rudolf Höss, his wife, Hedwig Höss, and their children as they live their lives next door to Auschwitz concentration camp where hundreds of thousands of Jews were killed. Whereas other movies about the holocaust have focused on the lives of victims, *The Zone of Interest* focuses on those committing crimes, while they carry on their lives, treating genocide as though it were simply a boring job. The movie begins with 3-minute black screen and the sound of a droning furnace that was a part of the genocide machine and remains consistently in the background for the entire film, creating a grating sense of unease. Periodically through the film, you will hear the cries of people being killed, which stand in marked contrast to the pleasant and pretty life of the Höss family. This juxtaposition of the calm and visibly beautiful and privileged life of the family with the sound of ethnic cleansing in the background occurs throughout the film. It makes explicit the concept of dehumanization; how out of touch with the humanity of others we need to be to both harm them and live a rich unbothered life at the same time. One prolonged scene focuses on Hedwig's beautiful garden, while the screams of dying Jews provide the soundtrack.

Though in many cases increased proximity to people we perceive to be different from us improves relatability and can reduce discrimination, Glazer's film demonstrates how, without examination of our own biases (in this case the dehumanization of Jews and other marginalized people), proximity achieves nothing (Abdulrehman, 2024). The film shows how the Höss family is intimately aware of the murder of people next door, receiving the spoils of ethnic cleansing. In an early scene, Hedwig is given a parcel of women's undergarments that she offers her servants ("only one per person!" she exclaims), and she happily receives the fur coat of a woman who had been incarcerated and then murdered. She finds lipstick in that fur coat and puts it on herself. The scene demonstrates how very close predators can come to their prey; Hedwig's lips touch the same intimate item a murdered woman's lips touched not so long ago. In another scene, Hedwig's young son plays with the golden dental implants of several dead people, and Rudolf himself treats a Polish woman like an object during a disturbing scene that shows the woman preparing to have sex with him. It is not just inanimate things that are objects to this family, but people themselves. Hedwig says to one of the Polish servants who is upset at her, "I could have my husband spread your ashes across the fields of *Babice*" (a village in southern Poland)! The family home and their lush life underscore the fact that Germany and the Second World War provided a good life for many Germans. In numerous scenes, the family is shown outdoors in their backyard, even entertaining by their pool, where just beyond their fence is the Auschwitz concentration camp, with its large chimneys billowing smoke from incinerated bodies.

Hedwig Höss is a particularly interesting character who represents both Nazi society during that time but also modern society complicit and silent on numerous atrocities happening around the world. Unlike her husband, who enthusiastically helps design the gas chambers with a consultant, Hedwig not only is passive and complicit in the genocide of the people directly in the concentration camp next to her home but fights to maintain the benefits associated with her husband's position. (For a more nuanced discussion of the real Hedwig Höss, see Heffer, 2024.)

It is also interesting to see the difference between Rudolf and Hedwig. Where Rudolf appears to be grappling with the "demands of the job," and his distress shows after he finds a human bone in a nearby river, Hedwig's resolve to remain living next to Auschwitz with all the rewards that go with her station remain stronger than ever. When Rudolf informs her that they need to leave, Hedwig is angry. She screams, reminding a "Polish girl," who we suspect is Jewish, that she needs to clean up a mess and notes, "need I remind you that you live in OUR house?" – reminding the girl of the rigid human hierarchy in which she now lives. This scene is an excellent demonstration of supremacy and privilege, and it illustrates how many people feel very uncomfortable giving up privilege, even in the face of harm to others. Hedwig successfully convinces Rudolf that he can go away while she and the family remain in the comfortable family home; aware he would not see her or the children anyway, because he would be "working all the time."

There are only brief signs of distress in the Höss family, and they come from the children. The baby, free of the socialization of hate, cries often, perhaps representing the missing social consciousness of the Höss family and German society. This metaphor is the clearest in the beginning of the film, when the baby becomes more distressed when her father, Rudolf, tries to hold her. The younger boy at one point hears the screams of someone at Auschwitz and then pulls back the curtain to look, only to shudder, close the curtains, and say, "I'll never do that again." Lastly, while the family sleeps there is an orange glow coming from the window, resulting from the mass incineration of bodies. Hedwig's mother pauses but says nothing.

Although the issues brought up in *The Zone of Interest* are specifically focused on Jewish people, the film reflects broader issues of power, privilege, complicity, and the **cognitive dissonance** many experience today that allow genocide and other human rights violations to persist in other parts of the world and even in modern times. There are scenes at the very end of the film that show Auschwitz as a museum, with the gas chambers empty and the halls filled with piles of shoes, luggage, and other personal items. The museum and the film are a reminder of what occurs when those with privilege forgo social responsibility for the **comfort of complicity**. This has certainly been the case with the genocide of the Palestinian people (Amnesty International, 2024), in which matters of social responsibility were lost by many involved in this modern-day Holocaust. And just as Hedwig's social responsibility and humanity are lost, using the lipstick and wearing the fur of the murdered Jewish woman, members of the Israeli military have been documented numerous times on social media parading around in the underwear of Palestinian women they killed or displaced (Berman, 2024). Acts of cognitive dissonance such as these have led to serious human rights violations and the death of countless people. And following the International Criminal Court's warrant for the arrest of Israeli Prime Minister Benjamin Netanyahu for his role in the genocide in Gaza, it was no surprise that the Polish government announced that he would be arrested if he attended the 80th anniversary of the liberation of Auschwitz, on January 27, 2025 (Jerusalem Post, 2024).

The film also shows several scenes in which a little girl, working inside the Höss house, sneaks out at night to plant apples in the fields where prisoners of the concentration camp work, placing herself at risk of being discovered by the Höss family, Hedwig in particular. That little girl symbolizes the risk of many who ally themselves with marginalized people and the danger they face for speaking up for human rights. These segments are filmed in reverse black and white to represent the stark difference between the normal life of complicity lived by most in the Höss household and the danger inherent in standing up for justice that many people of color and those from marginalized communities face in doing so. Glazer's intent for the film to have a broader impact was clear in his Oscar speech in 2023 (Schimkowitz, 2024), in which he said, "Right now we stand here as men who refute their Jewishness and the Holocaust being hijacked by an occupation which has led to conflict for so many innocent people, whether the victims of October the 7th in Israel or the ongoing attack on Gaza" (Thompson, 2023). Glazer's speech came under stark scrutiny (The Guardian, 2024) for allying himself with the marginalized Palestinians in Gaza. UN experts confirmed there were reasonable grounds to believe in the genocide of Palestinians (United Nations, 2024), and Glazer was called a "self-hating Jew" (Freund, 2024).

Prejudice, Discrimination, Oppression, Racism, and Ethnocentrism

Premiering first at the Toronto International Film Festival, **Farha** (2021) is a gut-wrenching film directed by Darin J. Sallam, based on the true story of 14-year-old Palestinian girl (played by Karam Taher) and her survival during the 1948 Palestinian **Nakba** (the displacement of the Palestinian people during the establishment of the state of Israel). The film begins by briefly showing what life was like for Farha and her father, Abu Farha (played by Ashraf Harhom), and her desire to continue her education rather than marry. Farha is torn between pursuing her personal ambitions and leaving her father behind. But her dreams and life are shattered as violence erupts when soldiers arrive, and people take up arms to defend their homes. Farha's father arranges for a friend to take Farha to ensure her safety, but, worried about her father, she runs out of the car to join him and fight. Concerned for his daughter's safety, Abu Farha locks Farha in a storage room promising to return soon, but she never sees him again. Waiting on pins and needles in the darkness of that storage room, she, and we, through her vantage point, witness the Nakba. A family trying to escape from soldiers takes refuge in Farha's home. She witnesses the pregnant mother give birth, and the parents trying to hide their

Farha: Do you know what I've decided? When I finish my studies in the city, I want to become a teacher. I will open a school here, just for girls.

Farida: When I grow up, I want to become... [*interrupted by gunfire*]

> A fourteen-year-old Palestinian girl, Farha, talks to her friend Farida about her future aspirations, just as fighting begins, commencing the first Nakba and the first violent expulsion of Palestinians from Palestine in 1948, in *Farha*.

three children. Eventually the family is discovered by soldiers, and Farha, trapped in the room, watches as every member of the family except the baby is shot execution style. But the senior soldier says to a younger soldier, "...we left the baby for you. A boy. ... Kill him and follow us. And don't waste a bullet on him." The young soldier looks distressed and attempts to crush the baby under his foot, but overwhelmed with grief, he is unable to kill the child, covering the baby's face with a handkerchief before running off. Unable to escape from the room, Farha is left helpless to watch; this reflects the helplessness of many Palestinians then and since that time. When she finally finds a handgun in a barrel of lentils, Farha escapes, only to find the baby dead and her home ravaged and empty.

Figure 10.2. *Farha* (2021, Talebox, Liaka Film, and Television Chimney). Produced by Deema Azar and Ayah Jardaneh. Directed by Darin J. Sallam. Farha, a 14-year-old girl, contemplates life without her best friend Farida. Farha hopes to escape her traditional village in Palestine to get an education and become a teacher.

Farha is a film that shares the perspective of a single person, but such experiences were common to many of the 750,000 Palestinians displaced from their homes and land in 1948 (United Nations, 2024). These experiences are also illustrated and explained by Israeli historians like Ilan Pappé (2006), who described the role of British colonialism and the impact of the Holocaust, not just for the European Jewish population, but also now for the Indigenous people of all faith backgrounds in Palestine. Although this film does not venture into politics, it does present a worthy historical perspective of a young girl surviving the *Nakba*, which is a worthy and necessary perspective in discussing the contagious nature of racism, hate, and oppression, their role in colonialism and eventual apartheid. While *The Zone of Interest* focuses on the perpetrators of genocide, *Farha* places the viewer on the opposite end of conflict; the innocent victims of colonialism. And rather than get caught up in broader false arguments of religious conflict, *Farha* brings us down to the granular experience of one person allowing us to appreciate her humanity. And as Malcolm X said in a 1964 speech in Cairo, "The problem that exists in Palestine is not a religious problem. It is a question of **colonialism**" (Bashir, 2021).

Cultural Identity, Acculturation, Assimilation

The United States is often described as a **melting pot**, while Canada is described as a **mosaic**. Similar metaphors are found in other Western countries, and the concept of acculturation or assimilation into the larger broader culture appears to be how we achieve equity. But it is also a means by which racial, ethnic, and cultural hierarchy and supremacy are maintained, sometimes by other people of color. For example, Governor Bobby Jindal (a South Asian man) said this in one of his campaign speeches: "We must insist on assimilation – immigration without assimilation is an invasion. We need to tell folks who want to come here, they need to come here legally. They need to learn English, adopt our values, roll up their sleeves and get to work" (Jindal, 2015).

Statements such as these don't just reflect Jindal's **internalized racism** but also suggest that those who were here first (typically perceived to be White people and not Indigenous people) worked harder and achieved more because of that, instead of succeeding due to systemic racism. His comments also suggest that those who immigrate (usually people of color and those from non-English-speaking countries) are further behind and must catch up to White people. But statements like these, and naive concepts of acculturation and assimilation into a broader monolith, are uninformed and blind to the basic reality of how racism and disparity work. As a part of a broader Netflix documentary series exploring a broad range of topics, *Explained: The Racial Wealth Gap* (2018) is a short documentary that clearly describes how and why the **racial wealth gap** exists in the United States (which can be extrapolated to other colonial countries as well as the global economy), relating it to slavery and racism. With special appearances by Senator Cory Booker (the first Black senator from the state of New Jersey), this documentary examines how the significant disparity of wealth, as a whole, between Black and White Americans was contributed to by slavery, **Jim Crow laws**, discriminatory housing practices (such as **redlining**), and unequal access to education and employment opportunities. The series documents that the racial wealth gap is more important than assimilation, as well as being the major contributor to inequity. The documentary opens our eyes to understanding how Black people, through slavery, were the real wealth in America, with an estimated value of three billion dollars in 1863. And even though as a whole, America has been able to break down some racial barriers, it has not addressed why the median savings of a White family are $171,000, while those of Black families are $17,600. This documentary makes clear that wealth begets wealth, and that without **reparations**, the wealth gap continues to widen as does the disparity between White and Black Americans. "Most people don't understand the power of housing, of where you live, of what opportunities exist in that community," says Booker in this documentary, and he shares his family's story of success that came because of finding better housing in a White community. That only occurred after a racist real estate agent pandering to economic racism physically attacked the Booker family lawyer and set his dog on Booker's father for purchasing his home with the help of a White family. The documentary makes it clear that the success of some Black people does not create freedom and equality for all, and that breaking some racial barriers does not mean we are approaching equity. In fact, the success of some people of color is sometimes based on the subjugation of other people of color. For example, critics of past President Obama highlight that although he was the first Black president (a substantial feat that indicated a breaking of racial boundaries in America after a history of slavery), he was also known as the "deporter in chief" due to deporting over 3 million people (primarily people of color) during his presidency (Chishti et al., 2017). Obama has also been criticized by those who believe that he did not do enough to address racism and police brutality (West, 2016); compared to President Bush, he conducted over 10 times more drone strikes in Muslim-majority countries (Purkiss & Serle, 2017). Ultimately, the underlying premise of *Explained: The Racial Wealth Gap* is that we cannot address issues of inclusion, equity, and even acculturation and assimilation while ignoring the practical and growing wealth disparity between White people and people of color. These are issues brought up by civil rights leader Malcolm X, as will be reviewed in the next section, and are reflected strongly in the culture and identity of many people of color, whose work to dismantle systems of oppression becomes a part of their cultural identity. As **Audre Lorde** (1984) said, "For the master's tools will never dismantle the master's house. They may allow us to temporarily beat him at his own game, but they will never enable us to bring about genuine change."

Value Conflicts, Value Orientations

The challenges of speaking up against oppression can be daunting, as is calling people to action, including those with privilege (racialized or not). This call to action requires pointing out that maintaining complicity and silence about human rights violations implies that people's value orientations align with racism and supremacy; this type of honesty would be offensive for most people. However, discussing value conflicts can be dangerous for racialized people or those who ally with them. For example, many Canadians of color speaking out for a ceasefire in the genocide against the Palestinian people since 2023 lost jobs and were harassed, where no such incidences were reported when White people spoke out in support of Israel (CBC News, 2023). In the case of Malcolm X, his speaking out for civil rights, saying things many others would not say, left him at odds with American values of that time. But as he progressed in his journey as a civil rights leader and upon his movement away from the Nation of Islam to orthodox Islam, he found himself at odds with the values of his former mentor and leader, Elijah Muhammed, and, as a result, at odds with the Nation of Islam. For Malcolm X, this conflict of values cost him his life as he was assassinated on February 21, 1965, in the Audubon Ballroom in New York City while preparing to deliver a speech to his supporters. The documentary mini-series *Who Killed Malcolm X?* (2020) explores not only Malcolm X's life and how he was at odds with the normative values of racism at the time, but also the question of who really assassinated him. The entire Netflix documentary includes six episodes, but Episodes 1 and 5, "Marked Man" and "Shotgun Man," provide a nice overview of the main issues discussed in this series.

Episode 1, "Marked Man," sets the stage for the documentary series investigation into Malcolm X's assassination and introduces the series central figure, Abdur-Rahman Muhammad (an independent historian whose day job is working as a tour guide). Muhammad's fixation on who really killed Malcolm X takes the viewer through a variety of sources of information including historians, convicted alleged assassins, former New York police officers, and ex-FBI agents. This episode reviews inconsistencies in the trial of the men accused, and notes that key information was ignored; however, most historians believe the confessed killers were a part of the Nation of Islam, and Malcolm's assassination a bid to terminate his influence as he left the Nation of Islam for a moderate view of orthodox Sunni Islam.

Episode 5, "Shotgun Man" (along with other segments throughout the entire series), reveals that Malcolm's activism for equality was seen as a threat to the government, in particular J. Edgar Hoover and the FBI. This episode digs deeper into the involvement of the FBI and NYPD in the events leading up to Malcolm's assassination. As it turns out, the eyewitness descriptions of who killed Malcolm do not line up with the faces of the persons incarcerated, and they add additional evidence suggesting that the FBI was aware of the murder plot but did not inform the NYPD. This episode also discloses how undercover officers were present in the Audubon Ballroom on the day of Malcolm's assassination and suggests key evidence had been mishandled. The conclusion of this episode is that law enforcement was, at very least, turning

Figure 10.3. *Who Killed Malcolm X?* Episode 4, "Showdown" (2020, Netflix). Produced by Arc Media. Directed by Rachel Dretzin and Phil Bertelsen. Making the pilgrimage (*hajj*) to the holy city of Mecca in Saudi Arabia is one of the five pillars of Islam (the other four are profession of faith, prayer, charity, and fasting). Muslims face Mecca when they pray each day, and every Muslim whose health and finances permit it must complete the *hajj* at least once. Malcolm X was profoundly influenced by his *hajj*, moving him from the Nation of Islam to Orthodox Islam. This scene from the mini-series depicts the *Kaaba*, the house that Abraham built to honor God.

a blind eye to the plot to murder human rights activist Malcolm X – and they were possibly involved in it. The episode also makes it clear that as Malcolm's influence was growing globally, particularly in the Middle East and Africa, he was quick to criticize US foreign policy and colonialism; thus, his views were considered to pose a threat to foreign and domestic plans of the US government.

The series implies that anyone who challenges the values of colonial White supremacy is at risk. This is not a historical artifact; currently, many academics and professionals using their privilege to speak up against colonial expansion and conflict in the Middle East are often subject to threat and censorship (Basu, 2023). As the falsely accused and imprisoned "Normal 3X" Butler says in this series, "White man says you're guilty, you're guilty. Why? Because he says so and he got a gun." We would like to believe that we as a Western society have moved past the chains of slavery, racism, apartheid, colonialism, and power disparities, but the evidence suggests this simply isn't true. Privilege is doled out for some, but at the cost of silence. As stated by the key figure in this documentary, Abdur-Rahman Muhammad, "Asking who killed Malcolm is a dangerous question," and "Folks tried to caution me, leave that alone man." The simple fact of what questions we can ask, and of whom, becomes a considerable threat to the people of color and those who ally themselves with them. For example, renowned American journalist and author **Ta-Nehisi Coates** (a Black man) wrote a book of essays, *The Message* (2024), based on his global travels. These essays address racism, colonialism, and apartheid in the contemporary world. However, CBS morning co-anchor Tony Dokoupil claimed that if all of Coates's successes and honors were stripped away, what Coates wrote could be found "in the backpack of an extremist" (Zakaria, 2024). Experiences like these for people of color, despite their expertise, confirm Muhammad's fear of asking questions. Stereotypes that come with people of color standing up for rights and asking questions can be dangerous as they are self-fulfilling prophecies that trap people of color into either subservience and silence or lead them to become perceived terrorists and extremists (as Malcolm X was labeled).

Social Norms and Norm Violations

Escape From Pretoria (2020)

Culture is an intersectional concept that impacts people both with and without privilege. If we begin to understand that our rights, our identity, and our culture are intertwined, our ability to resolve conflict and problems associated with all forms of systemic discrimination becomes greater. The film *Escape from Pretoria* (2020) deals with the concept of joint liberation as it follows the true-life story of White South Africans imprisoned for their work for liberation with the African National Congress, then alleged to be a terrorist organization. The main characters are Tim Jenkin (played by *Harry Potter*'s Daniel Radcliffe) and Stephen Lee (played by Daniel Webber), who were real-life political activists imprisoned for distributing anti-apartheid materials. The third character, Leonard Fontaine (played by Mark Leonard Winter), is another political prisoner in the movie, but this character is a composite of various other prisoners involved in the struggle against apartheid. The film revolves around their imprisonment, abuse, and degradation before their real-life escape. Freedom, as stated by Tim Jenkin in the movie, along with other concepts like justice and equality, "is a very simple idea. Which is why it can be so easily lost."

Several key themes are addressed by this film, the first of which is that change toward justice is not made by those affected alone but also *requires those with privilege to not just ally themselves but commit and be co-conspirators for the cause of justice.* The ability to see yourself in those who are impacted by marginalization, to see yourself as a part of their community, provides the critical proximity and intersecting identity necessary for not just cultural competence but also for impactful change for justice (Abdulrehman, 2024). Tim's girlfriend in the film is a Black South African, underscoring his sense of community and his dedication to the cause of justice.

This film has many nerve-wracking scenes, be it the prisoners witnessing harm to Black prisoners, experiencing abuse themselves for allying with Black South Africans, or in a major part of the film, escaping from Pretoria and the symbolic prison of apartheid. The film ends with the successful escape and with text about the eventual end of apartheid. But the tension experienced in this movie, the holding of breath experienced by the prisoners trying to escape, is not unlike the experiences of many fighting for justice and equity,

We didn't want a life based on lies and indifference. We wanted to join the ongoing struggle for a democratic and free South Africa, not based on racial discrimination.

ANC activist Tim Jenkin looks to the future
in *Escape From Pretoria.*

worried about the repercussions on their own lives. And it underlies a key question about urgency for change. Does change happen by force, or is it something we must wait for patiently? Though the key characters in this film are all White, the question of escape urgency is discussed. Do they all escape together, or, as some political prisoners think, wait out their time since they have done what they can for change? As the character of Denis Goldberg (played by Ian Hart), a real-life social campaigner against apartheid, says in the film, "a seed has to rot in the ground before you can enjoy its fruit." Do we all have the privilege and patience to wait for change, or must we push for it sooner?

As *Escape from Pretoria* suggests, the intersectional need for justice, peace, and equity cannot be an issue that belongs to one culture or group of people alone. We must all take responsibility for issues tied to injustice, rather than expecting the targeted group to resolve the problem. Examples include the little girl working in the Höss household delivering apples to the workers in Auschwitz, the little girl pushing a refrigerator past the checkpoint in *The Present* (discussed next), or the main characters imprisoned in Pretoria for standing with the African National Congress, presumed to be "terrorists." All the films in this chapter help us gain the sense of urgency needed to challenge the social norms of White supremacy, accepting the risks that come with that.

Stereotyping

The Present (2020)

The multiple award-winning short film, *The Present* (2020), directed by Farah Nubulsi, focuses on a day in the lives of a father, Yusef Khalidi (played by Saleh Bakri), and his daughter Yasmin (played by Maryam Kanj), in the occupied West Bank of Palestine. The pair set out to buy Noor (the mother, played by Mariam Basha) an anniversary gift (a replacement refrigerator for the one that is not working), but they must do this otherwise loving task by navigating the harrowing and humiliating Israeli occupation check points. Yusef faces harassment including being called a "dirty Arab," and being caged at one checkpoint, among other forms of dehumanization, all while his daughter fearfully watches. At one of the checkpoints, Yasmin loses control of her bladder, a symptom of **posttraumatic stress disorder** (PTSD; Geynisman-Tan et al., 2021). Research documents that up to 91% of Palestinian children have PTSD because of the brutal occupation they live under (Euro-Med

Figure 10.4. *The Present* (2020, Native Liberty, Philistine Films, and Doha Film Institute). Produced by Ossama Bawardi. Directed by Farah Nabulsi. In *The Present*, a young Palestinian girl wonders if her father, who is caged at a military checkpoint, will be safe.

Human Rights Monitor, 2021). The short film also shows both father and daughter being forced to be patient and tolerant, but eventually Yusef loses his temper when the refrigerator has to be forced through narrow gates. He starts shouting at the occupation soldiers, and the film demonstrates the trap of stereotypes: Yusef either must tolerate the abuse and racism or rage against it. In one case, he is subjugated; in the other, he fulfills the stereotype of the angry Arab, Palestinian, or Muslim. The occupation soldiers react to Yusef's anger by pointing their guns at him.

Stereotypes of how we see the world and those different from us can often become self-fulfilling prophecies and this film demonstrates not just how such stereotypes harm Palestinians, Arabs, and Muslims, but how they could impact all of us in systems of oppression. Yasmin, the character representing resilience and resistance, despite all her trauma, takes the brave step of pushing a fridge many times her size, around the narrow occupation checkpoint gates, defying the orders of the occupation forces, while her father risks being shot. Thanks to the humanity of one of the soldiers, father and daughter are permitted to pass with their refrigerator, but it requires an act of bravery from a child – someone with the least power and privilege.

The Present is a short but powerful film that shows Palestinians for who they are – everyday people trying to live their lives under apartheid (Amnesty International, 2022; Human Rights Watch, 2021). It is also a reminder that if you treat people as monsters, they become monsters, at least to you, no matter how human they may be.

Indigenous People and Cultural Identity, Acculturation, Assimilation

Little Bird (2023) is a Canadian miniseries by Jennifer Podemski and Hanna Moscovitch, produced by Jeremy Podeswa, about an Indigenous woman, Behzig Little Bird (renamed Esther Rosenbloom), who attempts to reconnect with her birth family and heritage after having been abducted and placed into a White Jewish family during the "Sixties Scoop." The **Sixties Scoop**, as explained at the beginning of Episode 1, refers to a settler-colonial practice (specifically in Canada, but such practices also occurred in other parts of the world), in which an estimated 20,000 Indigenous children were forcibly removed from their families and placed in foster care or adoptive homes of non-Indigenous, White families between the 1960s and 1980s. This occurred simultaneously with the growth of the residential school system, both of which were a means to break ties Indigenous children had with their culture, family, and identity for the purpose of Canada's broader assimilation policies. This miniseries is based on true events that took place during that time, which is critical to helping the broader public be more aware of the impact colonization had on Indigenous people in Canada. Co-creator and showrunner Jennifer Podemski, of Anishinaabe (Indigenous) and Ashkenazi (Jewish) descent, had this to say about the importance of *Little Bird* (Jennifer Podemski, personal communication, November 5, 2024):

> Telling stories about experiences and people to those who know nothing about that is a huge responsibility. It becomes more complex when the story is based on true events that illuminate harm caused by government and policy. The racism towards Indigenous people, in what we know as Canada today, is so deeply embedded in systems and its impact is most clearly presented in the under-representation of Indigenous people in **spaces and sectors of power** like Law, Justice, Education, Health, Child Welfare and Media. In *Little Bird*, centering Indigenous narratives, putting Indigenous people on screen and Indigenous directors at the helm was an act of resistance and anti-racism. Since the very first contact, policies were enforced that were designed to eradicate or assimilate Indigenous people. The Sixties Scoop was one of them. One of the reasons it was so critical to create a series around the topic was that the education system erased our true history. The important thing to know about systemic racism is that it's built on the foundation of white supremacy, but it's a system of policies that continue to be delivered and perpetuated by non-White people too. So, although *Little Bird* exposes one of many policies designed to eradicate Indigenous people, it's only a small example of a much bigger and more critical problem that impacts Indigenous people today. Regardless of someone's color or background, regardless of

how oppressed they were where they come from, there is nothing that prepares you for anti-Indigenous racism because it's deeply embedded and cemented into the system in which we live. And like the Jewish Holocaust survivor mother who adopted Esther, you may not realize that you are participating in an act of violence because it's being presented to you in a way that centers values that appear Canadian while in reality you are participating in harm and erasure of Indigenous people.

Although one must watch the entire series to understand the impact of assimilation and acculturation to White culture, and its impact on the loss of Indigenous people's identity, Episodes 1 and 2 ("Love Is All Around" and "So Put Together") begin an important conversation around the dangers of assimilation.

The two episodes alternate in time between Behzig Little Bird as a child and her as Esther Rosenbloom, an adult. "Love Is All Around" begins by showing the idyllic life Behzig had with her biological family in their Saskatchewan in their home and then transitions to her life as an adult with her adoptive family in Montreal at her engagement party. At the party she is wearing a necklace with the Star of David (also the name of her fiancé), and she gives a speech reflecting her adoptive Jewish identity and values, noting that she and David will have Jewish babies for a new Jewish generation. Following that, Behzig overhears her mother-in-law and other family members making racist comments about her, such as, "So she and David [her fiancé] are the answer to the Holocaust? She's like a regular Jew now?" And "You have one of the good ones. My cousin adopted one of them and he's into all the drugs and stuff." These comments trigger Behzig's long seated need to seek out her birth family as she begins to recall being ripped from her family. She has flashbacks of the horrific forms of racist child abuse that occurred because of many people working within the system, including the Royal Canadian Mounted Police, social workers, and childcare workers, shown throughout the episodes. The scenes that depict the abduction of Behzig and her siblings from her family are common to almost all Indigenous people of many generations (Truth and Reconciliation Commission of Canada, 2015). This colonial experience of cultural genocide through forced assimilation is so common that Canadian artist Kent Monkman depicted it in his well-known piece "The Scream" (2016).

When Behzig asks for information about her adult siblings, a social worker remarks, "You're so put together," as if this was surprising and uncommon for an Indigenous woman. It is almost as though Esther's adult sophistication justifies ripping Behzig from her family all those years ago. The key message in these episodes is the dangers of assimilation because it creates a

Figure 10.5. *The Scream*. Kent Monkman (Fisher River Cree Nation), *The Scream*, 2017. Acrylic paint on canvas: 84 x 132 in. Denver Art Museum: Native Arts acquisition funds, purchased with funds from Loren G. Lipson, M.D, 2017.93. © Kent Monkman. Image courtesy of the Denver Art Museum. This painting dramatically captures the horror of children being ripped away from their First Nations parents by Canadian Mounties.

hierarchy of culture, White culture being the most dominant and what Abdulrehman (2024) refers to as the "White measuring stick" by which all other racialized people must abide. Though the film focuses on problems with assimilation in the past, the issues are current and remain deeply troubling. As stated in text at the end of Episode 1, there are more (Indigenous) children in care in Canada today than there were in all its previous history. A TEDx Winnipeg speaker in 2024, Salena Starling, an Indigenous woman, outlines how she was apprehended and put into foster care as a young child and has since struggled with the impact of forced assimilation into White Canadian culture and her development of internalized racism. She speaks powerfully about looking in the mirror and wanting to "scrub the brown off her face" (Starling, 2024).

The show also highlights a key message: No matter how much you assimilate, Indigenous people and other people of color are never going to be treated the same as those who are White as long as we live in a society promoting White supremacy. And although the Indigenous community was specifically targeted in the systemic colonial practice of the Sixties Scoop, other **BIPOC** (Black, Indigenous, People of Color) communities in Canada face

Figure 10.6. *Little Bird*, Episode 1, "Love is All Around" (2024, Crave and Aboriginal Peoples Television Network [APTN]). Produced by Catherin Bainbridge, Tanya Brunel, Philippe Chabot, Dante Di Loreto, et al. Directed by Zoe Hopkins and Elle-Máijá Tailfeathers. Behzig (Little Bird) and her mother Patti, run from police and a social worker in front of their home on a reserve in Saskatchewan.

similar difficulties, with children of color who are more likely to be seen as lazy, unintelligent, and aggressive (Priest et al., 2018).

Recent case reviews confirm that social and legal systems and those who work within them have not learned anything from the forced assimilation of Indigenous children, and children of color still face serious problems caused by Canada's legal and social systems. In a review of cases of racial and cultural bias in legal systems, Williams et al. (2024) describe a situation in which a young child of color was not believed when he kept reporting abuse by a parent. Interestingly, the opposite can also be true in work with Indigenous communities; often, children are not believed when they say they want to stay with the families and are safe (as highlighted in Episode 1 of *Little Bird*), but instead are trapped into a position where no matter what they do, no matter how much they assimilate, they are often seen as outsiders and less valued than White people. Research on bias confirms that Indigenous people are seen as less likely to succeed and are believed to be perpetually tied to poverty, but both views reflect systemic racism (Abdulrehman & Clara, 2023). These beliefs are reflected in a statement by the social worker who abducted Behzig and her siblings, who noted, "you're saving them from a life of poverty."

Additional Films About Genocide, Apartheid, Civil Rights, and Colonialism

Thankfully, as much as these difficult topics are ignored by some, there are brave and insightful filmmakers and directors who have made powerful films on the topic. Some of our favorites include *Origin* (2023), *200 Meters* (2020), *Israelism* (2024), *Life Is Beautiful* (1997), *The Pianist* (2002), *Harriet* (2019), *Mississippi Burning* (1988), *The Hate U Give* (2018), *Not Your Model Minority* (2022), *Moffie* (2019), *Mandela: Long Walk to Freedom* (2013), *Twice Colonized* (2023), *Exterminate All Brutes* (2021), *Stuff the British Stole* (2022), and *Dirty Pretty Things* (2002). For a bit of a light-hearted but honest approach to racism and civil rights (which can be a necessary change after the heft of the serious movies to balance our responsibility with joy), consider comedy specials like *Baby Cobra* (2016) by Ali Wong (who addresses racism toward Asian people), *Fear of a Brown Planet* (2008), and *Fear of a Brown Planet Returns* (2011), which both star Aamer Rahman. You can also explore racism through satire in comedy miniseries such as *Ramy* (2019), *Mo* (2022), *Dear White People* (2017), and *Black-ish* (2024).

Critical Thinking Questions About Genocide, Apartheid, Civil Rights, and Colonialism

- Why do issues of civil rights of people of color in one part of the world correlate so strongly with the rights of a different group of people of color in another part of the world? For example, why was Malcolm X so interested in the rights of Palestinians?
- Have you paid attention to the role of colonialism in many global issues? If so, what have you noticed? If not, what has prevented you from noticing?
- Do you feel like in today's modern world we create exceptions for the application of human rights for all to some group of people? If so, why do you think that is? For example,
  - Do you believe that politics interferes with the basic human rights of people of color? Why or why not?
  - Do you believe that some governments and political systems use stereotypes of some people?
- How do politics sustain colonialism and apartheid, and how does political conflict lead to genocide of a people?
- There is criticism of how the Western world carries on with business as usual while people of color and the Global South are impacted negatively. What do you think contributes to the need to avoid these difficult issues?
- Indigenous people have been fighting for their basic human rights since contact with Europeans. What systems and beliefs have contributed to sustain their marginalization for so long?
- Dehumanizing terminology like "vermin" (used to describe Jews during the Holocaust); "savages" (used to describe Indigenous people); "chattel" and the N-word for Black people in America; "barbaric" and "human animals" to describe Palestinians; and "terrorists" to describe Arabs, Muslims, and the broader Middle East were all readily accepted by the broader public to manufacture consent to engage in harm and even kill many of these people. Why do you believe dehumanization of these and other people was so effective?

Further Exploration

If you only have time for one article, read:

Albanese, F. (2024, October 1). *Genocide as colonial erasure: Report of the Special Rapporteur on the situation of human rights in the Palestinian territories occupied since 1967.* United Nations. https://www.un.org/unispal/document/genocide-as-colonial-erasure-report-francesca-albanese-01oct24/

If you have time to read one chapter about the impact of racism on Black people, read:

Smith, A. (2006). Heteropatriarchy and the three pillars of white supremacy. In INCITE! Women of Color Against Violence (Eds.), *Color of violence: The INCITE! anthology* (pp. 66–73). Duke University Press.

If you have time to read an entire book, we recommend:

Coates, T-N. (2024). *The message*. One World.

References

Abdulrehman, R. (2024). *Developing anti-racist cultural competence*. Hogrefe. https://doi.org/10.1027/00515-000

Abdulrehman, R. Y., & Clara, I. (2023, February 3). *Testing bias: How the bias outside the box tool challenges the common conceptions of bias, and who carries them* [Conference session]. Society for Consulting Psychology Mid-Winter Conference, Manhattan Beach, CA.

Amnesty International. (2024, December 5). *Amnesty International investigation concludes Israel is committing genocide against Palestinians in Gaza*. https://www.amnesty.org/en/latest/news/2024/12/amnesty-international-concludes-israel-is-committing-genocide-against-palestinians-in-gaza/

Amnesty International. (2022, February 1). *Israel's apartheid against Palestinians: Cruel system of domination and crime against humanity*. https://www.amnesty.org/en/documents/mde15/5141/2022/en/

Bashir, A. (2021, May 19). What did Malcolm X say about Palestine, Gaza, and Zionism? *The New Arab*. https://www.newarab.com/news/what-did-malcolm-x-say-about-palestine-gaza-and-zionism

Berman, N. (2024, February 29). Violating intimacies. *Mondoweiss*. https://mondoweiss.net/2024/02/violating-intimacies/

CBC News. (2023, May 18). *Experts say online backlash against pro-Palestinian voices has chilling effect on free expression in Canada*. https://www.cbc.ca/news/canada/chilling-effect-pro-palestinian-1.7064510

Chishti, M., Pierce, S., & Bolter, J. (2017, January 26). *Obama record on deportations: 'Deporter-in-Chief' or not?* Migration Policy Institute. https://www.migrationpolicy.org/article/obama-record-deportations-deporter-chief-or-not

Coates, T-N., (2024). *The message*. One World.

Euro-Med Human Rights Monitor. (2021, July 2). *New report: 91% of Gaza children suffer from PTSD after the Israeli attack*. Euro-Med Human Rights Monitor. https://euromed-monitor.org/en/article/4497/New-Report:-91%25-of-Gaza-children-suffer-from-PTSD-after-the-Israeli-attack

Geynisman-Tan, J., Helmuth, M., Smith, A. R., Lai, H. H., Amundsen, C. L., Bradley, C. S., Mueller, M. G., Lewicky-Gaupp, C., Harte, S. E., Jelovsek, J. E., & Symptoms of Lower Urinary Tract Dysfunction Research Network (LURN) Study Group. (2021). Prevalence of childhood trauma and its association with lower urinary tract symptoms in women and men in the LURN study. *Neurourology and Urodynamics, 40*(2), 632–641.

Heffer, S. (2024, February 2). "Mass murder occurred over her garden wall": The evil of Hedwig Höss, the Auschwitz commandant's wife. *The Telegraph*. https://www.telegraph.co.uk/films/0/hedwig-hoss-the-zone-of-interest-auschwitz-holocaust-truth/

Freund, M. (2024, March 23). When Jews are antisemitic: Jonathan Glazer goes beyond self-hatred. *The Jerusalem Post*. https://www.jpost.com/opinion/article-793134

Human Rights Watch. (2021, April 27). *A threshold crossed: Israeli authorities and the crimes of apartheid and persecution.* https://www.hrw.org/report/2021/04/27/threshold-crossed/israeli-authorities-and-crimes-apartheid-and-persecution

Jerusalem Post Staff. (2024, December 21). Netanyahu will be arrested if he comes to Auschwitz memorial, Polish government confirms. *The Jerusalem Post*. from https://www.jpost.com/israel-news/benjamin-netanyahu/article-834302

Jindal, B. (2015, August 31). *Statement by Governor Bobby Jindal: Immigration without assimilation is an invasion.* The American Presidency Project. https://www.presidency.ucsb.edu/documents/statement-governor-bobby-jindal-immigration-without-assimilation-invasion

Lorde, A. (1984). *Sister outsider: Essays and speeches.* Crossing Press.

Pappé, I. (2006). *The ethnic cleansing of Palestine.* Oneworld Publications.

Purkiss, J., & Serle, J. (2017, January 17). *Obama's covert drone war in numbers: Ten times more strikes than Bush.* The Bureau of Investigative Journalism. https://www.thebureauinvestigates.com/stories/2017-01-17/obamas-covert-drone-war-in-numbers-ten-times-more-strikes-than-bush

Priest, N., Slopen, N., Woolford, S., Philip, J. T., Singer, D., Kauffman, A. D., Mosely, K., Davis, M., Ransome, Y., & Williams, D. (2018). Stereotyping across intersections of race and age: Racial stereotyping among White adults working with children. *PLoS ONE, 13*(9), e0201696. https://doi.org/10.1371/journal.pone.0201696

Schimkowitz, M. (2024, January 13). Jonathan Glazer's Oscars 2024 acceptance speech: Full transcript. *Vulture*. https://www.vulture.com/article/oscars-2024-jonathan-glazer-speech-full-transcript.html

Starling, S. (2024). *How reconciliation began with me: Overcoming internalized racism.* TEDx Winnipeg. https://tedxwinnipeg.ca/speaker/salena-starling/

The Guardian (2024, March 21). Jonathan Glazer's Oscars speech resonates deeply. (2024, March 21). *The Guardian*. https://www.theguardian.com/film/2024/mar/21/jonathan-glazers-oscars-speech-resonates-deeply

Thompson, A. (2023, October 12). Director Jonathan Glazer speaks out on Gaza at the Oscars. *Time*. https://time.com/6899602/jonathan-glazer-oscars-speech-gaza/

Truth and Reconciliation Commission of Canada. (2015). *Honouring the truth, reconciling for the future: Summary of the final report of the Truth and Reconciliation Commission of Canada.* https://nctr.ca/records/reports/

United Nations. (2024, January 13). *General Assembly Committee on the Inalienable Rights of the Palestinian People hears from civil society organizations on atrocities in Occupied Palestinian Territory, urges peaceful end to conflict.* United Nations Press. https://press.un.org/en/2024/gapal1467.doc.htm

United Nations. (2024, March 26). Rights expert finds 'reasonable grounds' genocide is being committed in Gaza. *UN News*. https://news.un.org/en/story/2024/03/1147976

West, C. (2016, July 14). Barack Obama, US racism, and police brutality: Why he failed victims. *The Guardian*. https://www.theguardian.com/commentisfree/2016/jul/14/barack-obama-us-racism-police-brutality-failed-victims

Williams, M. T., Faber, S., Zare, M., Barker, T., & Abdulrehman, R. Y. (2024) Intersectional racial and gender bias in family court. *Discover Psychology, 4*, 178. https://doi.org/10.1007/s44202-024-00282-8

Zakaria, R. (2024, October 14). Why the backlash against Ta-Nehisi Coates's Israel-Palestine comments is so telling. *The Washington Post*. https://www.washingtonpost.com/opinions/2024/10/14/coates-dokoupil-cbs-israel-palestine/

Afterword

One of the greatest benefits from writing this book was the opportunity to learn from each other and from the myriad stories told in films and television miniseries. In a world where conversations about culture (particularly those conversations that center on people of color, or diversity, equity and inclusion [DEI]) are increasingly met with anger, violence or, at the very least, a rolling of eyes, the process of writing this book provided a refreshing experience. Though we were friends and familiar with each other prior to writing this book, discussing which films and television miniseries to include and exploring what they taught us about culture certainly brought up different perspectives. But the benefit of film and television is that these media allowed us to make points to each other in a more elaborate form, appreciating the complex and nuanced points of view beyond the points we would have made simply by talking with one another. Our long discussions were compelling, heartwarming, and caused considerable introspection, allowing us, despite our differences, to better understand each other – as well as the communities and concerns we wrote about. Writing this book strengthened our friendship and our ability to relate to each other, and it even allowed us to find common ground on several of the global issues that occurred while we were writing this book (e.g., tariff and immigration policies, wars in the Middle East and Europe).

Our choices for the films and television series we reviewed reflect our deep concern over the current state of the world. We are US and Canadian authors, and each of us is the product of exposure to the variety of ethnic and cultural communities with which we interact. We recognize that the world values some perspectives more than others (e.g., White people over the people of the Global Majority, rich over poor, straight over queer and gay, West over East). Increasingly, the world is characterized by strife, inequity, genocide, and ethnic cleansing. While stories about those with great wealth dominate the news, we refuse to turn away from problems in Gaza and the West Bank, colonialism in the Congo and Sudan, and the sovereignty of independent nations (Greenland, Canada, Panama). Though some of these problems are the direct result of decisions by the current President of the United States, it is important to realize that US administrations before him, and many other

Western leaders and governments (including the Democrats, and also the Canadian government and political parties across the spectrum) contributed to these problems. This underscores the fact that complacency based on identity, political affiliation, gender, and our own personal strife in life can create blind spots (intentional or not) to the stories and struggles of others.

We were dismayed and deeply troubled by the election of Donald Trump and the chaotic political decisions he has made since the election. We have had similar concerns about previous presidents (remembering Biden was dubbed "Genocide Joe" for his support of what occurred in Gaza, and how US representatives to the UN vetoed a ceasefire against the votes of the rest of the world). These decisions are contrary to many of the core moral and ethical values that have guided and shaped our lives.

We have focused on discussion of film and television stories of diverse and marginalized people. Because some of our political leaders see little value in people living in "shithole countries," funding violence, removing DEI initiatives, seeing immigration as problematic, reducing the value of healthcare, including that needed by queer and trans people, and violating Indigenous rights, we chose to write about stories that helped oppose this erosion of human rights. In short, we chose to write about narratives that support building bridges instead of burning them.

We have been encouraged by the many film makers and authors who have addressed culture, anti-racism, and advocacy. As we prepared to wrap up the book, we found additional films, television programs, and books that we wanted to include, but we were running out of time. However, it was a sincere pleasure to see the recent Oscar winning documentary *No Other Land*, a collaboration between Palestinian activist Basel Adra and Israeli investigative journalist Yuval Abraham, get the recognition it deserved as Best Documentary in 2025. Documenting the Israeli military destruction of Adra's hometown, Masafer Yatta, in the West Bank, the film makers were at great risk, as they challenged colonial authority and culture to tell the stories that would help the world understand this complex situation. But it is through the allyship and support of fellow film-maker Yuval Abraham that this documentary becomes a success. This highlights the way in which film and television, when done through the intention of allyship and bridge building, can bring us together despite perceived differences, recognizing a problem for what it is through the understanding of perspectives and narratives otherwise seldom told. Similarly, the book *One Day, Everyone Will Have Always Been Against This* (El Akkad, 2025), a non-fiction book by award winning novelist and journalist Omar El Akkad, also addresses narratives of marginalized people, particularly those in Gaza. El Akkad reflects on his disillusionment with Western liberal values, expresses concern over contradictions it holds when these values are applied to issues of equity, inclusion, and human rights. He explores how these ideals often fall short in addressing the suffering of marginalized communities, including Black, Brown, and Indigenous populations. This book is an excellent supplement to the documentary *No Other Land*.

It is clear to us that there has been a historical and ongoing flagrant disregard for the experiences of marginalized people. However, there is convincing evidence that society benefits from the inclusion of diverse communities. Embracing people different from ourselves helps us understand that we should not be threatened by differences, by ethnicity, by immigration, by sex and sexuality, or gender. Likewise, we learn that we are not superior when we impose our values, our perspectives, or our narratives on others.

Storytelling has existed since the dawn of humanity. People gathered around a fire to tell and listen to stories. Modern day films and miniseries' stories fill this human need. Stories amuse, entertain, teach, and provide us with the motivation to be better allies and advocate across divides. Even more, they create magic and illumination needed at a time when political realities often feel very dim.

We hope this book is a light in the darkness that will encourage you to learn about others different from yourself. We hope this book allows you to understand narratives different from your own. And, finally, we hope this book empowers you to tell your story, in any form, understanding that the world and society will benefit from your lived experience.

Film Index

Peer Commentaries

By examining cinema from a cultural perspective, this book changes (and often challenges) the way we view contemporary narrative. It makes us re-think the stories we've seen before and deepens our understanding of the ways in which they reflect our culture. It's also an amazing journey through cinematic history, written with a profound love and depth of understanding.

Deborah Chow, Director and Executive Producer of the TV miniseries *Obi-Wan Kenobi*; Director of episodes of the TV series *The Mandalorian*

Movies, Miniseries, and Multiculturalism *highlights important contemporary social justice themes by providing insightful analysis of dozens of thoughtfully selected films and television shows and posing questions that push the reader to think critically about community, culture, equity, difference, values, and identity. Similar to Wedding's other texts, the accessibility of media is used to examine sociocultural concepts, build connections, and bring attention to the power and purpose of a story. While entertaining, the illustrated media examples and the stories they contain also prove to be valuable vehicles for acknowledging shared humanity, building compassion, and giving voice to the lived experiences of others, and bringing awareness of the viewer as an agent of positive social change. Kudos to the authors for delivering a lucid, well-structured, and unique teaching tool that will undoubtedly expand students' thinking and ability to make meaning of important stories in a creative, absorbing, culturally humble, and engaging manner.*

Jeremiah Dickerson, MD, Associate Professor of Psychiatry, University of Vermont – Larner College of Medicine

Reading Movies, Miniseries, and Multiculturalism *is like going to the movies with three experts on psychology, culture, and film. Comas-Diaz, Abdulrehman, and Wedding have curated an impressive range of films and miniseries on topics ranging from family and relationships to colonialism and social justice. The context and plot of films are offered without providing spoilers, which whets the reader's appetite to watch or rewatch these films. The authors discuss psychological principles (e.g., internalized racism, racial socialization, acculturation) illustrated in the films and provide references for those interested in an in-depth examination of the principles. Each chapter presents multiple questions to consider while watching the films to get the reader to think more deeply about the multicultural aspects of films. The authors are not afraid to discuss shortcomings of some of the films, including failures to realistically portray communities of color and to challenge stereotypes of groups. The book is of interest to multiple audiences, including psychologists, teachers, students, therapists, clients, filmmakers, and film enthusiasts.*

Gordon C. Nagayama Hall, PhD, Past President of APA Division 45: Society for the Psychological Study of Culture, Ethnicity and Race; Author of *Multicultural Psychology*

This book could not be more important! As our world grows increasingly interconnected, we find ourselves immersed in the richness of an immense variety of countless cultures. Nevertheless, we struggle to even sit in the same room as those who are different, let alone engage in curious and civil discussions. This book, therefore, is a gift. Through the magic of narrative and the universality of film in the theater or the living room, the authors remind the audience that art helps us to celebrate our similarities and to marvel at everything that makes us unique.

Steven C. Schlozman, MD, Medical Director Vermont Center for Children, Youth and Families at University of Vermont – Larner College of Medicine

What an extraordinary and outstanding treasure! If you love movies and miniseries and would like to increase your understanding of multiculturalism via those, you will be open to the magic in this book. I appreciated being reminded how multicultural themes in films can be enlightening and promote personal growth. Questions designed by the wisdom, expertise, and knowledge of three outstanding scholars/authors encourage critical thinking and inspired me to view some of the films again – and to discover new ones!

Melba J. T. Vasquez, PhD, ABPP, President, American Psychological Foundation; Former President, American Psychological Association